Cultural Pluralism

and Dilemmas

of Justice

Cultural Pluralism and Dilemmas of Justice

Monique Deveaux

Cornell University Press

ITHACA AND LONDON

First published 2000 by Cornell University Press

Printed in the United States of America

LIBRARY OF CONGRESS CATALOGING-IN-PUBLICATION DATA
Deveaux, Monique.
    Cultural pluralism and dilemmas of justice / Monique Deveaux.
      p. cm.
    Includes bibliographical references and index.
    ISBN 0-8014-3682-6 (cloth : alk. paper)
     1. Liberalism. 2. Toleration. 3. Pluralism (Social sciences)
  4. Multiculturalism. I. Title.
JC574 .D478 2000
305.8—dc21   00-010488

Cornell University Press strives to use environmentally responsible suppliers and
materials to the fullest extent possible in the publishing of its books. Such materials
include vegetable-based, low-VOC inks, and acid-free papers that are recycled,
chlorine-free, or partly composed of nonwood fibers. Books that bear the logo of
the FSC (Forest Stewardship Council) use paper taken from forests that have been
inspected and certified as meeting the highest standards for environmental and
social responsibility. For further information, visit our website at
www.cornellpress.cornell.edu.

Cloth printing   10 9 8 7 6 5 4 3 2 1

FSC FSC Trademark © 1996 Forest Stewardship Council A.C.
     SW-COC-098

For my parents

Contents

3
Neutrality, Justice, and Cultural Diversity
65

4
Cultural Pluralism from
Liberal Perfectionist Premises
109

5
Deliberative Democracy:
A Theory of Pluralism and Inclusion?
138

6

TOWARD A DELIBERATIVE LIBERALISM?

166

7

THE DILEMMA OF CULTURAL DIVERSITY IN POLITICAL THOUGHT

180

Acknowledgments

The concerns addressed in this book are ones that have captured the attention of many contemporary political theorists. Nonetheless, there is a sense in which I think of this project as distinctly Canadian or as emerging out of a set of concerns that preoccupy Canadian political theorists in particular. These include such questions as whether and how we might reconcile the competing claims of national linguistic and ethnic minorities and whether collective identities deserve greater, not less, attention in political life. It was while living and studying in Montréal in the mid-to-late 1980s, during a time of considerable and intense debate about the prospects of Québécois sovereignty and aboriginal self-determination, that I began to think more concertedly about the role of collective identity and language in political life in liberal democratic states. My teachers at McGill, especially Jim Tully and Charles Taylor, were at that time breaking new ground in scholarship on cultural pluralism and made an enormous impression on my thinking.

In the course of writing this book, I have been fortunate to receive much encouragement and support from many people. My greatest intellectual debt is to Onora O'Neill, who supervised my doctoral dissertation at the University of Cambridge and whose example as a scholar and thinker continues to inspire me. While at Cambridge, I also benefited enormously from discussions with faculty and students, including Susan James, Melissa Lane, Sharon Dolovich, David Kahane, and Sam Gibson. During a postdoctoral fellowship year at the Kennedy School of Government at Harvard University, I gained much from conversations with members of the Hilles Social Studies Seminar and with Tamara Metz, whose friendship helped sustain me through the revisions of this book. Simone Chambers provided innumerable valuable suggestions for improving the manuscript. I am also grateful to my colleagues at Williams College for providing a stimulating and supportive environment for finishing the book.

Though they were not always sure what I was up to, my family has encouraged me throughout the writing of this book. Indeed, the book has been shaped by my family in another respect: my approach to dilemmas faced by cultural minorities, indeed my very interest in these problems, has evolved out of my experience as a Canadian from a rapidly diminishing cultural group (the Acadians, from the French-speaking area of Nova Scotia), grappling with some of the issues that this identity inevitably raises. I thank my father for reminding me (with increasing frequency over the years) that I am indeed Acadian and for furnishing me with the Acadian flag which graces my office wall at Williams College.

I am indebted to the Social Sciences Research Council of Canada for both doctoral and postdoctoral funding, which made it possible for me to write this book. I am also grateful to the Association of Commonwealth Universities, which provided additional financial support.

Chapter 2 appeared in abbreviated form in the *Public Affairs Quarterly* 12, no. 4 (1998), and material from chapter 4 appeared in *Polity* 33, no. 4 (2000).

Finally, I thank my husband, Paul Voice, for his stubborn insistence on asking the skeptical liberal questions that needed to be asked of this book and for his unflagging encouragement and love.

MONIQUE DEVEAUX

Williamstown, Massachusetts

Cultural Pluralism

and Dilemmas

of Justice

Introduction

One of the ironies of growing economic globalization is the extent to which it has been accompanied by a persistence, even resurgence, of nationalist, ethnic, and linguistic struggles for recognition. Far from heralding an age of diminishing loyalties to ethnic, linguistic, and regional identities, the increased ease with which finance, capital, and commodities move across borders stands in sharp contrast to tenacious affective and cultural ties and identities. Liberal democracies are of course no exception to this trend. From the successful 1997 referendum in Scotland for devolution of power to the continued secessionist aspirations of Québécois nationalists and Irish Catholics and Protestants in Northern Ireland, there is little sign that regional economic cooperation and political integration have had a tempering effect on nationalist movements. Nor have these developments had any demonstrable impact on language-based struggles—except, perhaps, to accentuate them. The creation of the European Union (EU), for instance, has done nothing to diminish the separatist aspirations of Basques separatists or Catalán and Scottish nationalists or demands for recognition and respect (and calls for limited regional independence) by Welsh and Breton peoples. Nor do calls both for greater political inclusion by minorities with no nationalist aspirations and for limited local autonomy over issues such as education show any sign of abating in this age of economic globalization.

Our ethnic, cultural, and linguistic identities in liberal democracies continue to play an important role in political life despite the trend toward economic and regional political integration. Consequently, it is well worth examining how these identities figure in our political institutions and practices—how much credence is given to justice claims that invoke cultural identity and membership, whether cultural minority groups view themselves as having real access to political decision-making, and so forth. Yet although sociologists and political scientists have directed considerable attention to these questions (in discussions of nationalism and the salience of ethnic and linguistic identities), political theorists, on the whole, have until recently neglected to study the significance that struggles for cultural recognition hold for liberal and democratic theory and practice. Nor have they given sufficient consideration to the political importance of cultural identity and cultural membership in liberal democracies. Where they have addressed these features, recent thinkers have frequently stopped short of proposing ways to secure substantive respect and recognition for cultural minorities. The present work is thus an attempt to both evaluate and extend recent efforts in political theory to address the problem of justice for cultural minorities. In examining how liberal and democratic theorists have treated this issue, I pay particular attention to the following questions: How should justice for cultural minority groups be defined in socially plural, democratic states? How might it best be secured?

The task of this book is twofold. First, I try to show that much liberal political theory either fails to address or fails to respond adequately to crucial issues raised by cultural diversity in democratic states. And second, I argue that a more satisfactory approach to the justice claims of cultural minorities—what I call "respect for cultural pluralism"—must take fuller account of their demands for political respect and recognition. This in turn requires that we take questions of democracy more seriously than many recent liberal discussions have done, particularly the importance of political values of inclusion, consent, deliberation, and negotiation. I call this revised conception of liberal democracy "deliberative liberalism," and try to show that it provides a viable alternative to liberal and democratic theories that fall short of offering equal justice and full political inclusion for cultural minorities.

My discussion is informed by a broad view of the requirements of justice for cultural minorities in plural, democratic states that is best made explicit here. I begin from a set of claims, enumerated in chapter 1 and defended in the following chapters, about the features that a satisfactory account of *respect for cultural pluralism* minimally requires. These features reflect many of the justice claims of cultural minorities in democratic states. Chief among these is the demand by some ethnic, religious, and linguistic groups that they be permitted to help shape the political and wider public cultures of the societies in which they live. Often this justice claim is framed in terms of the desire to have a significant voice in the issues and institutions that affect one's own community, such as education, social policy, and legal and constitutional reform. For marginalized cultural and ethnic minority groups to have opportunities to help shape the public norms and practices that bind them, they will need to be granted a greater role in mainstream political institutions. In the case of national minorities, however, it may be that only some form of community autonomy—up to and including self-government—will meet their demands for political recognition. Securing justice for members of cultural minorities in democratic states will thus require either the reform of certain political institutions so as to secure permanent representation for national minorities (for example, through the introduction of group-based cultural rights) or a realignment of the state's internal power relationships (for example, by devolution of power or greater self-government for certain groups).

My claim that justice for cultural minorities in democratic states includes the right of these groups to help shape the public and political cultures of the broader societies in which they live stands in contrast to the views of many recent liberal theorists, such "neutral" or "political" liberals as John Rawls and Charles Larmore.[1] Unlike these writers, I suggest that helping to shape political norms and institutions will require that minority groups have a say in where the boundaries of public and nonpublic life are to be drawn. Ironically, my conclusions follow in part from taking seriously certain fundamental principles of liberal theory, particularly those of respect and consent. Thus, although I criticize recent liberal theories for their treatment (and neglect) of the justice claims of cultural minorities in democratic states, I do not advocate the wholesale rejection of liberal arguments and principles. Rather, I argue that some liberal norms are indispensable components of a more adequate response to ethnic, linguistic, and religious diversity. Crucially, however, these principles cannot be fully implemented in culturally plural polities without deploying a more robust conception of democracy, one that is at odds with the thinner conceptions of liberal democracy defended by many contemporary liberals.

The account of respect for cultural pluralism advanced in this book thus depends on a thicker conception of democracy than liberal the-

---

1. See especially Charles Larmore, *Patterns of Moral Complexity* (Cambridge: Cambridge University Press, 1987), and John Rawls, *Political Liberalism* (New York: Columbia University Press, 1993).

orists normally employ and draws on recent arguments by proponents of a deliberative approach to political life.[2] I shall try to show that aspects of a modified theory of deliberative democracy can be used to support and extend arguments for recognition and respect for cultural minority groups. In particular, the emphasis within deliberative democratic theory on the importance of the role of citizens in legitimating norms and assessing political proposals through public dialogue and decision-making may help ensure a greater political voice for cultural minorities. Certain aspects of deliberative democracy, if implemented, might encourage citizens and legislators to debate their moral views and practical disagreements in ways that encourage respect for one another's social differences and cultural identities. For these and other reasons, a modified account of deliberative democracy—one linked to liberal norms of respect and consent—may be more useful in addressing the demands of cultural minorities for respect and recognition than liberal conceptions of justice are.

Liberal theory alone, as usually developed, cannot provide adequate justification for valuing and protecting cultural membership and identity. Early modern and contemporary contractarian thinking, as well as recent liberal perfectionist approaches, do not supply satisfactory arguments for respecting and recognizing cultural minorities. Much neutral or political liberal writing, for instance, emphasizes the importance of protecting individual sources of difference, often expressed in terms of the protection of individuals' freedom to form, revise, and pursue a conception of the good. But neutral liberals also seek to prevent citizens from invoking their (controversial) moral views and social beliefs in debating what Rawls calls "constitutional essentials," a move that could make it difficult for certain cultural minorities to press their justice claims against the liberal state. Nor do recent liberal perfectionist arguments necessarily fare much better: in defending proposals for cultural membership rights and protections, liberal perfectionists point mainly to the role that cultural identity and membership play in furnishing the necessary context for personal autonomy, a value which stands in tension with the aspirations and values of some cultural minorities, especially traditional religious communities.

In contrast to these liberal strategies, respect for cultural pluralism, I argue, requires that we recognize the political significance of group-

---

2. By "thick," I mean more participatory, inclusive, and dynamic forms of democracy. The account of "thick democracy" for which I argue is not, however, related to theories of direct, participatory democracy, which emphasize the participation of individuals, not groups.

based, essentially nonvoluntary, social differences. One reason for this is that recognition of the value of cultural identities, and of their salience in practical political life is increasingly cited by minority groups as a requirement of justice as they perceive it. Sometimes such justice claims extend to demands for collective rights and even self-government; as I discuss, there are good reasons to think that respect for cultural pluralism will require that democratic states introduce more extensive collective rights and arrangements for cultural minorities than currently exist, and even extend formal autonomy or self-government to certain long-standing national minorities who seek it (such as aboriginal peoples). Some of these proposals appear to stand in tension with liberal commitments to individual rights and liberties and may in some instances pose real conflicts. It is perhaps unsurprising, then, that political theorists have been reluctant to endorse far-reaching strategies for cultural recognition.

Unlike the thin accounts of democracy associated with recent liberal theories, I suggest that a thicker account of democracy would require the introduction of certain collective cultural rights and special arrangements for cultural minorities and so could help secure a deeper form of accommodation for national and ethnic minorities.[3] A substantive, deliberative conception of democracy emphasizes the importance of citizens' participation in public life and the need to foster political relationships and practices based on reciprocity, political equality, and mutual respect—all crucial to meeting basic justice claims by national minorities and immigrants alike. These latter principles are clearly bound up with liberal theory, which has an important role to play in the development of strategies for the accommodation of cultural diversity. However, demands by cultural minorities for greater inclusion in political institutions and for powers of self-government

3. I use the terms "accommodate" and "accommodation" to denote the social and political inclusion of cultural, religious, and ethnic minorities in democratic states on terms acceptable to a significant majority of these groups. The idea of accommodation is not endlessly malleable: for instance, apartheid is a form of exclusion, not inclusion, and assimilation is not a form of accommodation, but rather a strategy for de-politicizing and ultimately eroding social and cultural differences. Assimilation, therefore, is largely incompatible with cultural claims for recognition. There are weaker and stronger variants of accommodation, corresponding to the degree of inclusion and respect accorded to minority groups. I also follow John Dryzek in using the term "political inclusion" to denote an aspect of the process of democratization in plural liberal states by which marginalized social and cultural groups come to be included in both local and national political decision-making. Political inclusion reflects demands for forms of participation that surpass "basic citizenship rights," such as voting rights. See John Dryzek, "Political Inclusion and the Dynamics of Democratization," *American Political Science Review* 90, no. 1 (1996): 475–87.

are evidence that the mere "macro-level democracy" afforded by liberalism—the basic political equality of citizens in representative democracies—cannot by itself secure justice for minority groups in culturally plural, liberal states. I shall argue that we also need to introduce democratic practices and structures at the "micro-level" of social and political life, in part to ensure that political deliberation and decision-making can take full account of citizens' cultural identities and memberships. Emerging conceptions of deliberative democracy can help facilitate these transformations.

The suggestion that meeting the demands of cultural groups for recognition and respect will require greater democratization at the micro-level of social and political institutions represents the end point, rather than the beginning, of my discussion. I start by assuming only a thin theory of democracy, one that includes universal franchise and formal political equality before the law. These principles are endorsed by contemporary liberal theorists as well as by proponents of deliberative democracy; they are also recognized by the democratic polities discussed here—Australia, Canada, the United States, the United Kingdom, and other countries of Western Europe. Though I move from a thin account of democracy to suggestions for a more robust model of democratic life, I do not purport to develop a thick theory of democracy in extensive detail; indeed, even my claim that we need such a conception requires considerable defense. Instead, I aim to offer reasons why a more inclusive and deliberative account of democracy—one that recognizes the importance of cultural identity and membership for many citizens—might help us to meet cultural minorities' demands for social and political accommodation.

The central claim of this book is that justice in democratic states must include respect for cultural pluralism. Unlike *cultural diversity*—a merely descriptive term denoting the presence of different cultures—a commitment to *cultural pluralism*, as I shall use the term, describes a normative position that accords basic respect and recognition to culturally diverse groups. The difference between cultural diversity and cultural pluralism in some ways parallels the contrast between ethical diversity and value pluralism or between moral diversity and moral pluralism. When we speak of moral (or value) diversity, we simply note the presence of different moral views or belief systems. By contrast, the term value pluralism expresses the thought that "value has fundamentally different kinds of sources,"[4] as well as conveying the normative view that diverse values are worthy of tolerance and protection. Analogously, the term "cultural diversity" merely denotes the existence of different cultural communities within a defined space, whereas respect for cultural pluralism implies the further belief that citizens' cultural identities and memberships merit basic respect and recognition (if not always admiration). On some accounts, a commitment to cultural pluralism may also require that we seek to protect existing forms of cultural diversity within a given territory. Proponents of cultural pluralism will of course differ on such questions as how we might best express respect and recognition, what kinds of protections and rights are warranted and for which groups, and where to draw the limits of inclusion and tolerance. However, no supporter of cultural pluralism could defend policies designed to accelerate the assimilation of cultural minorities, whether coercively or peacefully; nor could they advocate the imposition of a single, culturally specific way of life or set of values on a socially diverse populace.

Neither "cultural diversity" nor "cultural pluralism" makes much sense in the absence of a definition of what is meant by "cultural." In the discussion that follows, I use the terms "cultural" and "cultural group" in a narrow sense. When referring to "cultural groups," I mean those communities that share an identity based on nonvoluntary features and ways of life, such as a specific nationality, ethnicity, race, language, a common history and collective memory, religion, and social customs.[5] These are frequently constitutive features of one's identity. Membership in a cultural group in this narrow sense is normally through birth and to a much lesser degree through marriage and formal induction (e.g., religious conversion). The term "cultural *minorities*," not surprisingly, refers to ethnic, racial, and religious groups who form a minority of a given population and frequently identify as such. In liberal democratic states, minority status is often linked to social and economic disadvantage, political marginalization, and even political subjugation.

My discussion of cultural groups does not extend to newly constructed or voluntary communities whose members may share a culture

4. Thomas Nagel, "The Fragmentation of Value," in *Mortal Questions* (Cambridge: Cambridge University Press, 1979), 132.

5. My definition of cultural groups is sufficiently broad so as to include not merely long-standing national minorities but also recent immigrant communities. For a narrower account of national identity, one that includes many of the same features listed here, see David Miller, "In Defense of Nationality," *Journal of Applied Philosophy* 10, no. 1 (1993): 3–16.

in the sense of a set of views, lifestyle, political interests, or common ex-
periences of discrimination and oppression. Rather, the cultural groups
that I address are made up of individuals who share a common ethnicity, language, or a specific, enduring historical identity that is largely understood as "given" and transmitted across time and generations. Thus,
collectivities that organize mainly to further a particular social or political cause, or to establish a new religious community, are not under discussion here. South Asian Muslims in Britain and the Amish in the
United States are clearly cultural groups under this description—for
their social identities are essentially involuntary, a function of the families and communities into which they are born—but new social movements, such as gay and lesbian communities and recent religious groups
such as the Scientologists, are not. Of course, this distinction is not always easy to make. There are borderline cases of recently formed communities that now transmit religion to the next generation, such as the
Mormons of Utah, who can claim cultural group status under the description I have given above. In general, however, I argue that recently
and largely voluntarily established social and religious groups have different sorts of claims on the liberal state and should be considered separately from those groups whose members share a common ethnicity,
language, or long-standing historical identity.

Of course, communities that are not cultural groups in my more demanding sense may and do also press their justice claims against states
on the basis of perceived discrimination and lack of recognition. Nothing in my discussion of justice for more narrowly defined cultural
groups precludes the possibility of arguments for respect or positive
forms of protection for other kinds of collectivities. Such a discussion,
however, is beyond the scope of the present project. Although there is
some overlap in the principles and reasons appealed to by cultural
groups and voluntary or "constructed" communities, I suggest that
there are good reasons to treat their claims separately; we have little to
gain in conflating disparate types of groups and struggles and much to
lose.

There are two main categories of cultural groups seeking forms of
recognition within the liberal democracies of North America, Western
Europe, and Australia: territorial and nonterritorial minorities. Territorial or national minorities, such as Basques, Québécois, Scots, and native or aboriginal peoples, press claims that are different in both kind
and scope from those of territorially dispersed minorities. The latter are
either relatively recent immigrant communities that have settled in
large urban centers or long-standing but for the most part territorially
dispersed racial minority groups, such as African Americans and Lati-

nos. Territorially concentrated minorities frequently demand devolution of power and forms of self-government—including anything from selective veto powers within a federal state to outright secession.[6] Sometimes claims for self-determination are combined with secessionist aspirations, as in the case of Québécois separatists; but equally, these demands for self-rule may attach to calls for unification, as evidenced by the case of Ireland.[7] By contrast, territorially dispersed minorities rarely press for self-determination, though when they form a local majority they may demand autonomy in such spheres as education. The attempt by Satmar Hasidim in the upstate New York village of Kiryas Joel to establish their own state-supported school district for disabled children in their community, for example, stands out as a well-publicized example of such a demand. Oftentimes the claims of territorially dispersed groups express a desire for greater respect and inclusion in mainstream social and political structures or some amendment to facilitate such inclusion. The call for race-conscious redistricting in U.S. electoral districts where blacks constitute a majority of voters but are not well represented in political office reflects just this sort of aspiration.

As a preliminary response to the question "How should we define justice for cultural minorities in democratic states?" I propose the following. Minimally, justice for cultural minorities includes respect for the dignity and rights of members of cultural groups, as well as recognition of the "standing" of distinct cultural communities.[8] In many cases, it is not possible to respect individuals even in a basic sense unless we also recognize and in some sense affirm the value of their primary cultural identities, attachments, and forms of community. It may also be necessary to acknowledge and come to respect (at least in a thin or formal sense) peoples' core moral beliefs. These expressions of respect, which

6. In some cases, such as Québec, we find both aspirations for full political independence and more limited calls for greater voice within the federal state. There is also a strategy that seeks to combine both of these goals: the idea of "sovereignty-association," as proposed by some Québec nationalists.

7. I will not examine in any detail the social ideologies of nationalism nor the machinations of different secessionist struggles—since my concern is how liberal and democratic theories can be employed to better accommodate cultural diversity within liberal states.

8. I use the term "standing" in a manner similar to that suggested by Judith Shklar in her discussion of the expansion of citizenship rights in modern America. Shklar employs "standing"—as in her phrase, "citizenship as standing"—to denote civic rights, dignity, and real political inclusion in a specific state. Although I use this term to connote respect for one's rights as a citizen, I believe it also captures aspects of the demands of cultural minorities for recognition of the dignity and value of their communities. See Shklar, *American Citizenship: The Quest for Inclusion* (Cambridge, Mass.: Harvard University Press, 1991), esp. 2–23.

derive from the principle of respect for persons, in turn require certain social and political policies that demonstrate and help secure "cultural recognition." Some degree of cultural recognition often already exists in liberal democracies, as evidenced by explicit policies affirming the multicultural heritage of citizens and the introduction of certain collective, cultural rights for national minorities. A deeper degree of recognition may also be achieved by making small modifications to existing public arrangements—say, by funding first-language education for national minorities or by allocating state resources for religious schooling for certain groups of recent immigrants (as has been demanded by some South Asian Muslims in Britain). Reforms to the structure and composition of representative political institutions so as to afford national minorities in particular a greater political voice are other possible strategies for meeting cultural demands for respect and political inclusion. Recognition of national minorities may require changes in a state's constitutional arrangements, especially devolution of power: Inuit peoples living in the Eastern Arctic region of Canada (formerly the Northwest Territories), for instance, successfully argued that justice for their communities required the creation of a territory with extensive powers of self-government: the result was the creation of the Nunavut in 1999, a new, autonomous administrative territory.[9]

In the minds of some critics, contemporary struggles by cultural minority groups for recognition and inclusion in democratic states are evidence enough that political theorists need to revise key aspects of liberal democratic thought. I share this view. In particular, I argue that we need to rethink the role that citizens' social and cultural identities and practices play in moral and political life. Insofar as liberal theory is concerned, we need to revise and in some cases look beyond central assumptions in liberal thought and attend more closely to the question of how to deal democratically with the claims of cultural minorities. I suggest that meeting the minimum requirements of justice, equality, and fairness as these categories are typically understood by many recent liberal thinkers can provide only partial solutions to some of the dilemmas posed by cultural diversity. Nor are these shortcomings merely a matter

9. The proposal for the creation of the administrative territory of Nunavut, which covers a region roughly the size of Europe, was ratified at the circumpolar conference on Inuit affairs in 1995. Starting in April 1999, Nunavut has been treated essentially as a province of Canada, governed by a combination of traditional native law and Canadian federal and provincial law but with wide internal powers of self-government for Inuit peoples.

of the incomplete or partial application of liberal principles to institutions and practices: rather, there are an ever-increasing number of demands by cultural groups that are inappropriately and inadequately addressed by recent accounts of liberal justice and the liberal state as necessarily "neutral" vis-à-vis citizens' particular identities and attachments. Instead of viewing citizens' group-based claims as in some sense tangential to justice in democratic states—thereby meriting provisional, strategic responses such as state neutrality and mere toleration—I suggest that political theorists, liberals in particular, must engage in a more fundamental questioning of the relationship between citizens' social and cultural identities and political norms and practices. The account of respect for cultural pluralism for which I argue is fully compatible with many core liberal principles, but will require that we rethink conventional liberal assumptions about the moral and political status of citizens' cultural identities and memberships. It will further require that we think harder than liberal theorists have traditionally done about how democratic institutions and practices might better accommodate these identities.

A corollary of the approach to cultural pluralism argued for in this book is thus the claim that we cannot meet legitimate cultural demands for respect and recognition merely by incorporating *individual* members of cultural communities into existing liberal political structures or by better protecting their individual rights. Consequently, my arguments are not likely to persuade readers who view cultural identity and cultural membership as wholly irrelevant dimensions of political life in contemporary liberal democracies. Nor, most probably, will I convince those who consider strategies of cultural assimilation to be the only appropriate response to the presence of conflicting cultural norms and frameworks. However, I aim to show that cultural minority groups have legitimate justice claims and that these claims can be defended in part by delineating the reasons why cultural identity and membership are important to individual members of cultural groups as well as to their communities as a whole. Moreover, if we endorse liberal principles of consent and respect, then we are committed to making good the promise of these principles by ensuring the political inclusion of all citizens who seek it, even those members of groups who challenge some of the norms and procedures of prevailing liberal political institutions. More generally, I also seek to show that democratic states have reasons to value and to seek to protect existing forms of diversity within their borders. There are numerous advantages to social and cultural diversity, yet these benefits are frequently overlooked by writers concerned with devising strategies for alleviating conflicts that often attend such diversity.

Even readers who share my view that justice in contemporary, pluralistic democracies requires that we meet some of the claims of cultural
minorities may balk at the perceived dangers of according a greater political voice to these groups. What about the threats posed by illiberal
minorities who reject individual rights or who undermine the agency
of their own members? How can we respect ethnic or religious groups
that are intolerant of others? I try to address these worries by acknowledging that democratic states must also draw limits to the political inclusion and indeed to the toleration of some minority groups. However, the best criterion for rejecting demands for recognition, greater
political accommodation, or, alternatively, greater political autonomy,
is not likely to be a simple test to determine the liberal character and
credentials of a minority group. Fears about the specter of anti-liberal
cultures too readily prevent political theorists from considering
whether and how we might meet the justice claims of cultural minorities.[10] A better criterion for determining whether to accommodate a
group's demands for recognition and accommodation, as I suggest in
the next chapter, is whether the agency rights of members of a minority community (including less powerful members) are respected—that
is, whether individuals have the capacity and opportunity to affirm as
well as to refuse the ideals and social and political arrangements of the
group as whole.

The discussion proceeds as follows. In chapter 1, I discuss certain mistakes that recent liberal political theorists have made in addressing issues of cultural identity, membership, and diversity. I suggest here that
liberals will have to make three main conceptual shifts if they are to
contribute usefully to debates about dilemmas of cultural difference. I
also enumerate and offer a preliminary defense of the conceptual and
practical features that an adequate account of respect for cultural pluralism minimally requires.

In chapter 2, I examine both "weak" and "strong" liberal conceptions
of toleration from the vantage point of demands by cultural minorities
for greater respect and recognition. Although the notion of toleration

---

10. We need to distinguish between merely nonliberal cultural minorities—i.e., those
whose values and forms of community do not cohere with liberal ideals and norms—and
actively *anti*liberal cultural groups, many of whose practices may require censure in democratic states.

does not play as pivotal a role in contemporary liberal theory as it did in early modern liberal thought, I suggest that it continues to shape some liberal responses to cultural diversity. Toleration, I argue, is an indispensable feature of liberal theory and practice, but political theorists often fail to recognize its limitations. Aimed as it is at regulating relationships between unequals (religious majorities tolerate vulnerable religious minorities, but not vice-versa) the principle of toleration rarely challenges the social, economic, and political power relations that perpetuate such inequalities. Since the justice claims of cultural minorities include demands for the transformation of unequal public relationships, a toleration-based approach to dilemmas of diversity simply may not reach far enough. Moreover, the idea of toleration encourages us to view dilemmas of cultural difference through the narrow lens of basic individual liberties and equal political or civic rights. By contrast, meeting the justice claims of certain national minorities in particular will require that we look beyond notions of individual rights to positive kinds of recognition, in the form of greater inclusion in political institutions and support for certain collective, cultural rights.

In chapter 3, I assess an influential contemporary liberal account of justice, that of neutral or political liberalism. As advocated by Rawls and Larmore, political liberalism proposes that liberal political institutions and procedures should be based on morally neutral principles of justice in general and an ideal of neutral, public reason in particular. Political liberals think they eliminate the need for *special* recognition of citizens' social differences by ensuring that the basic constitutional principles and institutions of political life reflect norms that all citizens could accept. So long as key public norms are "merely" political—in the sense of meeting the test of neutral, public reason—citizens' diverse conceptions of the good can be accommodated and protected in social and private life. Crucially, however, political liberals fail fully to grasp the importance of citizens' social and cultural identities to public and political arrangements. Neutral liberal justice, I shall argue, purchases political legitimacy and stability through a dual strategy of *assimilation*—of culturally diverse citizens to a neutral liberal political culture—and *exclusion,* by requiring that citizens not invoke their particular moral views and identities when debating political fundamentals. The requirements of liberal neutrality may further prevent some cultural groups from voicing their communities' concerns. To demonstrate how liberal norms of neutral justification and "reasonableness" may disadvantage minority communities, I discuss the example of aboriginal women in South Australia whose traditional cultural norms of privacy prevented them from supplying the information and public justification required in a land-claim dispute from the early 1990s (known as the "Hindmarsh case").

In chapter 4, I address liberal perfectionist approaches to the issue of cultural diversity, in particular the arguments of Joseph Raz and Will Kymlicka.[11] In contrast to neutral liberals, liberal perfectionists demonstrate a genuine appreciation of the importance of cultural identity and membership and of their role in human flourishing. These writers recognize, moreover, that conceptions of the good are not simply to be bracketed. Although their acknowledgment of the value of cultural identity and membership represents an advance over neutral or political liberal approaches, liberal perfectionists make numerous undefended assumptions that could limit the scope of their proposals for greater respect for cultural minorities. The main justification Kymlicka and Raz offer in favor of state support for cultural groups is what I call the "argument from autonomy," which views cultural identity and membership as important insofar as these furnish agents with the capacities and context necessary for personal autonomy. Although this argument may supply reasons for protecting vulnerable cultures that are liberal in character, it precludes the prospect of accommodating nonliberal cultural groups whose practices and beliefs conflict with liberal ideals. I illustrate this problem by examining recent demands by South Asian Muslims in Britain for state-supported Muslim independent schools, as well as dilemmas raised by customary arranged marriages in South Asian immigrant communities.

In chapter 5, I turn away from liberal perspectives and examine a perspective that has evolved in part as a response to the failures of liberalism: deliberative democracy. Although much more concerned with values of political inclusion and normative agreement than the liberal theories examined here, proponents of deliberative democracy have yet to offer a systematic examination of how members of cultural minorities could better be accommodated in democratic political life. Indeed, some aspects of theories of deliberative democracy give us cause for concern that ethnic, linguistic, and religious communities could be further marginalized within such a framework than is currently the case. For instance, one of its most troubling aspects is the view that since democratic discourse is socially mediated discourse, it may merely

---

11. The main texts I examine here are Joseph Raz, *Ethics in the Public Domain: Essays in the Morality of Law and Politics* (Oxford: Clarendon Press, 1994); Will Kymlicka, *Liberalism, Community, and Culture* (Oxford: Clarendon Press, 1989); and Kymlicka, *Multicultural Citizenship: A Liberal Theory of Minority Rights* (Oxford: Clarendon Press, 1995).

reflect—or even reinforce—citizens' social, political, and economic in-equalities. The disadvantages that norms of consensus, agreement, and publicity—central to many accounts of deliberative democracy—may pose for cultural minorities in democratic states are brought into relief by a discussion of some of the obstacles to political participation faced by Canadian aboriginal groups as well as immigrants from traditional, deeply religious cultures. It is therefore essential to revise deliberative conceptions of democracy so as to minimize the effect of these dis-advantages on citizens' access to, and participation in, deliberative procedures.

In the sixth chapter, I argue that a suitably modified conception of deliberative democracy—what I propose to call deliberative liberal-ism—can better meet the requirements of justice for cultural minori-ties in democratic states than can the liberal approaches examined in earlier chapters. When linked to liberal principles of respect and con-sent, deliberative liberalism requires and can also foster the inclusion of diverse cultural groups in political deliberation and decision-making. Moreover, the thicker account of democracy that informs this perspec-tive meets many more of the requirements of respect for cultural plural-ism than thin forms of liberalism, such as those based on notions of tol-eration and neutrality.

In the seventh and concluding chapter, I review the requirements of respect for cultural pluralism (as proposed in chapter 1) and give a cap-sule summary of the shortcomings of toleration-based approaches to di-versity, neutral liberal strategies, liberal perfectionist arguments for cul-tural membership rights, and prevailing deliberative democratic treatments of the issue of cultural pluralism. I then reflect again on some of the main conceptual shifts that liberal theorists would need to make in order to begin to meet some of the justice claims of ethnic, lin-guistic, and religious minority groups. This is followed by a brief discus-sion of the key potential strengths and merits of the modified concep-tion of deliberative democracy that I call deliberative liberalism. I conclude that respect for cultural pluralism will require political the-orists to move toward a more robust model of democracy, one that takes seriously the importance to political life of citizens' social and cultural identities and memberships.

FAFO+
now age history

ONE

Difference and Diversity in
Liberal and Democratic Thought

The State consists not merely of a plurality of men, but of different
kinds of men; you cannot make a state out of men who are all alike.

—ARISTOTLE, *The Politics*

If there is a country in the world, where concord, according to
common calculation, would be least expected, it is America. Made up,
as it is, of people from different nations, accustomed to different forms
and habits of government, speaking different languages, and more
different in their modes of worship, it would appear that the union of
such a people was impracticable; but by the simple operation of
constructing government on the principles of society and the rights of
man, every difficulty retires, and all parts are brought into cordial
unison.

—THOMAS PAINE, *Rights of Man*

Aristotle's ideal of an internally differentiated yet socially viable
Greek polis and Thomas Paine's vision of a frontier society com-
prising multiple nationalities and religions living harmoniously
under the protection of universal rights have long since been displaced
by a more pessimistic picture of the implications of social and cultural
diversity. Although the universal principles and individual rights held
up by Paine remain central commitments of liberal states, the breezy

16

optimism he expressed about the capacity of democracy to harmonize citizens' social and cultural differences would today strain belief. Myriad challenges from social and cultural minority groups in liberal democratic states have ushered in a new "politics of recognition."[1]

Liberal theory, historically viewed as the natural ally of pluralism, has borne the brunt of these recent challenges. This may seem surprising. Unlike communitarian and republican thinkers, some of whom openly endorse an ideal of a cohesive community with shared norms, values, and ends, liberals start from the premise of diverse ends, plural values, and the fact of multiple—possibly even incommensurable—conceptions of the good.[2] From seventeenth-century doctrines of religious toleration onward, liberalism has been conceived of as a political theory uniquely capable of securing tolerance and respect for people's differences.[3] Most contemporary contractarian liberals, especially since the 1971 publication of John Rawls's *A Theory of Justice*, claim that a liberal account of justice uniquely permits citizens of diverse beliefs and backgrounds to form, revise, and pursue their own conceptions of the good. Nonetheless, as I shall argue, liberal approaches to issues raised by social and cultural diversity are lacking in numerous respects.

Liberal theories and institutions confront an ever-increasing array of demands from ethnic and cultural minorities for respect and recognition. As is by now evident, the problem of how to respond to

1. Charles Taylor, "The Politics of Recognition," in *Multiculturalism: Examining the Politics of Recognition*, ed. Amy Gutmann (Princeton, N.J.: Princeton University Press, 1994).

2. The extent to which liberalism is, *au fond*, committed to pluralism is a contested issue. Isaiah Berlin has argued that both liberalism and pluralism reject monism in questions of value. See Berlin, *The Crooked Timber of Humanity*, ed. H. Hardy (London: John Murry, 1990), and also his "Does Political Theory Still Exist?" in *Concepts and Categories*, ed. H. Hardy (London: Hogarth Press, 1978), esp. 153–54. For a succinct restatement of this position—and an argument for why value pluralism is not the same thing as moral relativism—see Berlin and Bernard Williams, "Pluralism and Liberalism: A Reply," *Political Studies* 42 (1994): 306–9. A minority view suggests that value pluralism and liberalism are not natural allies, on the grounds that liberals are ultimately committed to determinate liberal values and ideals whereas pluralists can have no such commitments. This is John Kekes's argument in "The Incompatibility of Liberalism and Pluralism," *American Philosophical Quarterly* 29, no. 2 (1992): 141–51, and in *The Morality of Pluralism* (Princeton, N.J.: Princeton University Press, 1993).

3. Most early liberals restricted the scope of tolerance considerably, just as they advocated selective citizenship. Locke, for instance, drew in part on theistic beliefs and prudential arguments that precluded extending tolerance to Catholics and atheists. Pierre Bayle, who argued in favor of extending tolerance even to atheists, was the notable exception. See the discussion in James Tully's Introduction to John Locke, *A Letter Concerning Toleration* (1689), ed. Tully (Indianapolis: Hackett, 1983), 8. I take up the limitations of tolerance below, in chapter 2.

these claims has come to preoccupy leading political theorists.[4] Long
accustomed to taking for granted the compatibility of pluralism and
liberalism, liberal political philosophers now face allegations that liberal justice and liberal democratic citizenship, far from delivering
color- and gender-blind justice, do not treat women and members of
ethnic and cultural minorities as equal citizens.[5] The bulk of these
criticisms emphasize liberalism's inattention to social and cultural
particularity—and citizens' constitutive attachments—and its alleged
failure to secure justice for certain groups. To a limited extent, recent
criticisms of liberalism's neglect of cultural identity, and membership
in particular, echo earlier, communitarian and neo-Aristotelian challenges to liberal theory.[6] Where such thinkers as Alasdair MacIntyre,
Michael Sandel, and Charles Taylor criticized contemporary liberals
for neglecting in moral and political theory the significance of identity, community, and notions of human flourishing, today some theorists concerned about the marginalization of cultural and ethnic minorities doubt whether liberal thought can fully appreciate the
importance of cultural identity and membership to citizens' conceptions of the good and to political life.

As a consequence of these practical and conceptual challenges, liberal theorists in particular find themselves at a critical crossroads.
They may continue to affirm individual rights and culture-blind forms
of justice—thereby rejecting many claims by cultural groups—and
hope that cultural conflicts recede. Alternatively, they may acknowledge the political salience and legitimacy of some cultural claims
for recognition and seek ways to meet minority groups' demands for
greater inclusion in existing political institutions and their calls for
forms of community autonomy. One thing is certain: whichever route
is taken—the rejection of cultural group claims or their recognition—neither liberal theory nor liberal democratic institutions will
emerge unchanged.

4. Some key examples include Gutmann, ed., *Multiculturalism: Examining the Politics of
Recognition*; Will Kymlicka, *Liberalism, Community, and Culture*, and *Multicultural Citizenship*;
Joseph Raz, *Ethics in the Public Domain*; James Tully, *Strange Multiplicity: Constitutionalism in
an Age of Diversity* (Cambridge: Cambridge University Press, 1995); and Iris Marion Young,
Justice and the Politics of Difference (Princeton, N.J.: Princeton University Press, 1990).

5. Some prominent feminist critiques of liberalism's neglect of substantive justice
and equality for women include Susan Moller Okin, *Justice, Gender, and the Family* (New
York: Basic Books, 1989); and Carole Pateman, *The Sexual Contract* (Stanford, Calif.: Stanford University Press, 1988).

6. Michael Sandel, *Liberalism and the Limits of Justice* (Cambridge: Cambridge University Press, 1982); and Alasdair MacIntyre, *After Virtue* (Notre Dame, Ind.: University of Notre Dame Press, 1981), and *Whose Justice? Which Rationality?* (Notre Dame, Ind.: University
of Notre Dame Press, 1988).

The Political Context of Cultural Minority Claims

Though this book focuses on the conceptual difficulties and strengths of different approaches within liberal and democratic theories to dilemmas of cultural difference, no such discussion can take place in a theoretical vacuum. The claims of diverse minority groups in liberal democratic states (such as aboriginal peoples, Québécois, Scots, and Basques, as well as comparatively recent immigrant communities such as South Asian Muslims in Britain) are set within an international context of struggles for group recognition and self-determination, some peaceful, many not. Although I limit my discussion to groups in liberal states, it is worth noting that these are not wholly untouched by movements for national self-determination and ethnic and religious secession in nondemocratic or semidemocratic states.

To begin to understand why cultural diversity has come to pose such pointed challenges to contemporary liberal and democratic thought, we must look at the changing character of the modern nation-state. Until recently, political theorists have tended to assume—often counterfactually—that there exists or should exist a direct coincidence of national identity and citizenship (and statehood). This relationship finds its expression in the model of the nation-state. Although the nation-state has never been the sole or even the predominant model of statehood in modern Europe,[7] it is no longer a tenable design for contemporary, socially plural democracies. The politicization of social and cultural cleavages in democratic states has been accompanied by threats to national unity in the form of claims for regional autonomy and, in some cases, even secession.[8] The culmination of these developments is spoken of within political studies as the "crisis of the nation-state."[9]

---

7. Of contemporary European states, only Portugal, Poland, and Germany can be called nation-states (the latter two in part by genocide and assimilation). Greece purports to be a nation-state, but can qualify only by denying its sizable Macedonian minority. Nor has the nation-state been dominant elsewhere; for instance, the Ottoman millet system, which lasted for nearly five centuries until the collapse of the Ottoman Empire in World War I, gave functional community autonomy to Greek Orthodox and Armenian Orthodox peoples and the Jews; internal ethnic and linguistic differences within these communities were recognized by the establishment of smaller units. For an overview, see Will Kymlicka, "Two Models of Pluralism and Tolerance," *Analyse & Kritik* 13 (1992): 33–56.

8. Throughout the book, I use the term "democratic states" to denote states that guarantee liberal individual rights and freedoms—i.e., including, but not limited to, basic civic and political rights—and whose representative institutions feature a well-developed multi-party system. I focus primarily on the liberal democracies of Canada, the United States, Australia, and Europe but exclude other democracies, notably India and South Africa. I recognize, moreover, that other political systems may have democratic features and that a multi-party political format is neither a guarantee of a democratic political culture nor necessarily appropriate for all societies.

9. See articles by Istvan Hont, Neil MacCormick, James Tully, and others in a special

Current challenges to the sovereignty and legitimacy of existing liberal states by cultural and ethnic minorities derive from a number of sources. In Canada, aboriginal peoples—Inuit groups in the former Northwest Territories, First Nations peoples in the rest of Canada—have called repeatedly for constitutional recognition and forms of self-government, citing the injustice of colonization and the incompatibility of traditional native values with the norms and institutions of the Canadian state.[10] The imperial yoke of English-speaking Canada and the distinctness of Québec society are pointed to by the separatist political party, the Parti Québécois, whose ongoing bid for secession has not yet met with success. Nonetheless, nationalist sentiments continue to run high in Québec, and federalism is far from flourishing. The ongoing conflict between Loyalists and Republicans in Northern Ireland is nominally religious in its origin, but the cultural identities of Northern Irish Catholic and Protestant communities are also manifestly political and as such require a political solution. The most important negotiated political solution of recent years, the Northern Irish peace accord of 1998, may yet bring a permanent end to the violence in this beleaguered state (it is still too soon to tell), but it is unlikely to diminish the acrimonious relations between Loyalists and proponents of Irish nationalism anytime soon. The recent successful Scottish referendum on the issue of devolution of power may hold out an example for Irish nationalists in particular.

Nor do struggles by European communities asserting their linguistic and ethnic identities show any sign of waning, despite the creation of the European Union with its goals of economic integration, coordination of social policies, and political cooperation. The European Union is certainly changing the face of citizenship for European nationals, though not by any means strictly in the direction of pan-European unity. The transference of what were once exclusively matters of national concern and jurisdiction to the broader EU structure has far-reaching implications for national and regional identities, state autonomy in economic and social affairs, and even broader questions of sovereignty. Indeed, the European Union promises to alter the relationship between nationality, statehood, and political sovereignty in fundamental ways, as noted by Neil MacCormick:

---

issue of *Political Studies* 44 (1996), edited by John Dunn, titled "Constitutionalism and the Crisis of the Nation-State."

10. In the Canadian context, the terms "native," "aboriginal," "First Nations peoples" and "Native Indian" are often used interchangeably. Of these, only the term "aboriginal" also includes Inuit peoples.

In the traditional legal sense of "sovereignty", member states of the European Union no longer constitute legally sovereign entities. Nor does the Union, nor its internal pillar the Community, constitute a sovereign entity. The distribution of sovereignty rights at various levels of course leaves a compendious "external sovereignty" of all the member states intact and even in a sense strengthened.

Politically, the same goes. Political sovereignty cannot be ascribed to the Union as a political association of member states, nor to that part of it, the Community, which does constitute a distinct legal order. But the constraints of economic co-operation, even short of economic and monetary union, of maintaining a common market, and of observing even to an imperfect extent the obligations of a common body of law, also deprive member states of that full freedom of action which was traditionally taken to be the hallmark of politically sovereign states.

On this view, we confront in Western Europe now a politics "beyond the sovereign state." Old conceptions of state sovereignty and of the absolutism of the nation state are now radically challengeable.[11]

Whether EU states will welcome the cultural, ethnic, and linguistic differences of other member states remains to be seen. Although the EU nominally affirms the differences reflected in the national cultures of the individual member states—and accepts the implications of such differences for social and, to a more limited extent, economic policies—it has done little to formally affirm or support minority cultures within these states. The ambivalence of the EU agencies regarding the claims of Bretons, Basques, Alsatians, and the Catalán should come as no surprise in the light of the stated aims of economic and social integration and broad political cooperation. Nationalist groups that invoke parochial ethnic and linguistic identities are clearly no natural ally to the EU, for they frequently challenge the sovereignty of their "host" states and reject incorporation into pan-European structures on this ground. Nor are such regional minorities likely to find the European Union an effective political body within which to express their claims, for the voices and concerns of the political leadership of dissenting member states are more likely to be heard. But both interstate disputes and intrastate cultural conflicts pose important challenges to the success and legitimacy of the EU as a whole. Regional struggles by internal ethnic or linguistic minorities may pose a less dramatic threat than serious disagreements between member states, but they serve as a for-

11. Neil MacCormick, "Liberalism, Nationalism, and the Post-sovereign State," *Political Studies* 44 (1996): 561–62.

midable reminder that democratic, individual rights and universal citizenship—even the pluralistic citizenship of a common European Union—are not a panacea for social and cultural conflicts.

The most important contemporary solution proposed for deep cultural cleavages in European states (in the period prior to the advent of the EU) is that of consociationalism, a form of power-sharing between two or possibly among three major cultural or linguistic groups within a state.[12] Variants of this model have been adopted in several European states: consociational regimes in Austria, the Netherlands, Switzerland, and Belgium have enjoyed limited success. It is unclear, however, just how EU structures will affect the internal political arrangements of democratic states that feature consociational regimes. More generally, consociationalism is only suitable for certain kinds of societies—namely, those with only two ethnic or linguistic groups—and there is evidence that it may tend to reinforce cultural and linguistic cleavages in politically and socially disadvantageous ways.

The defining feature of nation-states is the way in which they link citizenship to membership in the dominant national or ethnic group. Today, few democratic states consider nationality or ethnicity as the primary basis for citizenship. In purely pragmatic terms, large, pluralistic states with permeable boundaries can maintain nationality as the criterion for citizenship only with great difficulty. Moreover, states that *do* insist on ethnicity or nationality as a condition of citizenship face much international and domestic criticism for the precarious status that they accord to non-nationals within their borders. Germany and Greece are two of the last remaining examples of liberal democratic states that impose a requirement of nationality (traceable through the bloodline) for acquiring citizenship, and they are widely criticized for using this to deny full citizenship rights to immigrants, refugees, and migrant workers.

Democratic states that do not link citizenship to ethnicity or nationality are still sometimes accused of failing to meet the justice claims of national and cultural minorities. States that embrace an explicitly political or civic conception of citizenship, as do France and the Netherlands, often ignore the specific political demands of their cultural and ethnic minorities in part because they perceive these claims as a threat to a culture-blind conception of universal citizenship and to national unity

12. Arend Lijphart lists as the four main features of consociational democracy: "government by a grand coalition of the political leaders of all significant segments of the plural society"; "mutual veto or 'concurrent majority' rule" to protect minority interests; proportionality in political representation; and considerable autonomy for each segment. See his *Democracy in Plural Societies* (New Haven: Yale University Press, 1977), 25.

more generally. It is not surprising that such states typically eschew multicultural policies altogether and choose instead to pursue a strategy of assimilation. For instance, modern France, which embodies the idea of the "civic" nation, notably requires immigrants to abdicate their own nationality and, to a certain extent, their own culture as a condition of full French citizenship.[13]

It is instructive that against this uneven background of state strategies for addressing citizens' national, ethnic, and cultural differences, concern for safeguarding the rights of national and ethnic minorities in international law has increased steadily since World War II. International treaties and covenants that address the question of protections for minorities—although not reflecting a single, specific liberal doctrine—incorporate such ideals as tolerance, freedom of conscience, freedom of association, and respect for dignity and human rights. Moreover, such agreements (whose effectiveness is a matter of much debate) have moved gradually in the direction of endorsing not merely negative rights but also positive rights for minorities. This is not to say that earlier agreements did not make strides toward positive rights and protections for minorities. The Paris Peace Conference Treatises created by the League of Nations in the immediate post-World War II period specified numerous positive rights for the protection of national minorities in Europe; but these treatises, which mainly bound defeated states, also incorporated unrealistic enforcement procedures. For this and other reasons, they soon collapsed.[14] Subsequent agreements were not so ambitious and dropped the language of positive rights: the 1950 European Convention for the Protection of Human Rights and Fundamental Freedoms, for instance, reverted to requiring more conventional liberties for minorities, stating only (in article 9) that such persons are entitled to freedom of thought, conscience, and religion.

The much more recent shift toward far-reaching and positive protections for minority populations in international law incorporates some of

13. As Catherine Audard notes, ethnic and racial minorities in France typically do not enjoy the full benefits of citizenship even once they become French nationals. However, Audard's view, with which I do not wholly agree, is that neutrality or *laïcité* is not in itself the wrong strategy for mediating cultural conflicts in democratic societies, but that rather "it is when the process of assimilation is forced upon the people without the compensation of full citizenship that things go wrong." See Catherine Audard, "Political Liberalism, Secular Republicanism: Two Answers to the Challenges of Pluralism," in *Philosophy and Pluralism*, Royal Institute of Philosophy, suppl. 40, ed. David Archard (Cambridge: Cambridge University Press, 1996), p. 167.

14. For a comprehensive account of these events, see Jay A. Sigler, "Defining the Majority," in *Minority Rights: A Comparative Analysis*, ed. Sigler (Westport, Conn.: Greenwood Press, 1983).

the protections that the earlier Paris Treaty sought to secure. To appreciate the significance of these changes, it is useful to compare the wording of the relevant section of the United Nations Covenant on Civil and Political Rights (1966)—still the main international legislation dealing with the issue of national and cultural minorities—with a more recent UN effort. Article 27 of the 1966 Covenant states:

> In those states in which ethnic, religious, or linguistic minorities exist, persons belonging to such minorities shall not be denied the right, in community with other members of their group, to enjoy their own culture, to profess and practise their own religion, or to use their own language.

By contrast, the 1992 United Nations Declaration on the Rights of Persons Belonging to National or Ethnic, Religious or Linguistic Minorities emphasizes the benefits of protecting rights of individual members of minorities, stating that "the promotion and protection of the rights of persons belonging to national or ethnic, religious and linguistic minorities contributes to the political and social stability of states in which they live." A more notable change is that this document recognizes the importance of preserving group identities and ways of life. Article 2 of the 1992 Declaration states:

> States shall protect the existence of the national or ethnic, cultural, religious and linguistic identity of minorities, within their respective territories, and *shall encourage conditions for the promotion of their identity.* (Emphasis added.)

The stronger language of the 1992 Declaration, although cause for optimism in some quarters, must be interpreted in the light of the fact that it incorporates (or at least does not counteract) a problematic feature of the 1966 Covenant. Simply put, this latter document is ineffectual if states deny the very existence of their national minorities, as exemplified by Turkey's denial of its Kurdish minority. Nor do the 1966 and 1992 documents address instances in which states admit the existence of national minorities but deny that these groups seek to maintain their distinct identities and cultures.

Even if the discrepancy between accounts by states of the status of national minorities and the actual claims of these latter communities could be resolved—say, by requiring independent reporting on national minorities—the problem of how to secure justice for other ethnic groups, especially for recent immigrants and refugees, remains. Significantly, the UN definition of cultural minorities, as political scientist Jay Sigler notes, effectively excludes "aliens from its coverage by its limitation to 'nationals of the state.' Thus guest workers, refugees, and immigrants, in general, are not covered."[15] Although the claims of temporary workers and refugees are different in kind and degree from those of national minorities, it is worrying that these groups are assumed to have forfeited the protection of their culture, language, or ways of life on entering the "host" country. The deterioration of race relations in contemporary France in the wake of immigration from former African colonies illustrates the social instability and racial ghettoization that can result from a state's refusal to permit those immigrants and refugees who so wish to maintain their cultural identities. By contrast, when the initiatives of recent immigrants and refugees to develop and maintain their distinct identities and certain ways of life have been met with supportive state policies, these groups have generally had a smoother transition to life in their new countries. Following the adoption in 1988 of the Canadian Multiculturalism Act, for instance, not only did immigrants receive greater recognition and financial support from the state, but even refugee groups such as Tamils and Ethiopians were able to set up cultural services and programs to provide critical support for recent arrivals and help foster a greater sense of community.

Precisely why some democratic states prefer not to devise arrangements that could help protect the cultural identities and ways of life of their minority communities is a complex matter. States frequently have political and economic interests that prevent them from acknowledging national and cultural minorities, as well as from meeting their claims for cultural rights and special constitutional provisions. A detailed examination of the specific policies and political ideologies of different liberal democratic states is not possible here. What is important for present purposes is that we bear in mind the discrepancies between what states or international laws *actually* recognize (i.e., choose to recognize) as legitimate claims by minority groups and what cultural groups and political theorists think *ought* to be recognized as morally legitimate claims.

Perhaps the most significant discrepancy between normative analyses by legal and political scholars and the actual policies of many demo-

---

15. The UN definition of minorities, as Sigler notes, was drawn up by the Special Rapporteur of the UN Sub-Commission on Prevention of Discrimination and Protection of Minorities; it states that minorities are groups "numerically inferior to the rest of the population of a state, in a non-dominant position, whose members—being nationals of the state—possess ethnic, religious or linguistic characteristics differing from those of the rest of the population and show if only implicitly a sense of solidarity, directed towards preserving their culture, traditions, religion, or language." Ibid., 4.

cratic states concerns the issue of negative versus positive rights for cultural minorities. Whereas negative rights merely protect minorities
from discrimination, positive rights help secure access to protections
and resources they need in order to flourish. For numerous reasons,
many states are clearly reluctant to accord minority groups positive
rights. By contrast, the conclusion that negative rights do not supply
sufficient protection for cultural groups marked an important turning
point for political scientists, international lawyers, and human rights activists addressing these issues in the 1970s and 1980s. Interestingly, the
same insight has taken much longer to make an appearance in conceptual discussions within political theory of justice for cultural minorities:
only since the late 1980s have substantive arguments for and against
positive social and cultural rights for ethnic minorities come to the fore
of liberal theory, probably starting with Will Kymlicka's 1989 argument
that liberal justice requires positive protections for minority cultural
membership.[16]

Prior to publication of Kymlicka's *Liberalism, Community, and Culture,*
many legal scholars and political scientists had come to the conclusion
that merely negative rights were ultimately ineffective in securing adequate justice for national and cultural minorities. Nearly fifteen years
ago, positive rights—that is, social, cultural and economic rights—were
widely endorsed by numerous scholars of law and political science. Nor
did they deny that positive rights express a determinate normative view.
As Sigler notes:

> Minority rights imply more than nondiscrimination. It is insufficient to
> say that the government does not make distinctions based upon race,
> religion, language, or ethnicity. Minority rights begin with nondiscrimi-
> nation, but they must extend to protective activities and promotional
> activities.[17]

Just what protections for minority groups democratic states should
provide and whether these should be understood in terms of negative
or positive rights or both are matters to which I return in subsequent
chapters. For now, however, I seek only to note that the trend in international law (and in some areas of political science) is toward recognizing not only negative rights—basic protections against persecution and
cultural annihilation—but also positive rights that enable individual
members of cultural minorities to maintain their identities and ways of

16. Kymlicka, *Liberalism, Community, and Culture.*
17. Sigler, "The Future of Minority Rights," in *Minority Rights,* 199.

life, as well as to have a greater political voice in the states in which they live.

Liberal Theory and Political Practice

The relationship between normative discussions of cultural pluralism in political theory and the actual policies of democratic states (and international law) is not a direct one. As noted above, contemporary discussions of *cultural pluralism*—as opposed to moral and value pluralism— emerged not in political philosophy, but in legal theory and formal political science. Studies of different varieties and forms of pluralism by such writers as Arend Lijphart and Robert Dahl were among the first and most influential works in this area.[18] Although these authors tended to neglect the broader, normative implications of social diversity, especially its relevance to theories of justice, they supplied critical and timely discussions of actual and possible political models for dealing with conflicts between ethnic groups.

Studies by Lijphart, Dahl, and others are rarely taken up in current writing on cultural diversity by political theorists and political philosophers. This is regrettable, for discussion of different types of plural democratic societies and the formal political models developed to deal with these could lend a much-needed practical focus to political theorizing on cultural diversity. For instance, Lijphart usefully distinguishes between different kinds and levels of pluralism: societies that are relatively homogeneous in religious and linguistic terms may nonetheless be described with respect to their constitutional structure as either nonplural (e.g., Denmark and Iceland), semiplural (France), or plural (Austria and Israel). Similarly, religiously or linguistically heterogeneous societies may be described as nonplural in their constitutional arrangements (Australia), semiplural (Canada), or fully plural (Belgium and the Netherlands).[19] Lijpart also enumerates several possible state

18. Robert Dahl, *Democracy, Liberty, and Equality* (Oslo: Norwegian University Press, 1986); Arend Lijphart, *Democracy in Plural Societies* and *Democracies: Patterns of Majoritarian and Consensus Government in Twenty-One Countries* (New Haven: Yale University Press, 1984).

19. Lijphart, *Democracies*, 43. Some of Lijphart's categorizations seem out of date and frankly implausible: for instance, he considers Britain nonplural in structure, despite the existence of a Scottish legal structure and educational system. Moreover, he views the United States as semiplural, despite its clearly assimilationist constitutional framework; indeed, in studies of comparative constitutionalism, the U.S. model has been referred to as "assimilative secularism." See the discussion by Gary J. Jacobsohn, "Three Models of Secular Constitutional Development: India, Israel, and the United States," *Studies in American Political Development* 10, no. 1 (1996): 1–68.

responses to ethnic and cultural diversity—such as federalism, consociationalism, state partition, and assimilation—and reminds us that the type and degree of pluralism in a society to a large extent determines the possible and appropriate solutions. The success of consociationalism as a possible strategy for mediating the effects of certain conflictual forms of pluralism depends very much on what kind of cleavages—"religious, ideological, linguistic, regional, cultural, racial, or ethnic"—a particular state encompasses.[20]

Contra the tendency in much political theory of the 1990s to conflate distinct types of social diversity, I suggest that there are good reasons to distinguish varying forms and sources of social and cultural difference. Quite simply, these differences give rise to a wide range of justice claims with varying degrees of legitimacy. In particular, it is important not to collapse diverse claims by national, cultural, and ethnic minority groups: demands by national minorities for sovereignty should be distinguished, for instance, from those of certain recent ethnic immigrant groups for greater inclusion in the liberal democratic state. It matters a great deal what kinds of states and what types and degrees of diversity one has in mind when discussing possible approaches to cultural pluralism. Too often, contemporary political theorists fail to specify the particular type of diversity they mean to address: whether their concern is with moral and ethical diversity in a general sense or with cultural difference; and if the latter, whether they intend their discussion to address dispersed minorities, such as recent immigrants, or territorially concentrated groups, such as national minorities and long-standing communities.[21]

Failure to specify the particular form of social or cultural difference in question may lead to situations in which political theorists debate the merit and justice of political proposals while assuming quite disparate kinds of social differences. For instance, the default subject of many European and Canadian discussions of diversity and pluralism is that of national (including ethnic, cultural, and linguistic) minorities, usually concentrated in a particular region. These discussions consider the merits of such arrangements as federalism, secession, consociationalism, devolution of power, structures of economic and political unification, and pan-cultural models of citizenship (e.g. pan-European citizenship). By contrast, American political theorists (and legislators) have

---

20. Lijphart, *Democracy in Plural Societies*, 3–4.

21. An example of the tendency to elide diverse types of social, ethical, and cultural differences is to be found in William Connolly's *Identity\Difference: Democratic Negotiations of Political Paradox* (Ithaca, N.Y.: Cornell University Press, 1991).

tended *not* to focus on national and regional minorities such as those found in many European states and instead address the claims of territorially *dispersed* racial and ethnic minorities. American thinkers are particularly concerned with the claims of minority groups living in the United States, such as African Americans, Latinos, and Asian Americans; they also ask how institutions and procedures within existing (U.S.) constitutional arrangements might be made more just in the face of citizens' moral, religious, and ethnic differences.[22]

The specific type of diversity one sets out to address thus matters very much to discussions of cultural pluralism. Both the constitutional approach, typified by many European, Indian, South African, Australian, and Canadian discussions of cultural and ethnic minorities, and the more diffuse emphasis on "difference" and the "politics of difference" or "diversity" by some U.S. writers (such as Iris Young and William Connolly) are nonetheless instructive in different ways.

It is essential to bear in mind the practical political contexts within which theoretical discussions about citizens' differences and debates about the legitimacy and feasibility of group claims and collective rights take place. Which cultural claims can be recognized and which differences accommodated—and how this can be done—will depend very much on the concrete interests, capacities, and limitations of a particular modern state and its political leadership.[23] Globalization renders these issues still more complex: Will increasingly permeable state boundaries change the very character of democratic citizenship, as is happening in Europe with the growth of the European Union? Should

22. An instructive contrast is found in the different discussions of diversity and identity in works by leading U.S. and European democratic theorists. In her influential book *Justice and the Politics of Difference* the American philosopher Iris Young deals almost exclusively with questions of political inclusion and exclusion in liberal democratic political institutions as these pertain to territorially dispersed social and cultural minorities. By contrast, in his "Citizenship and National Identity: Some Reflections on the Future of Europe" (*Praxis International* 12, no. 1 [1992]: 1–19), Jürgen Habermas argues for a pan-European political conception of citizenship, one divorced from specific national identities. Clearly, these writers have in mind very different sorts of societies as the basis for their proposals: Habermas is thinking of Western Europe and mentions Germany most frequently, whereas Young has in mind the socially and politically marginalized minorities in contemporary U.S. politics, such as African Americans, Latinos, and women. I offer a critical assessment of aspects of both Young's and Habermas's views in chapter 5.

23. The tendency of political theorists to neglect the practical constraints on modern states when proposing different social and political arrangements is an important theme in the work of John Dunn. Dunn has written extensively on the failures of exercises in "ideal" political philosophy that do not recognize practical, real-world interests and "political causality." See, for example, his "The Future of Political Philosophy in the West," in *Rethinking Modern Political Theory: Essays, 1979–1983* (Cambridge: Cambridge University Press, 1985).

democratic states be looking to regional and international law for direction when devising their own internal policies regarding cultural and ethnic minorities, or indeed, should these international agreements replace them? Too often it is the very lack of attention to concrete political claims, developments, and practical restrictions that lead some political theorists to suggest ineffectual and even implausible ways of arranging our political affairs.

Some Limitations of Liberal Thinking on Difference

Despite the way in which early writers conceived of liberalism as a doctrine uniquely able to contain (or at least deflect) social and religious conflicts, many liberal theories are ill-equipped to respond to demands for cultural recognition and group rights.[24] Liberal scholars who reject suggestions that it is within the proper purview of the state to provide resources which will help citizens flourish have difficulty conceiving of positive, "cultural" rights as legitimate and indeed integral to liberal justice. But even liberals who are not specifically hostile to perfectionist concerns face at least three limitations when addressing issues of cultural identity, cultural membership, and diversity—limitations that derive from conceptual difficulties and blind spots within liberal theory.

First, liberals since John Stuart Mill have tended to conceive of pluralism in terms of the diversity of *individual* preferences, opinions, moral views, and beliefs, rather than *collective* social and cultural identities and belief systems. In contemporary liberal thought, the bias toward individual forms of difference is reinforced by the use of the term "value pluralism," which often connotes individual moral and ethical differences. Although many liberals recognize that individuals' values and beliefs emerge from determinate social and cultural backgrounds, discussions within liberal moral and political philosophy about value pluralism and ethical diversity rarely emphasize these broader social contexts. The habit of treating issues of diversity and pluralism in terms of individual differences in belief has made it easier for some liberals to overlook the significance of collective identities and group differences.

Second, the emphasis that contractarian liberal theorists (including recent political liberals) place on *individual rights and freedoms*—and on

---

24. With the partial exception of deliberative democracy—which has its origins in Habermas's discourse ethics—the approaches I examine in this book are easily classified as liberal theories. The variant of deliberative democracy for which I argue is, I believe, still within the reach of liberalism.

the individual as the locus of moral agency and consent—has made it difficult for them to appreciate the importance or even the feasibility of collective protections and entitlements. Because demands for *group rights* lie at the heart of many current struggles for cultural recognition, the liberal focus on individual freedoms and entitlements may prevent some liberal thinkers from conceding the legitimacy of certain collective rights claims.

Third, most liberal theories distinguish too sharply between the public and political realms, on the one hand, and social and private realms, on the other.[25] Although liberal thinkers themselves are not unaware of citizens' diverse situations and conflicting loyalties, many conceive of citizens' public identities as wholly independent of their social and cultural identities. Because it is these features of persons and groups—namely, ethnic, religious, and cultural identity, membership, and language—that constitute the foundation of many collective claims for cultural recognition, it is no surprise that liberal theories which view the political and social realms as wholly separate should fail to recognize the importance of citizens' cultural identities. Individualist forms of liberalism, which stress the rights and responsibilities owing to individual agents, have particular difficulty conceding that citizens' social identities and memberships may also form the basis of *legitimate* political claims. Indeed, as I shall argue in coming chapters, it is only by fundamentally reconceiving the boundary between public and private life that liberals can come to appreciate the intimate relationship between these realms.

Perhaps in response to these difficulties, some liberal thinkers have recently attempted to rethink key liberal categories and commitments by acknowledging the political significance of cultural identity and membership. These writers have turned their attention to the issues of group identity and group justice claims, and they have even attempted to develop liberal justifications of collective cultural rights.[26] Some such proposals can be argued from modified liberal premises, for instance, by expanding the liberal idea of the social bases of self-respect. These efforts notwithstanding, few would deny that there exist numerous tensions between the liberal emphasis on individual rights and liberties, on

25. John Rawls, for instance, draws a sharp distinction between the public/political and social/private spheres in both *A Theory of Justice* (Cambridge, Mass.: Harvard University Press, 1971) and *Political Liberalism*. I take up this feature of Rawls's work at length in chapters 2 and 3, below.

26. I have in mind here Raz, *Ethics in the Public Domain*, and Kymlicka, *Liberalism, Community, and Culture* and *Multicultural Citizenship*. See also Kymlicka's "The Rights of Minority Cultures: Reply to Kukathas," *Political Theory* 20, no. 1 (1992): 140–46.

the one hand, and collective, cultural rights and claims for group self-determination, on the other.[27]

Whether liberal theory can be successfully reformulated so as to recognize the full political importance of cultural identities and membership remains to be seen. However, in response to these and other limitations of liberal thinking on questions of social difference, I suggest liberals will need to make at least three broad conceptual shifts if they are to contribute usefully to discussions of cultural pluralism.[28]

Reconceiving Diversity

The first and broadest of these changes is the need to shift from conceiving of diversity in terms of the interests, capacities, and beliefs of *individuals* to viewing certain politically important differences as socially constituted and collective in form. In Mill's day, it made sense to discuss diversity in terms of respect for individual differences in thought and belief. Government abuse of authority and the specter of the tyranny of the majority over the minority help to explain nineteenth-century pleas by Mill and others for respect for individuality. In our own time, however, some of the most politically important differences—those most in need of recognition—are those that distinguish ethnic, religious, racial, and cultural communities. Some citizens demand not so much an end to their mistreatment as individuals

27. Many liberals remain unsympathetic to the idea of developing special rights and arrangements for cultural minorities. Some still reject the idea that cultural identity and membership are relevant to political morality and political principles. See, for instance, Jeremy Waldron, "Minority Cultures and the Cosmopolitan Alternative," *University of Michigan Journal of Law Reform* 25, nos. 3–4 (1992): 751–93, and Waldron, "Legislation and Moral Neutrality" and "Particular Values and Critical Morality," both in *Liberal Rights: Collected Papers, 1981–1991*, ed. Jeremy Waldron (Cambridge: Cambridge University Press, 1993). Similarly, Chandran Kukathas rejects cultural rights in favor of an uncompromising individual rights-based liberalism: "People from particular religious or cultural or intellectual or moral backgrounds should have every right and the freedom to speak or to play a role in public affairs. But they enjoy these rights and freedoms as individual citizens, rather than as members or representatives of particular groups"; that is, "there is no call for any particular cultural community to be given explicit recognition and to play a special role in public affairs; nor is there a call for all cultural communities to be granted explicit recognition." See Kukathas, "The Idea of a Multicultural Society," in *Multicultural Citizens: The Philosophy and Politics of Identity*, ed. C. Kukathas (St. Leonards, Australia: Centre for Independent Studies, 1993), 28–29. Kukathas's liberal position against cultural group rights is also made clear in "Are There Any Cultural Rights?" *Political Theory* 20, no. 1 (1992): 105–39.

28. I do not intend for these proposed shifts to correspond precisely to the limitations noted above.

as respect for and recognition of their collective identities and ways of life.

From Moral to Cultural Pluralism

Second, to appreciate the importance of cultural claims for recognition, liberal theorists need to shift from thinking about pluralism merely in terms of the diversity of citizens' *views, preferences, and beliefs* and recognize that these represent only some of citizens' salient differences. Discussions of *value pluralism* and *moral pluralism* do not exhaust all the important features of social and cultural diversity. Whether moral pluralism is construed in terms of contrasting ethical attitudes and principles—as by certain Kantians—or as a matter of diverse preferences (or ranking of preferences) and beliefs—as by some liberals and all consequentialists—this notion cannot help us to grasp all or even most of citizens' important differences. The reduction of issues of cultural diversity to conflicts among individuals' views and preferences leads political theorists to overlook a range of important social differences that fall outside these descriptions. Variations in conceptions of value, in social and domestic arrangements, and in material and cultural practices are ill-captured under the heading of divergent preferences and beliefs. Even the notion of "diverse conceptions of the good" fails to grasp all that is at stake in debates about cultural diversity.

Equally impoverished are attempts by consequentialists (such as utilitarians and social/rational choice theorists) to cast discussions about social diversity strictly in terms of conflicting interests and to suggest that interest-group pluralism is a satisfactory response to issues raised by cultural diversity. To shift from thinking about social diversity in terms of individuals' divergent moral beliefs, preferences, and interests, political theorists need to acknowledge that it is often people's broader cultural contexts that shape and constitute these and other kinds of salient differences and also form the basis of many justice claims.

Recognizing the Value of Diversity

Finally, if political theorists are to offer proposals for meeting cultural minorities' claims for respect and recognition, they will need to shift from thinking about diversity strictly as a problem to be mediated or contained and come to recognize that we also have reasons to *value* existing forms of social and cultural diversity in democratic states. They do not have to agree on what all of these reasons are but must minimally acknowledge that citizens' social and cultural differences, in addition to posing numerous practical dilemmas, may also contribute positively to social and political life. Beyond the importance of cultural identity and membership to citizens' self-respect, dignity, and well-being (which of course cannot provide reasons for valuing diversity per se), the existence of a plurality of cultures may enrich democratic societies in numerous ways. Exposure to different normative frameworks and conceptions of value may help individuals think more reflexively about their views and life plans. Educating children both in their own cultural traditions and in the ways of minority cultures (especially those within their societies) may help broaden their horizons and knowledge of possibilities.[29] A context of social and cultural diversity may make individuals and groups more aware, and possibly even critical, of their own belief systems and social practices—and therefore more tolerant of others.

There are also potential political benefits to cultural diversity: the presence of citizens of diverse social and cultural backgrounds brings different moral perspectives into political life and may enhance debate and decision-making in the context of deliberative, democratic arrangements.[30] Finally, there is also a strong argument to be made for the idea that a constitutional democracy made up of different cultural communities is greater than the sum of its parts, enriched by the traditions, moral insights, and civic practices that diverse cultural groups may bring to the "constitutional association."[31]

These three shifts—reconceiving diversity in terms of collective, not individual, differences; looking beyond the issue of moral pluralism to the broader cultural character and sources of diversity; and coming to appreciate the positive value of citizens' cultural differences—are closely related to the requirements of an adequate conception of respect for cultural pluralism, to which I now turn.

---

29. This Millian argument is also made by C. L. Ten, "Multiculturalism and the Value of Diversity," in *Multicultural Citizens: The Philosophy and Politics of Identity*, ed. Chandran Kukathas (St. Leonards, Australia: Centre for Independent Studies, 1993), 7. Yael Tamir similarly argues that one of the ways in which "individuals can benefit from cultural plurality" is that cultural diversity "ensures that reflections about one's own culture take place within a genuine context, one offering models for imitation and even options for assimilation." See Tamir, *Liberal Nationalism* (Princeton, N.J.: Princeton University Press, 1993), 30.

30. An analogous argument is made by Amélie Oksenberg Rorty (though with reference to the value of ethical diversity rather than cultural diversity), who suggests that "decision-making bodies need representatives with different types of ethical character." See her "The Advantages of Moral Diversity," in *The Good Life and the Human Good*, ed. Ellen Frankel Paul (Cambridge: Cambridge University Press, 1992), 53.

31. Tully, *Strange Multiplicity*, 177.

Some Requirements of Cultural Pluralism

Any discussion of the merits and failures of normative approaches to cultural diversity must adopt yardsticks, however provisional, with which to assess these various theories. In developing these yardsticks, I have found it useful to enumerate some conceptual and practical requirements of an account of cultural pluralism. I suggest that an adequate notion of respect for cultural pluralism must minimally include four conceptual features.[32] In particular, such a conception recognizes: (1) the importance and *value* to individuals of cultural identity and of membership in a respected cultural community; (2) that liberal democratic states (and citizens more generally) have reasons to value, and to protect, cultural diversity within their boundaries; (3) that respect and justice for cultural minorities includes their right to challenge and to help shape the public and political culture of the society in which they live; and (4) that liberal democratic states cannot (justly) define which differences they have reason to recognize politically without first deliberating with those involved.

To contribute usefully to the task of securing justice for cultural minorities, a conception of cultural pluralism must also include two further features: (1) a satisfactory defense of the importance of certain group cultural rights and limited forms of community autonomy and of the need for allocation of state resources to support such special arrangements; and (2) an adequate account of where to draw the "limits of tolerance" and how we are to decide which cultural practices democratic polities cannot protect or accept.

The four conceptual requirements of cultural pluralism set out above stand in tension with liberal policies that require citizens to "bracket" their ethnic and cultural identities from many aspects of political life. In the coming chapters, I defend the view that strategies which approach diversity from the standpoint of notions of toleration, neutrality, assimilation, and the "management" of differences are at best problematic and at worst reflect a failure to respect the cultural group in question.

My claim that liberal theorists and liberal institutions ought not to set pre-deliberative limits on either the scope or the nature of differences they may have reason to recognize politically is also at odds with recent "neutral" or "political" liberal arguments. Political liberals such as Rawls and Larmore hope to minimize moral disagreement in political debate by requiring that no political norms or institutions instantiate controversial normative ideals. In their view, citizens should avoid invoking

---

32. These features are defended in subsequent chapters.

their own moral views, as well as aspects of their social and cultural identities, when debating constitutional essentials. In setting this requirement, neutral and political liberals unjustly delimit the kind and scope of arguments citizens may introduce in public debate and so also restrict the social differences we may have reason to recognize politically. Consequently, they also ignore the possibility that justice for cultural minorities might well require the transformation of liberal-democratic institutions and practices so as better to include groups currently marginalized from public life.[33]

Full democratic citizenship, as the third conceptual requirement noted above states, includes the right to take part in shaping the public culture of one's society. Citizens need to have input in existing political structures but must also have opportunities to criticize and help transform those institutions and public practices. To deny cultural groups the right to do so is to ignore the critical role that cultural identity, beliefs, and practices occupy in the normative frameworks of citizens. If national and cultural minorities are to have opportunities to criticize and help shape public institutions, they may require formal rights of political representation, such as guaranteed seats on committees reviewing political institutions and a voice in top-level constitutional negotiations. In some cases, absence of this type of representation makes a farce of the liberal principle of consent, as well as of democratic norms of political inclusion and public debate. Securing formal group representation—which is only one way of meeting cultural communities' claims for respect and recognition—will require that we rethink the boundaries between public, political culture (i.e., public norms and institutions), on the one hand, and citizens' social and private identities and arrangements, on the other. If cultural minorities are to have the right to shape the public culture of their societies, they must also have some say in where to draw these boundaries.

The Limits of Inclusion

Some of the claims, beliefs, and practices of minority groups in democratic states inevitably clash with the interpretation and application of important liberal principles. These conflicts merit serious consideration. Nonetheless, their existence by no means demonstrates the untenability of certain liberal and democratic norms or the illegitimacy of fundamental rights and duties of citizens. To urge political theorists to

---

33. I elaborate on this view in chapters 2 and 3.

take cultural identity and membership seriously does not imply that they should capitulate to cultural relativism, much less to political relativism.[34] It would be foolhardy, for instance, to suggest that the best response to the claims of specifically *illiberal* cultural minorities is simply to urge institutional toleration or protection of their practices and beliefs, regardless of the consequences.

Misapprehensions about what cultural pluralism requires are reflected in three objections commonly raised by contemporary political theorists in connection with proposals for special rights and provisions for cultural minorities. First, some fear that by tolerating illiberal minorities and including them and their views in political deliberation, we may well jeopardize the stability and democratic culture of our political institutions.[35] If illiberal minorities do not regard norms of mutual respect, reciprocity, and freedom of speech as worthy of their allegiance, will not their inclusion in political debate tend to erode the very democratic practices and principles that are the precondition for meeting cultural minorities' justice claims? A second objection suggests that group rights conflict with individual rights and responsibilities and may compromise or even jeopardize the latter.[36] Finally, some political theorists (notably communitarian and republican thinkers) worry that by extending formal recognition and especially collective rights to cultural groups we will undermine the social bases for broader, national solidarity and civic-mindedness in democratic states.

These are not irrelevant concerns. However, fears about the effect of greater political inclusion of cultural minorities on the democratic culture of liberal states are partly premised on undefended assumptions. One such assumption is that cultural minorities are usually antiliberal

34. For insightful examinations of the flawed logic of many culturally relativist positions and contrasting arguments in favor of the cross-cultural application of political norms, see Martha Nussbaum, "Human Functioning and Social Justice: In Defense of Aristotelian Essentialism," *Political Theory* 20, no. 2 (1992): 202–46; and Amy Gutmann, "The Challenge of Multiculturalism in Political Ethics," *Philosophy and Public Affairs* 22, no. 3 (1993): 171–206. Recent work by Bikhu Parekh on the possibility of a pluralist universalism also suggests a way to avoid cultural relativist positions; see his "Non-ethnocentric Universalism: A Preliminary Sketch" (paper delivered to the conference on "Multiculturalism, Minorities and Citizenship," European University Institute, Florence, April 1996).

35. Even writers who endorse collective rights for some national minorities, such as Will Kymlicka and Joseph Raz, make plain that the toleration and inclusion of illiberal minorities pose certain threats to liberal institutions. I discuss their views on this issue in chapter 4.

36. For instance, Kukathas expresses a combination of objections 1 and 2: he voices a common concern about the freedom of exit from communities and suggests that this and other democratic liberties are best protected by "a liberal political culture." See his "Are There Any Cultural Rights?" 134.

(as opposed to merely nonliberal), which is not necessarily the case. Of course, identifying just what "illiberal" and "antiliberal" mean in the context of a commitment to cultural pluralism is bound to be a politically contested task; but it does not serve us to collapse myriad groups into a morass of antiliberal communities.

To some extent, such worries also reflect the fictitious notion that meeting the justice claims of cultural minorities in democratic states requires, or is tantamount to, unreflective capitulation to all such demands and to a wholesale surrender of liberal and democratic principles. In the democratic states that I consider, the prospect of eroding formal commitments to democratic principles and individual rights is not a real possibility. As far as meeting the claims of cultural minority groups for collective rights and special constitutional arrangements is concerned, these have been—and will continue to be—hard-won political gains, subjected to considerable scrutiny, limitation, and endless political negotiation. For instance, land claims and demands for collective rights of self-government by native peoples of Canada have taken many years of debate, negotiation, and political activism to yield partial, provisional settlements. The newly created Inuit territory of Nunavut is the culmination of years of countless multilateral talks. Moreover, concerns about the rights of non-Inuit residents have prompted guaranteed civil and political protections for these citizens.

This is not to deny that cultural pluralism may pose uncomfortable challenges for democratic states. There clearly exist some tensions between collective cultural rights and certain individual rights and freedoms, as the problem of rights of "exit" from traditional (especially closed religious) communities demonstrates. Concerns about whether women's gender equality rights—which are typically protected as individual rights in contemporary democratic states—are safeguarded by cultural, collective rights also loom large.[37] Moreover, there is a real possibility that recognizing cultural groups in formal, political terms might serve to accentuate the different interests and aims of diverse groups. But we should not therefore conclude that these tensions and potential conflicts automatically trump the claims of cultural minorities for respect and recognition, or interpret difficulties as evidence that the introduction of special group rights and protections for minorities is inevitably impracticable.

37. For a discussion of the tensions between gender equality rights and proposals for collective rights and self-government for native peoples of Canada, see my "Conflicting Equalities? Cultural Group Rights and Sex Equality," *Political Studies* 48, no. 3 (2000): 522–39.

The problem of whether to tolerate (or to introduce positive protections for) nonliberal and antiliberal cultural minorities is one that I address at some length in chapter 4 in my discussion of liberal perfectionist approaches to cultural diversity. As a provisional response to fears about the "specter" of illiberal minorities, however, I suggest that we consider the requirements and duties that attend the principle of respect, at least on the familiar Kantian version of respect. As Kant argued, the duties of respect are fundamentally reciprocal: "Every man has a legitimate claim to respect from his fellow men and is in turn bound to respect every other." Demonstrating this respect is a way of acknowledging another agent's dignity; the duties of respect prevent one from acting "contrary to the equally necessary self-esteem of others.... [Therefore, we are] under obligation to acknowledge, in a practical way, the dignity of humanity in every other man."[38] In cases where cultural minorities seek to undermine the agency, dignity, or humanity of their own members or that of other members of society, they will forfeit the special recognition and forms of community autonomy previously granted them. That is, democratic states must demand basic reciprocal duties of respect: it is a condition of according respect and recognition to cultural minorities (illiberal and otherwise) that they themselves demonstrate respect for the basic dignity and agency of their own members and of other citizens. How to conceive of respect in ways that are appropriate for ethically and culturally diverse polities is of course a difficult question and one to which I return in chapter 2 (on toleration) and again in chapter 4 (on liberal perfectionism).

38. Immanuel Kant, "The Doctrine of Virtue," book 1, part 2, sections 37 and 38, in *The Metaphysics of Morals*, trans. Mary Gregor (Cambridge: Cambridge University Press, 1991), 255.

Toleration and Respect

Toleration is not the *opposite* of Intolerance, but is the *counterfeit* of it. Both are despotisms. The one assumes to itself the right of withholding Liberty of Conscience, and the other of granting it.

—THOMAS PAINE, *Rights of Man*

Tolerance ... involves an attitude that is intermediate between wholehearted acceptance and unrestrained opposition.

—T. M. SCANLON, "The Difficulty of Tolerance"

Perhaps toleration will prove to have been an interim value, serving a period between a past when no one had heard of it and a future when no one will need it.

—BERNARD WILLIAMS, "Toleration: An Impossible Virtue?"

Modern liberalism, as is well known, grew out of arguments for religious toleration in the wake of the sixteenth- and seventeenth-century wars of religion. Liberal thinkers argued that state toleration was both a rational and prudential response to religious diversity, the most volatile and politically significant (though of course not the only) form of social difference in Europe in those centuries. The Reformation and wars of religion ensured that religious conflict and its implications for state sovereignty and stability were uppermost in the minds of early modern and modern liberal thinkers.

Toleration was widely credited as a key aspect of enlightened strategies for dealing with religious strife. Today, few would contest the idea that toleration, along with liberty and political equality, remains a key principle of liberalism. Indeed, Judith Shklar went so far as to rank toleration as the highest liberal virtue.[1] Not only is toleration central to liberal theory and practice, but it is typically thought to define the very essence of the liberal disposition. As David Strauss asserts:

> These are the liberal virtues: the capacity to be tolerant and respectful toward those with whom one disagrees; and the capacity to welcome, rather than fear or find unsettling, the availability of a wide range of choices about central issues in one's life. Liberalism cannot be justified unless one accepts these traits as virtues.[2]

The biggest single difference between early liberal accounts of toleration and contemporary liberal discussions is that toleration is no longer held to apply solely or even mainly to instances of religious diversity. In the past half-century, new axes of social difference have come to the fore in democratic states, many of which are now the subject of appeals to tolerance—race, ethnicity, and sexual orientation, to name just a few. Dramatic immigration shifts, geopolitical changes, economic globalization, the increased permeability of state borders, the gradual decline in importance of organized religion (especially in Western Europe), the advent of mass media, and the proliferation of social movements have all contributed to the development of democratic societies in which religious diversity is now just one of many salient social differences among citizens. Once seen as a strategy for mediating religious conflicts alone, toleration has gradually been extended as a possible solution for other kinds of social conflicts. Consequently, it is well worth asking what role, if any, the principle and practice of toleration should play in democratic responses to current dilemmas of cultural diversity and the justice claims of citizens of different national and ethnic minorities.

In this chapter I ask whether toleration can, and should, be stretched to address contemporary dilemmas of cultural difference that are prevalent in socially plural, democratic states. My concern is with institutional forms of toleration—what we might call formal, state forms of tolerance and accommodation—rather than with toleration as a per-

---

1. Judith Shklar, *Ordinary Vices* (Cambridge, Mass.: Harvard University Press, 1984).
2. David Strauss, "The Liberal Virtues," *Nomos* 34: *Virtue*, ed. John Chapman and William Galston (New York: New York University Press, 1992), 198.

sonal disposition or virtue. Although not unimportant, expressions of tolerance by individuals—and the idea of toleration as a personal trait—do not address in any very direct way the broader social and political dilemmas facing cultural minorities, much less purport to satisfy such groups' demands for respect and recognition. The questions that guide the discussion that follows are all concerned, therefore, with the political and institutional dimensions of tolerance. What forms of diversity can different notions of toleration accommodate? Can either weak or strong toleration, and the practices that they foster, help secure substantial respect for cultural (ethnic, religious, and linguistic) minority groups? And can the principle of toleration ground *positive* measures to support the flourishing of distinct cultural communities, such as laws for the protection of minority languages and special mechanisms for the political representation of cultural minorities?

These questions reflect some of the main requirements of respect for cultural pluralism, as set out in chapter 1. A commitment to cultural pluralism in democratic state requires, among other things, the inclusion of cultural groups in existing political institutions and decision-making structures (for those who seek it); and positive forms of state assistance and special arrangements for cultural communities who seek to preserve their distinct identities, languages, and ways of life. Sometimes, as in the case of long-standing, territorially concentrated national minorities, cultural recognition may require that the state devolve certain powers of self-government. A commitment to cultural pluralism thus reflects a substantive, normative position, one that accords value and respect to cultural communities.[3] Liberal responses to dilemmas of cultural diversity which appeal solely or mainly to the principle of toleration, I argue, cannot readily secure many of the requirements of respect for cultural pluralism as sketched above (and set out in chapter 1).

Whether certain aspects of toleration are deemed a useful response to contemporary claims for cultural recognition will depend in part on the conception or conceptions of toleration under consideration. In the sections that follow, I examine variants of both weak toleration—which implies merely negative tolerance, such as freedom from reli-

---

3. If the term were not so easily misconstrued, we might say that cultural pluralism, in some circumstances, entails an endorsement of multiculturalism, as opposed to mere tolerance. Lawrence Blum offers a useful discussion of the requirements of multiculturalism, which he says must include "respect for and interest in the cultural heritage of members of groups other than one's own." See Blum, "Multiculturalism, Racial Justice, and Community: Reflections on Charles Taylor's 'Politics of Recognition'," in *Defending Diversity*, ed. L. Foster and P. Herzog (Boston: University of Massachusetts Press, 1994), 181.

gious persecution and racial discrimination—and strong toleration—which refers to positive measures that assist or support specific practices or ways of life in question.

Groundwork: Lockean Toleration

Toleration, both historically and today, refers to the principle and practice of noninterference. A person or institution exercises tolerance by refraining from interfering with, and / or by extending a kind of permission to, practices or beliefs with which they disagree.[4] Tolerance is not to be confused with indifference to a particular custom or belief. Nor is toleration mere powerlessness in the face of moral disagreement or indeed moral indignation: since toleration follows from a conscious choice to tolerate as opposed to suppressing *x*, it must be within the power of those who tolerate to quash or at least to hinder *x*. We do not necessarily have to be in a position to exercise *coercive* power in order to be capable of tolerance, however; even publicly denouncing or lobbying against a custom or belief with which we disagree in such a way as to damage the dignity or standing of the "offending" group or to precipitate restrictions on a practice could count as intolerance. Nonetheless, the most typical instance of tolerance is one in which *the state* possesses the coercive power to prevent or suppress objectionable views and acts, but refrains from imposing legal restrictions, sanctions, or other obstructions.

These three background conditions for the exercise of toleration—the presence of clashing moral, religious, or social beliefs and practices; strong disapproval; and the power to hinder practices—were well understood by Enlightenment thinkers. These factors are also reflected in the two main kinds of justifications they offer for toleration, namely, rational and prudential reasons. Rational and epistemological arguments for tolerance typically suggest that since we cannot know for sure whether or not certain ideas will turn out to be true or false, it is rational and prudent to tolerate a range of different beliefs and views. The epistemological benefits of tolerance (in both a falsifying and verificationist sense) are also often stressed in accounts by early liberals,

4. Whether toleration pertains strictly to situations of *moral* disagreement and disapproval, or can characterize situations of mere dislike, is a matter of much dispute; however, certainly one or the other must be present. As Susan Mendus notes, this question is part of a "general philosophical debate about the very status of moral judgements, and the nature of the distinction between such judgements and judgements of taste or preference." See her *Toleration and the Limits of Liberalism* (London: Macmillan, 1989), 10.

who thought that the free circulation of clashing beliefs and worldviews was more likely to produce accurate explanations of phenomena or truth than the systematic suppression of opinions.

This skeptical line of reasoning is central to John Locke's argument for tolerance. Locke considered our judgment to be fallible and argued that it is rational to tolerate opposing views as these might better help us to uncover truth; only "Light and Evidence ... can work a change in Mens Opinions."[5] Mill later developed the skeptical-rational argument in favor of tolerance in *On Liberty*, in which he asserts that when opinions are suppressed, we forfeit the clarifying benefits that false hypotheses and the process of falsifying them can bring us.[6] Locke appeals to another aspect of rationality in justifying toleration: that it is irrational to try to persecute people for holding particular religious views, since it is virtually impossible to change the minds of people in matters of conscience. This is so not only because we consider our religious beliefs to be true but also because we view them as the basis for our own personal salvation after death. It is in the nature of religious belief that it cannot be compelled by force.[7] The tenacity of private faith—in particular among the dissenters, who so impressed Locke—thus reflects the fact that these views represent the "inward persuasion of the Mind." Locke's suggestion that law simply cannot compel beliefs that emanate from a sense of inner judgment or force[8] is an opinion echoed by Voltaire in the following century.[9]

Locke's argument also invokes aspects of a prudential and pragmatic justification of tolerance. Prudence, on his view, suggests that states have an interest in maintaining civil peace, not least because of the high costs of suppressing rather than tolerating social differences. Intolerance, not false beliefs, is the main cause of war and dissolution and the greatest threat to civil and political progress.[10] Locke is doubtless the most prominent early modern defender of toleration who combined appeals to rationality with prudential justifications of tolerance, but he was by no means the only one. Less than a century later, Voltaire

---

5. John Locke, *A Letter Concerning Toleration* (1689), ed. James Tully (Indianapolis: Hackett, 1983), 27.

6. John Stuart Mill, *On Liberty* (1859; Indianapolis: Hackett, 1985), 16–19.

7. Locke, *A Letter Concerning Toleration*, 27. See his discussion of the tension between our salvation and the dictates of the "Civil Magistrate," 26–27. Locke argues here that religion pertains to the "inward persuasion of the Mind," whereas the Magistrate's power is merely "outward force."

8. Ibid., 26–28.

9. Voltaire, *A Treatise on Tolerance*, trans. B. Masters (1763; London: Folio Society, 1994), 121.

10. Locke, *A Letter Concerning Toleration*, 55.

condemned intolerance as irrational, part and parcel of superstition and bigotry, and a major cause of war: "Yet of all superstitions is not the most dangerous that which demands we hate our neighbour on account of his opinion?"[11]

Appeals to general liberal principles are associated much more with nineteenth- and twentieth-century arguments for toleration than with the polemics of earlier advocates of tolerance. To the extent that earlier thinkers provided "principled" justifications, it was in connection with a specific ideal of liberty—that is, religious liberty and liberty of conscience—and the emerging doctrine of the rights of man. This historical context suggests that early modern and Enlightenment arguments, insofar as they invoke mainly rational and prudential—rather than principled—reasons for tolerance, cannot take us very far in meeting contemporary claims for cultural recognition and respect. Locke's thesis might persuade us to tolerate certain expressions of religious diversity and to adopt a skeptical stance toward different ethical views (though Locke's own position is not one of moral, but rather epistemological, skepticism). However, the rational and prudential justifications he offers for toleration cannot—nor should they be expected to—provide arguments for protecting the goods of cultural identity and cultural membership, nor for introducing positive measures to ensure the survival of distinct but vulnerable cultural communities.

There are other features of early liberal accounts of toleration that render them unsuitable for addressing contemporary struggles for cultural recognition. Most obviously, early conceptions of toleration were highly limited in their scope of application. Locke and Voltaire reassure their readers that they do not expect states or citizens to extend tolerance to all groups: Catholics and atheists, in Locke's view, were not to be tolerated, and Voltaire hastens to assure us that he does not suggest that non-Catholics "should share in the places and honours available to those who are of the prevailing religion."[12] Nor do early conceptions of toleration assign any particular value to social differences: religious differences are viewed merely as regrettable, a source of conflict that states must attempt to contain. Religious minorities deserved to be protected by state policies of toleration, early modern thinkers argued, but very possibly on terms that reflected their powerlessness and marginalization. Understandably, then, early liberals do not suggest how we might integrate and fully include different social and cultural groups in public life in equitable and just ways.

11. Voltaire, *Treatise on Tolerance*, 120.
12. Ibid., 25–26.

The sources of diversity and the kinds of claims made by cultural minority groups today are clearly not reducible to the paradigm of religious tolerance presupposed by early modern accounts of toleration. Both conceptually and practically, the negative rights that weak toleration seeks to secure do not capture the substance of many claims by cultural minorities, who demand full inclusion in democratic institutions and processes and the right to shape the political culture of their societies. Weak toleration is perhaps best suited to the contexts of nondemocratic states, where discrimination and persecution on religious and ethnic grounds are still much in evidence. Although calls for civil peace and religious toleration still persist in democratic states—we have only to look at Northern Ireland for an example of this—demands for social inclusion and political recognition are much more characteristic of contemporary, culturally plural liberal polities. Although we might consider demands for antidiscrimination laws as a contemporary analogue to earlier pleas for tolerance, today's demands by citizens of cultural minorities for respect and inclusion are best understood as transcending demands for religious liberty and freedom of conscience.

Locke's argument for toleration, based as it is on appeals to prudence and rationality, seems, if not to preclude, at least to bracket normative evaluations, and specifically affirmations, of social diversity. As Bikhu Parekh notes in connection with Locke's and Mill's thought, the objects of toleration as construed by these authors have moral claims to the "protection of their *rights and interests*, but not to the inviolability of let alone a basic respect for their *ways of life*."[13] This goes some distance in explaining why prudential and rational justifications of toleration have gradually receded and given way to more principled arguments.[14] Lockean weak toleration thus does not fare well on any of the criteria for an adequate response to demands for cultural recognition: it does not foster democratic inclusion of a wide range of cultural minority groups; it cannot inculcate practices of mutual respect between different cultural communities (though it does not necessarily preclude these); and it cannot supply arguments for the introduction of positive protections and assistance for cultural communities in democratic states. Where negative or weak toleration is justified by appeals to ra-

13. Bhikhu Parekh, "Moral Philosophy and Its Anti-pluralist Bias," in *Philosophy and Pluralism*, Royal Institute of Philosophy, suppl. 40, ed. David Archard (Cambridge: Cambridge University Press, 1996), 125.

14. The older arguments have not entirely disappeared, but epistemological skepticism no longer plays a prominent role in justifications of toleration or of rights. Friedrich Hayek's thought is a notable exception, as he invokes epistemological skepticism to argue for liberal ends.

tionality or to prudence, the aim is to prevent persecution and to secure civil peace and some form of basic political rights. Locke's conception of toleration neither attempts nor purports to accommodate a wide range of socially and culturally diverse groups; nor does it welcome diversity, even in Mill's later utilitarian sense.

The evident and unsurprising unsuitability of Locke's and other early accounts of toleration to contemporary dilemmas of diversity has led some contemporary political philosophers to rethink their views of tolerance. As we shall see, today's liberals more typically combine notions of tolerance and *neutrality* in proposing principles of justice for culturally plural societies. Others appeal to the role of state toleration in securing the conditions for personal autonomy. On the whole, recent liberal thinkers do not want to dispense with toleration so much as reform it: Susan Mendus, for example, suggests that since weak, or legal, toleration alone may not be enough to secure social integration and accommodation, we should conceive of toleration not merely as negative in character but also as requiring "a positive welcoming of difference."[15] In response to this quandary of tolerance, some scholars today tend either to argue for the rehabilitation of weak tolerance—married to a conception of neutrality—or, following Mill, to argue for a stronger conception of tolerance on the basis of comprehensive or liberal perfectionist premises. I now turn my attention to examining the merits of the former strategy.

Political Liberalism and Weak Toleration

Locke's view of toleration as a set of negative restrictions, or "forbearance" on the part of the state or "Magistrate," is echoed to a certain degree in the work of contemporary "political" or "neutral" liberals.[16] Political liberals conceive of toleration in terms of freedom from state perfectionism (i.e., freedom from the state's imposition of a particular ideal of the good and state interference in the private lives of citizens). However, where Locke appealed to the rationality and prudence of toleration, political liberals are more apt to link tolerance to liberal principles of justice, equal concern, and respect. In a broad sense, the neutral or political liberal endorsement of the principle of toleration reflects liberals' recognition of the diversity of citizens' values and beliefs in liberal polities and of the need to accord basic respect to different concep-

---

15. Susan Mendus, *Toleration and the Limits of Liberalism*, 5.
16. I use the terms "political liberal" and "neutral liberal" interchangeably here.

tions of the good. Political liberals, notably John Rawls, believe that a conception of justice for socially plural societies should reflect only widely acceptable political norms rather than comprehensive moral ideals.[17] To this end, Rawls in his recent work elaborates a constructivist conception of political justice which he claims is based on practical reason and observations about the actual political intuitions of citizens in liberal states. This political conception of justice is the "focus of an overlapping consensus" among reasonable citizens of democratic polities, which refers to their tacit agreement to a particular conception of "justice as fairness," and to the norm of neutrality.[18]

Rawlsian toleration follows from the terms of political liberalism, which prevent the state from favoring any particular conception of the good or comprehensive moral doctrine. Toleration of a variety of comprehensive views is required by public reason and justice as fairness generally, in part because the basic structure of social and political life must not reflect a particular (and necessarily partial) conception of the good. Consequently, toleration plays a pivotal role in Rawls's account of justice: political liberalism "expresses [citizens'] shared and public political reason. But to attain such a shared reason, the conception of justice should be, as far as possible, independent of the opposing and conflicting philosophical doctrines that citizens affirm. *In formulating such a conception, political liberalism applies the principle of toleration to philosophy itself.*"[19] State intolerance toward a particular reasonable doctrine would indicate that the state illegitimately favors a comprehensive ideal of the good in its institutions and procedures. Nor is the adoption by the state of a particular moral ideal justifiable from the standpoint of public reason. Rawls thus views toleration and the closely related principle of political neutrality as essential features of justice as fairness.

A central aim of a merely political liberalism is to ensure that the state accords maximum tolerance to citizens' moral or comprehensive views in the private and social realms, consistent with adherence to principles of justice. So long as citizens' beliefs and ways of life do not jeopardize other basic liberties required by justice as fairness, they should be tolerated. Rawls's view affirms Mill's belief that people must be free to form and pursue their own conception of the good and to hold whatever private beliefs they so desire. In this way, Rawls's neutral or political liberal argument for tolerance claims to be able to tolerate a *greater*

17. Rawls intends his distinction between a merely "political liberalism" and a "comprehensive liberalism" to capture the difference between plural and nonplural liberal models of justice. See Rawls, *Political Liberalism*, xxvii–xxviii and 196–200.

18. Ibid., 90 and 97.

19. Ibid., 9–10. Emphasis added.

range of social and cultural differences than comprehensive versions of liberalism, which endorse a particular conception of human flourishing. Since Rawls's theory does not appeal to a particular comprehensive moral view, he is confident that it affords the maximum toleration of diverse conceptions of the good permissible within a stable and just liberal state.[20] In addition to claiming that political liberalism accommodates a greater range of social diversity than comprehensive liberalism can allow, Rawls suggests that its practice helps foster mutual respect among citizens. More generally, Rawls understands toleration to be deeply bound up with equality and social justice.[21] These features place Rawls's account of toleration somewhere ahead of those of Locke and Voltaire, neither of whom suggests that toleration should inculcate respect or that it reflects on the social conditions that make tolerance necessary.

Despite his good intentions, there are reasons to doubt that Rawls's account of toleration provides a sufficient basis for justifying positive recognition and respect for cultural minorities. Because he cannot invoke moral comprehensive beliefs to justify toleration, Rawls must instead appeal to some combination of principles of justice and public reason: he cannot, say, point to the importance of toleration in supporting individual autonomy, since to do so is to invoke a nonpolitical norm.[22] This introduces tangible restrictions on the scope and kind of differences that Rawls's view can accommodate: in particular, our public, political beliefs and proposals are constrained by the "burdens of judgment" and the terms and procedures of neutral liberal political deliberation.[23] Rawls expects his notions of reasonableness, fair terms of social cooperation, the "burdens of judgment," and the requirement of neutral public reason to help set the limits of tolerance.[24] These features of a "well-ordered society" both make possible practices of toleration in a general sense (by aiding in the construction of a political culture bound by principles of public reason) and help determine what will qualify as reasonable, comprehensive doctrines worthy of toleration.

Besides failing to secure the robust form of respect required by a commitment to cultural pluralism, Rawls's conception of justice as fairness and his account of toleration may also pose tangible obstacles to

20. Ibid., 198–99.
21. Ibid., 122.
22. In Rawls's view, the good of individual autonomy is an element of a comprehensive, moral view and thereby cannot be appealed to in a (merely) political conception of liberalism.
23. *Political Liberalism*, 54–58.
24. Ibid., esp. 10, 44, 49–62, 81–82, 100, and 118–19.

the positive recognition of cultural minorities. In particular, Rawls's notion of public reason requires and assumes that "reasonable" citizens accept a basic division between their private, particular moral views and arrangements and public and political norms, principles, and procedures. Only noncontroversial, truly public norms may inform the basic institutions of the liberal state (or "constitutional essentials"). Moral comprehensive views, although not officially excluded from political debate, do not meet the test of neutral, public reason and so are unlikely to be politically persuasive.[25] Citizens and their representatives are thus discouraged from arguing from their own partial perspectives in public life, and political institutions are to be structured according to "the guidelines and procedures of public reason."[26] In debating and voting on matters of constitutional essentials, we are to refrain from making normative political claims that appeal to the beliefs, identities, or ways of life of our social and cultural communities.

For political liberals such as Rawls, then, the limits of toleration coincide with the limits of public reason; as Parekh suggests, "[Rawls's] reasonable pluralism is pluralism within the limits of liberalism, and excludes a wide variety of ways of life while claiming to be neutral."[27] Ethnic and religious minority groups whose political views are intertwined with their moral and religious beliefs may well be excluded from this model of neutral liberal politics, for they may not agree to follow the norms of neutral public reason as required by Rawls. Even Rawlsian toleration could not counter the effect of highly constrained political deliberation on the political participation of cultural minority groups.

Rawls's notion of tolerance is limited in a further way: since justice as fairness cannot invoke comprehensive norms or goods, Rawls cannot appeal to the importance of cultural identity and cultural membership to human flourishing in order to justify instances of "strong toleration," such as the introduction of collective cultural rights and other arrangements.[28] Without an account of why cultural identity and membership may be valuable to citizens, and therefore worth protecting, it is difficult to see how Rawls's political conception of justice could per-

25. Ibid., 137 and passim.
26. Ibid., 62.
27. Parekh, "Moral Philosophy," 124.
28. Some liberals argue that Rawls's project can be reformulated so as to support collective rights for cultural minorities. Both Will Kymlicka and Daniel Weinstock have argued that Rawls's idea of the social bases of self-respect could be interpreted as requiring the introduction of group rights so as to protect the identities and viability of cultural communities. See Kymlicka, *Liberalism, Community, and Culture*; and Weinstock, "The Political Theory of Strong Evaluation," in *Philosophy in an Age of Pluralism*, ed. James Tully (Cambridge: Cambridge University Press, 1994).

mit (let alone require) positive protections for the survival and flourishing of cultural minorities. Just as Locke appeals to rationality and prudence to show why we should tolerate certain religious dissidents, Rawls invokes both practical and rational-theoretical reasons to justify toleration: he argues both that citizens of contemporary liberal democracies show actual regard for justice as fairness (in which toleration figures prominently) and that the "burdens of judgment" and terms of a well-ordered society make state toleration a reasonable and rational strategy for dealing with citizens' diverse interests and beliefs. Like Locke, Rawls relies on a negative or weak conception of toleration; his notion of "reasonable pluralism" simply confirms the *fact* of diverse conceptions of the good but makes no comment as to its desirability, quite possibly because he thinks affirming the value of social and cultural differences would take his theory too far in the direction of comprehensive liberalism.

Rawls's failure to concede the value of social diversity is reinforced by his tendency to view citizens' salient differences as individual in character rather than social or group-based.[29] Although in *Political Liberalism* Rawls speaks more directly to the issue of our social differences than in his earlier work, even here he emphasizes the importance of citizens' individual, and in some sense voluntary, differences—namely, their diverse and at least partially personal conceptions of the good. This may make it easier for Rawls to assume that rational and reasonable citizens will agree to bracket their moral comprehensive views from debates on constitutional essentials: it is easier to stand back from one's individual preferences, beliefs, and / or account of the good than it is to stand back from an entire cultural context of social mores and norms.

Weak toleration as advanced by Locke and Rawls thus cannot ground strategies for the democratic inclusion of cultural minorities as required by a robust commitment to cultural pluralism. Nor does weak toleration succeed in securing adequate respect for cultural minorities: Rawls's theory is concerned to inculcate mutual respect among citizens strictly *as citizens*, in abstraction from their specific identities and memberships. Although this basic respect among citizens is surely indispensable, it cannot replace the more substantive respect and recognition that some social groups demand for their distinct group identities and memberships. To meet demands for group-based forms of respect and recognition, Rawls would need to amend his theory so as to concede the importance of citizens' cultural identities and memberships to political life.

29. For a parallel discussion of this problem, see Anna Galeotti, "Citizenship and Equality: The Place for Toleration," *Political Theory* 21, no. 4 (1993): 594.

Mill's Argument for Tolerance

Contemporary "comprehensive" and perfectionist variants of liberalism, unlike merely political conceptions of justice—such as that of Rawls—appeal to moral worldviews and beliefs to defend liberal political principles and arrangements. Some of the accounts of morality and conceptions of the good embraced by contemporary comprehensive and perfectionist liberals derive from the thought of John Stuart Mill.[30] Mill's argument for toleration is arguably "comprehensive" (in the sense employed by Rawls) in that it entails an appeal to a comprehensive moral theory, within which the specific good of a highly self-directed life plays a prominent part. Nonetheless, he depends heavily on rational and epistemological reasons for toleration. Indeed, Mill begins his defense of toleration by reaffirming reasons offered by earlier proponents: like Locke and Voltaire, he praises the falsifying and clarifying benefits of "false opinions" and hypotheses and the ways in which these lead us to revise our opinions and rectify our mistakes.[31] Mill's concern that we not reject ideas that might well be correct led him to assert that "Heretical opinions ... are generally some of these suppressed and neglected truths."[32] Here his position is underscored by the view that truth often lies somewhere in between two conflicting, extreme doctrines.

Above all, of course, Mill was concerned to defend toleration because of his fear that the state might "dwarf" men's individuality and diversity, and so their liberty. Mill's view that individual freedom (which he defines as "pursuing our own good in our own way") is secured by toleration is the aspect of his thought most readily incorporated by contemporary comprehensive liberals and liberal perfectionists. Also echoed today is Mill's notion of the revisability of beliefs, or the idea that we are able to reflect on and alter our options and rectify our mistakes so long as knowledge and diverse opinions circulate freely.[33] It is precisely this thesis connecting diversity of thought, opinion, and character to personal liberty and the revisability of ends that undergirds some recent arguments for toleration of diversity and freedom of speech.

Unlike Locke or Rawls, Mill offers reasons—instrumental, utilitarian reasons—for *valuing* social diversity, as opposed to merely tolerating and accommodating differences. Not only is the presence of diverse

---

30. I do not include in this category the majority of perfectionists, who are not specifically liberal.

31. Mill, *On Liberty*, esp. 16–19.

32. Ibid., 44.

33. Ibid., 12 and 19.

opinions and beliefs linked to discovery of truth, but it crucially contributes to the "cultivation of ... individuality," which Mill in turn links to intellectual and social progress.[34] Mill follows the German philosopher Wilhelm von Humboldt in citing "freedom and variety of situations" as key requirements of human development and flourishing; he laments that "the second of these two conditions is in this country every day diminishing."[35] Mill's understanding and appreciation of diversity, however, is highly individualistic, as befits some of his philosophical leanings; his interest is in developing and preserving the uniqueness of individual character and thought, not group differences or collective identities. Despite his inattention to these latter differences and his inability to supply all or even many of what we might now consider the most important reasons for valuing group differences, Mill's argument signaled an important turning point in discussions of toleration. In particular, Mill was one of the first modern thinkers to suggest that toleration is essential not simply to civil order and liberty but, equally, to individuality and human flourishing. His arguments for toleration and individual diversity also show that appeals to comprehensive views of the good need not be synonymous with a political commitment to social homogeneity or ethical monism (as with some communitarian views). Contemporary comprehensive liberals follow Mill in viewing diversity and value pluralism as important not in spite of but rather precisely because of their perfectionist commitments, especially to the value of personal autonomy.

Raz's Comprehensive Liberal Defense of Toleration

Joseph Raz's comprehensive liberalism centers on the liberal perfectionist ideal of the flourishing, self-directed moral agent who makes valuable life choices. This norm, which invokes aspects of both Mill's and Kant's moral theories, depends in large part on agents' capacities for independence and the presence of conditions that help sustain autonomy.[36] Among these conditions is the availability of a range of worthwhile options from which agents may choose, thereby exercising judgment and personal autonomy. Raz's ideal of the self-directed agent provides the basis for his defense of "strong toleration," or toleration

34. Ibid., 61.
35. Ibid., 70.
36. This is an abbreviated version of Raz's "autonomy-based doctrine of freedom," which he advances in *The Morality of Freedom* (Oxford: Clarendon Press, 1986).

that entails positive state duties rather than the merely negative duty to refrain from hindering a belief or practice.

His view is developed in several parts. First, Raz suggests that personal autonomy is an important feature of a flourishing life. Although personal autonomy need not be directed toward worthwhile choices to count as autonomy, valuable expressions of autonomy must be so directed. Yet in order to make valuable choices, we must have available diverse, worthwhile options from which to choose (i.e., it is not enough to have a single valuable option available). Our options / choices are bound up with public goods; this circumstance in turn necessitates the state's involvement in supplying and managing these goods. Together, these thoughts inform Raz's suggestion that "autonomy ... requires pluralism but not neutrality."[37] To help secure the conditions necessary both for autonomy and for moral pluralism, the state is obliged not only to tolerate a range of different views, beliefs, and preferences in plural societies but also to ensure the availability of valuable options.[38] Raz thus endorses strong, or positive, toleration rather than mere negative tolerance.

Where neutral and antiperfectionist liberals normally appeal to ostensibly neutral principles of justice and fairness to justify "weak" toleration—and combine this with an argument for state neutrality—liberal perfectionists such as Raz interpret the endorsement of valuable forms of autonomy and moral pluralism as implying a commitment to strong toleration.[39] Recently, Raz has extended his perfectionist defense of autonomy and moral pluralism to argue for limited cultural group rights, and it is here that some of the central difficulties in his conception and justification of toleration come to light. Raz's account of a flourishing life is far from uncontroversial; his view that "people prosper through a life of self-definition consisting of free choices among a plurality of in-

37. Joseph Raz, "Liberalism, Autonomy, and the Politics of Neutral Concern," in *Midwest Studies in Philosophy*, vol. 7, ed. Peter French et al. (Minneapolis: University of Minnesota Press, 1982), 324.

38. Raz does not use the "strong" versus "weak" toleration distinction, but his views support a strong, or positive, conception of toleration. See especially Raz, "Autonomy, Toleration, and the Harm Principle," in *Justifying Toleration: Conceptual and Historical Perspectives*, ed. Susan Mendus (Cambridge: Cambridge University Press, 1988), 161. Similar arguments are made in his *The Morality of Freedom* and "Liberalism, Scepticism, and Democracy," in *Ethics in the Public Domain*.

39. Here "weak toleration" denotes a situation in which a person or state institution merely refrains from interfering with a practice or belief found disagreeable and / or morally repugnant. "Strong toleration" refers to instances where a person, or, more typically, an institution, not only refrains from hampering a belief or practice but also contributes to the viability of that practice by introducing positive or protective measures.

compatible but valuable activities, pursuits, and relationships ... (and) forms of life" is decidedly liberal in tone and could possibly lead to disadvantageous policies toward cultural *groups*.[40] His further claim that cultural membership is good because it enhances citizens' personal autonomy is equally problematic. Raz states that his liberal defense of multiculturalism "emphasizes the role of cultures as a precondition for, and a factor which gives shape and content to, individual freedom."[41] This is a big assumption, however, and one that may not be compatible with the idea of being embedded in a particular cultural community—especially a traditional religious one.

Raz understands toleration as an important component of "liberal multiculturalism," which he takes to express a positive commitment to the preservation of cultural communities. In his view, a state should seek to secure the conditions for cultural group membership through special rights and protections because such membership bears directly on individuals' capacities for independence and opportunities to flourish. For Raz, it is in virtue of our cultural membership that we have access to opportunities, feel a sense of belonging, and enjoy dignity and self-worth—all necessary components of a valuable life.[42] However, although many cultural groups will indeed provide these benefits for their members, some, we must assume, will not. Yet because Raz links the value of cultural identity and membership so closely to the liberal good of autonomy, he gives us no reason to value or protect cultures that do not actively support their members' independence. Indeed, Raz tries to set limits to his endorsement of pluralism so as to preclude state sponsorship for ways of life that may actually undermine personal autonomy: he cautions that the state need only support "worthwhile," autonomy-enhancing options and suggests that we should accord respect to persons in view of their "reasonable choices."[43]

Although few would dispute Raz's claim that the state is not obliged to tolerate, much less support, all ways of life, his assertion that the state is bound only to tolerate and make available (through various forms of assistance) *valuable*, worthwhile options begs numerous questions, par-

40. Raz," Liberalism, Scepticism, and Democracy," 105.

41. Raz, "Multiculturalism: A Liberal Perspective," in *Ethics in the Public Domain*, 163. See also Raz's "National Self-Determination" (esp. 115, 121) in the same volume. Will Kymlicka supplies another example of an expanded argument in favor of positive state duties of tolerance. See his "Liberal Individualism and Liberal Neutrality," *Ethics* 99 (1989): 903; *Liberalism, Community and Culture*, 169; and *Multicultural Citizenship*, 105–6.

42. Raz, "National Self-Determination," 115.

43. Raz, "Liberalism, Scepticism, and Democracy," 108, and *Morality of Freedom*, 411–12.

ticularly in the context of culturally plural societies. Who is to decide what is valuable? Why should options that enhance agents' autonomy receive preferential support from the state? And do illiberal cultures ever merit more than mere toleration, if indeed they merit that? Raz's view also introduces important restrictions on the toleration and recognition of citizens' social and cultural differences. One possible implication of his theory is that cultural groups whose beliefs and practices do not foster or reinforce personal autonomy may not be deemed worthy of state support, much less greater political inclusion.[44] Given that Raz attributes intrinsic value to (and seeks to preserve) cultural membership, his implicit requirement that groups foster a liberal ideal of a self-directed life makes little sense: as political theorist Jonathan Chaplin notes, if communities "become liberal, they may thereby have lost much of their distinctiveness."[45]

These difficulties aside, Raz's account of toleration and his defense of liberal multiculturalism surpasses the arguments of Locke, Rawls, and Mill in several respects. For Raz, toleration is only one part of the broader goal of affirming the importance of moral pluralism in general and cultural identity and membership in particular. Raz understands that politically significant differences are socially constituted and collective in form, not strictly a matter of our individual moral, ethical, and normative views, preferences, and beliefs. Like Mill, he offers some (instrumental) reasons for valuing and not merely accepting or tolerating diversity—instrumental reasons which derive from the supposed relationship between individual autonomy, diversity, and cultural membership. Raz's accounts of tolerance and multiculturalism transcend the minimal rights and protections that weak tolerance of the Lockean variety affords; his argument also avoids the extreme reductionism of the Millian thesis on individual liberty and diversity (as well as Mill's phobia of collective forms of socialization, such as public education). Despite the evident advantages of Raz's argument, however, it is not as tolerant or accommodating of social differences as it purports to be. His view is tainted by the same instrumental view of the value of diversity attributed to Mill's defense of toleration: the idea that diversity is primarily useful insofar as it helps to secure worthwhile choices for agents, which they need in order to flourish.[46] So although Raz's view is far beyond Mill's

44. Kymlicka confirms this restriction when he writes of the need to liberalize certain minority cultures within democratic states. See *Liberalism, Community, and Culture*, 170–71.

45. Jonathan Chaplin, "How Much Cultural and Religious Pluralism Can Liberalism Tolerate?" in *Liberalism, Multiculturalism, and Toleration*, ed. J. Horton (London: Macmillan, 1993), 43.

46. Mill, *On Liberty*, chapter 3, "Of Individuality."

understanding of diversity as *individuality* (as expressed in the cultivation of individual thought and character), he fails to see that cultural identity and cultural membership might be important even in cases where they do not explicitly support members' autonomy. In sum, as Susan Mendus has noted, the narrowness of Raz's justification of toleration may indicate that "autonomy-based liberalism is far less open, plural and tolerant than its advocates would have us believe."[47]

Raz's expanded Millian, autonomy-based argument for tolerance and cultural diversity may represent the best that a conception of *strong tolerance* can offer us: namely, proposals for a wide range of state protections and forms of assistance for cultural minority groups. Why should this not be enough? If it is not, does this suggest that there are intrinsic limitations to the concept of tolerance or merely with its practical application? It seems clear that Mill's and Raz's arguments for toleration cannot fully meet cultural claims for recognition: even strong, or positive, forms of tolerance cannot deliver the respect necessary to intercultural dialogue and cooperation. To understand why, it is useful to juxtapose toleration with a more substantive principle invoked frequently by cultural minority groups themselves, that of respect.

Beyond Toleration: Intercultural Respect

That political philosophers commonly distinguish between respect and tolerance seems instructive and lends support to my claim that respect is the more robust form of concern for persons.[48] Amy Gutmann states the difference as follows: "Toleration extends to the widest range of views, so long as they stop short of threats and other direct and discernible harms to individuals. Respect is far more discriminating. Although we need not agree with a position to respect it, we must understand it as reflecting a moral point of view."[49] Gutmann is speaking here specifically of respect for beliefs, not persons, but the distinction she draws is nonetheless helpful in getting at the contrast between respect and mere tolerance. In

---

47. Mendus, *Toleration and the Limits of Liberalism*, 110.

48. The relationship between respect and toleration is of course considerably more complex than my comment suggests. Some writers view toleration as a "sub-category of respect," as David Heyd has recently argued in his introduction to *Toleration: An Elusive Virtue*, ed. D. Heyd (Princeton, N.J.: Princeton University Press, 1996), 12. Raz also appeals to a particular conception of respect for persons to ground his argument for toleration. But for reasons cited earlier, the respect Raz cites is not conducive to the substantive, intercultural respect with which I am concerned.

49. See Amy Gutmann, Introduction to *Multiculturalism: Examining the Politics of Recognition*, ed. Gutmann (Princeton, N.J.: Princeton University Press, 1994), 22.

particular, we might say that respect for cultural communities is in many senses "more demanding than toleration"[50] because it requires some understanding of, as well as engagement with, a group's beliefs and ways of life. Formal political toleration requires little engagement with the community that is to be tolerated, the members of which may simply come under a particular description of persons whose presence and / or practices are to be tolerated. By contrast, respect requires much more: it demands that institutions and individuals take some account of the *content* of different cultural groups rather than merely viewing them from the outside. In short, respect requires concrete knowledge of, and sometimes actual engagement with, the group in question.

A related, equally important difference between respect and tolerance is that whereas the former typically requires the faculty and practice of judgment, the latter need not. Indeed, tolerance may involve very little reflexivity. As Barbara Herman has recently argued, we need to distinguish between mere toleration—which she suggests does not require much reflection and interaction with others—and practices of judgment, which do (or should) require such engagement. Whereas toleration is a "laissez-faire virtue," judgment demands much more of agents in terms of dialogue and understanding. Herman's Kantian approach emphasizes the idea of a "community of moral judgment" and a "deliberative field" into which local values enter and are assessed.

Herman's deliberative model has several advantages: it demonstrates ways to develop practices of respect at the same time that it provides a basis for public, critical assessments of cultural practices.[51] More importantly, deliberative practices of judgment preclude simply invoking liberal values to settle conflicts of belief, as some comprehensive liberals propose we do. Equally, deliberative judgment imposes minimal standards of openness and reflexivity;[52] as such, it is potentially both more inclusive of social differences and offers a better model of fostering respect than either weak or strong toleration.

Why might it be important to encourage greater understanding of the norms and beliefs of cultural minorities that make justice claims against the liberal state? In the first place, more direct knowledge of the content of a culture (and if possible, engagement with particular groups) is necessary if we are to avoid treating collective social differences as mere difficulties to be overcome, as problems to be mediated. In the absence

50. Gutmann, "Civic Education and Social Diversity," *Ethics* 105, no. 3 (1995): 576.

51. Barbara Herman, "Pluralism and the Community of Moral Judgment," in *Toleration: An Elusive Virtue*, ed. David Heyd (Princeton, N.J.: Princeton University Press, 1996), 63–74.

52. Ibid., 77.

of critical reflection on the content of cultural differences, stereotypes of minority groups are perpetuated and crucial distinctions lost.[53] Informed deliberation about the justice and practicability of accommodating certain practices—or alternatively, restricting these—requires concrete knowledge and understanding of citizens' different contexts and identities. We cannot hope to make fair political judgments about which practices are simply unacceptable in a plural, democratic society without some understanding of the moral landscapes and traditions that form the backdrop to these disputed practices.

The norm of institutional respect thus demands and perhaps even facilitates a more thorough understanding and interaction with cultural minority groups. In some sense, it sets the goal post much further than does toleration, which neither promises nor purports to secure more comprehensive understanding or deeper forms of recognition. It is difficult to imagine how such recognition could get off the ground in the absence of greater engagement with a group's normative beliefs and social arrangements. Similarly, appreciation and admiration—one step beyond recognition and inevitably rarer—surely require that we inquire into the cultural meanings of different practices or beliefs and the role these play within particular cultures and sub-cultures. The state may tolerate a nonliberal group (say, aboriginal peoples) for purely formal reasons to do with a commitment to liberal freedom and political neutrality, but that group may still well demand an understanding and appreciation of its distinctness, its norms and beliefs, and social practices and arrangements. How to determine whether (and which) groups are deserving of such admiration and respect is a matter I shall take up shortly.

Toleration, unlike the norm of respect, may also be at odds with the suggestion that we have reasons to value existing forms of cultural *diversity*. Let me clarify this claim. To suggest that cultural diversity (as opposed merely to *specific* cultural identities and groups) is valuable in a general sense is not to say that "more diversity is always better" or that states should actively seek to create *new* forms of diversity, such as new languages and identities. Equally, it does not follow that liberal states should seek to preserve all social differences at *any* cost. Rather, my claim that democratic states (and citizens generally) have cause to value cultural diversity is a more modest one, consisting of the follow-

53. This is well illustrated by the example of the 1989 expulsion from French state schools of Muslim girls wearing the traditional headscarf. As one critic notes, in this case the principle of toleration invoked by French authorities failed "to differentiate meaningfully between wearing the Islamic veil and wearing a funny hat at school." See Galeotti, "Citizenship and Equality," 592.

ing points.[54] First, democratic states have reason to value the actual and potential contributions of many of their *existing* multicultural communities—as well as to consider the benefits of culturally diverse immigrants—whose presence enriches the social and cultural possibilities available to all of us. Second, a culturally plural social context provides a good background against which one may reflect on (and assess) one's own norms, beliefs, and culture.[55] Third, valuing cultural diversity provides an essential argument for "multicultural" policies in education, which aim to introduce children to diverse cultural and religious beliefs; this sort of concrete interaction with members of different cultural communities provides children (and parents) with a direct and valuable basis of knowledge and understanding. Educating children to appreciate different ways of life and perspectives may help to encourage respect for cultural minorities, as well as helping children to develop the powers of critical reflection later necessary to good practices of citizenship.[56]

Two further reasons for valuing diversity speak to the political benefits of a society in which different cultures coexist. In many instances, cultural diversity contributes to a certain degree of *ethical* diversity, which democratic states have reason to value (as well as, of course, to fear). The presence of citizens with contrasting political sensibilities and judgments is surely critical to the health of democratic politics. As Amélie Rorty notes, deliberative institutions "need representatives with different types of ethical character."[57] The presence of moral differences and moral disagreement in democratic political life—closely related to cultural and ethnic differences—also serves to underscore the need for more consultative, deliberative political procedures that can take serious account of these. And finally, a constitutional democracy made up of diverse groups may be greater than the sum of its parts: cul-

54. I take this issue up at greater length in chapter 4.

55. Yael Tamir also recently has argued this point in *Liberal Nationalism*, 30, 32.

56. Amy Gutmann's account of the reason why civic education should reflect social diversity is a good one: "At issue here is not mere exposure to different ways of life for the sake of giving children more choices among good lives but, rather, teaching future citizens to evaluate different political perspectives that are often associated with different ways of life." See her "Civic Education and Social Diversity," 577.

57. Rorty, "The Advantages of Moral Diversity," 53. Although public decision-making that involves citizens of different ethical perspectives is inevitably more difficult, it is also potentially richer. A parallel argument about the merits of ethical diversity can be found in writings by some neo-Kantian theorists that address the theme of judgment. For instance, Barbara Herman suggests that citizens' social and ethical differences contribute in valuable ways to the development of what she calls (reconstructing Kant's theory) a critical and reflexive "community of moral judgment." Herman, "Pluralism and the Community of Moral Judgment."

tural communities bring to the constitutional association valuable resources, traditions, and decision-making practices that may enhance public life.

For all of these reasons, respect—which requires and encourages greater understanding of and engagement with cultural minority communities—seems a more appropriate norm and goal than toleration for plural democratic states. This is especially so where claims for cultural recognition give voice to the sense that one's group is not in fact respected and where minimal forms of institutional tolerance simply have not sufficed (for example, as in the case of certain national minorities in liberal societies, such as aboriginal peoples in the United States, Canada, Australia, and New Zealand, and ethnic and linguistic minorities in Europe and Canada). A conception of respect that directly reflects this requirement for deeper recognition of one's personhood is articulated by Kant, who defines respect as the "recognition of a dignity in other men, ... of a worth that has no price."[58] Because Kant's account of respect highlights the importance of moral regard for agents' dignity and self-esteem, it has an affinity with contemporary claims for cultural respect and recognition. In contrast to toleration—which may, but does not necessarily, involve concern for persons' dignity and self-esteem—the duties of respect require that we treat others in ways that show regard for their dignity and humanity. Applied to the issue of cultural diversity, we might say that social and institutional regard for cultural groups' identities and ways of life is central to the self-respect of their members, as well as to the dignity and standing of groups themselves.

The suggestion that the norm of respect is a more adequate principle for liberal democratic societies invariably meets with the objection that many groups do not deserve such respect, either because they are intolerant of others or because their internal practices and arrangements are oppressive or unjust. But to say that *some* groups will not merit formal respect for these or other reasons is not to say that other cultural minority groups—say, those that do not violate their members' basic rights—are not entitled to such respect, both morally and politically. Surely it is possible to determine which groups have forfeited their claims to recognition and respect based on a set of criteria that derives broadly from liberal democratic norms but reflects the demands of culturally plural societies. Here too, a Kantian perspective on respect is helpful, for it incorporates the criterion of reciprocal duties of respect.

58. Kant, "The Doctrine of Virtue," *The Metaphysics of Morals*, book 2, part 2, sec. 37, p. 254.

As mentioned in chapter 1, the requirement that persons treat others—
including members of one's own group, however defined—with respect
if they are to deserve such respect themselves provides us with at least a
preliminary mechanism for rejecting claims for greater accommodation
by groups with evidently oppressive practices.[59]

An account of respect for persons that derives from Kant's view is different from toleration in numerous ways. Practices of toleration *may* secure a kind of grudging respect, if any at all; but they cannot deliver
substantive, "intercultural" respect, which requires concrete knowledge
of, and very likely dialogue with, cultural communities. Philosopher
Lawrence Blum's account of the kind of respect crucial in a culturally
plural society comes closest to capturing this notion: "the active sense of
informed respect for cultures other than one's own."[60] The Millian account of toleration, as we have seen, does not inquire into the *content* of
the particular beliefs and practices being tolerated. Likewise, Raz's account is less interested in the content of culture than in the way that
certain features of cultural membership and identity furnish members
with the capacities for autonomy and with worthwhile options and
choices. By contrast, respect for members of cultural communities—
and for the standing of these groups—is best understood as the recognition that their identities, attachments, and ways of life are valuable
and may give rise to legitimate social and political needs.

On the view sketched here, the cultivation of intercultural respect requires concrete dialogue between cultural communities and between
cultural groups and the state, the terms of which minority groups themselves must help shape. This is because it is only through practical discussions that citizens can come to understand others' cultural differences as anything more than opposing or perhaps simply opaque
viewpoints. Intercultural dialogue may occur both through such formal
structures as representative and consultative government bodies and in-
formally in civil society through cultural associations, media, commer-
cial life, and more informal interaction. Such respect may not always be
possible in public life, in which case legal and institutional forms of respect and tolerance will have to suffice; but it is premature and politically cynical to assume that opportunities for intercultural dialogue do
not exist or that they cannot be created or expanded.

We may want to press further and ask whether, and why, justice in liberal democratic states should require that we understand and engage

59. I address this issue at greater length in chapter 4.
60. Blum, "Multiculturalism, Racial Justice, and Community," 186.

with, much less respect, different cultural beliefs and practices. The simplest answer to this is that liberal states today face a range of demands by cultural, ethnic, and religious minorities that cannot be understood, much less settled, without attending to the content of those demands and the cultures they reflect. Practices of toleration do not normally require that we engage critically and respectfully with the normative substance of different cultures, beliefs, and practices, much less reflect on or revise our views about the rightness or wrongness of those beliefs and practices. This gives rise to two sorts of problems. First, it means that, in practice, the objects of toleration—whether beliefs, practices, or groups of persons—are too readily treated as an undifferentiated mass, so that religious sects are tolerated in the same breath and with as little reflection as are religious and ethnic minorities. And second, without attending to the content of cultures, we cannot come to appreciate others' views and ways of life or accord them or their communities adequate respect and recognition.

Michael Sandel, in his discussion of homosexual rights, nicely illustrates the importance of respecting persons as opposed to merely tolerating them. Sandel suggests that a 1969 U.S. Supreme Court decision (*Stanley v. Georgia*) which granted "privacy" rights to homosexuals merely extended tolerance to homosexual practices but made no attempt to understand or convey respect for the "minority goods" at issue.

> The problem with the neutral case for toleration is the opposite side of its appeal; it leaves wholly unchallenged the adverse views of homosexuality itself. Unless those views can be plausibly addressed, even a Court ruling in their favor is unlikely to win for homosexuals more than a thin and fragile toleration. A fuller respect would require, if not admiration, at least some appreciation of the lives homosexuals live.[61]

From this account, we can see that the underlying views by which a practice comes to be labeled "wrong" or aberrant may be left wholly unchallenged by practices of toleration. As Sandel notes, "*Stanley* tolerates homosexuality at the price of demeaning it; it puts homosexual intimacy on par with obscenity—a base thing that should nonetheless be tolerated so long as it takes place in private."[62] Surely a democratic theory of cultural pluralism should not replicate this mistake.

---

61. Michael Sandel, "Moral Argument and Liberal Toleration: Abortion and Homosexuality," *California Law Review* 77 (1989): 537.
62. Ibid.

I have argued that the different accounts of toleration discussed here cannot supply strategies for meeting cultural minority groups' demands for recognition and respect in plural, liberal states. To meet many of these claims, democratic polities (and citizens generally) need to appreciate the content—and contexts—of different values, beliefs, and practices, in part through reflective engagement and concrete dialogue with minority cultural communities. Toleration does not direct us to inquire into the *content* of different beliefs or practices, though toleration may be a necessary requirement of, or pre-condition for, such inquiries. Nor does toleration require that we accord substantive respect to the persons or views that are its objects. Practices of toleration may also reflect and reinforce assumptions and social relations that are incompatible with the aspirations and claims of cultural minority groups, in particular their quest for mutual respect and greater social and political inclusion.

Proponents of weak or negative toleration do not purport to secure a robust form of respect for persons, much less for persons in the context of their cultural identities, attachments, and memberships. Defenders of strong toleration propose to deliver more in the way of positive protections for citizens' differences. But Mill, as we have seen, offers an argument for tolerance that is fundamentally about protecting individual diversity and liberty; his is *not* a plea for respect for groups or collectives, nor for individuals whose sense of identity derives from membership in those groups. Although Raz's expanded Millian argument includes some good proposals for cultural rights and the protection of group cultural membership, the reasons he offers for these measures construe culture and autonomy in problematic ways and can promise to include only those groups whose beliefs roughly conform to a restrictive, liberal moral view.

To the extent that toleration can play a role in shaping policies for meeting cultural claims and mediating cultural conflicts, it will be a limited one. Toleration is not a redundant principle or virtue, but it offers too little. Perhaps tolerance is best viewed as a strategy that individuals or government bodies may take up when there is no hope for more extensive exchange and dialogue or when avenues for more reciprocal engagement are closed. At any rate, the conceptions of liberal tolerance I have addressed here are limited in ways that recommend against the adoption of toleration as overall strategy for meeting the challenges posed by cultural diversity in democratic states.

THREE

Neutrality, Justice, and Cultural Diversity

> The problem of political liberalism is: How is it possible that there
> may exist over time a stable and just society of free and equal citizens
> profoundly divided by reasonable though incompatible religious,
> philosophical, and moral doctrines? ... How is it possible that deeply
> opposed though reasonable comprehensive doctrines may live
> together and all affirm the political conception of a constitutional
> regime?
>
> —JOHN RAWLS, *Political Liberalism*

Contemporary contractarian liberals appeal to the idea of neutrality more readily than to the notion of toleration to suggest how we might mediate conflicts arising from citizens' diverse views of the good. Their view that the state should be neutral about the good life expands and extends the principle of toleration by situating it within a broader framework of liberal political norms and principles. As might be expected, there are several different contested interpretations of liberal neutrality. The core idea it expresses, however, is simply that political principles, procedures, and state institutions should not favor any particular, controversial comprehensive conception of the good, but rather should reflect only those political norms that are in fact shared by citizens (or which citizens could accept as reasonable). Liberal legitimacy, in this view, depends on securing the reciprocal agreement of citizens who may have diverse and even incommensurable moral and social beliefs and values.

Crucially, neutral or political liberals posit that if liberal principles and institutions are to reflect only those public norms that are widely shared in plural liberal states—or which are justifiable by a process of neutral, public argumentation—then we must exclude issues about the good life from the scope of political principles. For this reason, neutral liberalism may seem well designed to cope with dilemmas presented by social and cultural diversity in democratic states. A theory of justice that makes no appeal to controversial moral norms should logically secure the agreement of a wider range of citizens than comprehensive moral and political theories (be they liberal, utilitarian, Marxist, etc.).[1] Indeed, to underscore this point, Rawls suggests that citizens' agreement on a merely political conception of liberal justice forms an "overlapping consensus" of citizens' "reasonable comprehensive views."[2] Despite the evident appeal of the idea of a neutral or merely political liberalism, I shall argue that it is not likely to secure equal justice for cultural minorities living in democratic states. To show why, I assess the principle of neutrality and the claims of its liberal defenders from the vantage point of cultural minorities' claims for recognition, greater democratic inclusion, and respect. The coherence of neutral or political liberalism does not depend solely on whether the principle of neutrality can help to meet the special claims of all cultural groups, of course. Nonetheless, if norms and procedures endorsed by neutral liberals can be shown to be biased against the political approaches, aspirations, and claims of some cultural communities in democratic states, this surely casts into doubt the adequacy of neutral liberalism as a conception of justice for socially plural societies.

In the discussion that follows, I ask whether liberal institutions centered on a commitment to political neutrality can foster greater recognition and democratic inclusion of cultural minorities. My concern is that proposed transformations to democratic institutions along the lines suggested by neutral or political liberals could pose unfair burdens to some cultural minorities, particularly those that do not fit a liberal profile.[3] Such burdens might in turn translate into formidable obstacles

---

1. Contemporary theories of "neutral" justice can be viewed in part as an attempt by liberal thinkers to revive and secure the legitimacy of liberal theory amid competing socialist, Marxist, and especially utilitarian political doctrines. Since these latter political theories rely on comprehensive conceptions of the good and/or perfectionist accounts of state obligation, they are particularly ill-placed, so their liberal critics argue, to meet the challenges posed by value pluralism in socially plural democratic states.

2. John Rawls, "The Priority of the Right and Ideas of the Good," *Philosophy and Public Affairs* 17, no. 4 (1988): 261–62, and *Political Liberalism*, passim.

3. Both John Rawls and Charles Larmore endorse a political conception of liberalism that centers on the idea of neutrality. Although he does not use the term political liberalism, Bruce Ackerman also appeals to the principle of neutrality in political deliberation.

to the representation and participation of cultural minority communities in democratic politics. I offer two main reasons to support this claim. First, despite the claims of its proponents, the key principles and procedures of neutral liberal justice are sometimes covertly predicated on controversial norms and assumptions about idealized moral agents—especially about their reasonableness and motivations—that favor citizens with liberal values and views. These norms presuppose that agents are motivated by the goal of securing neutral, democratic justice and have social and moral allegiances and attachments that are compatible with this conception of justice. Yet these assumptions are especially tendentious in the context of socially and culturally plural societies and may be incompatible with the sorts of institutional changes that may be necessary to foster greater inclusion of cultural minorities—especially aboriginal peoples and immigrant communities with traditional cultural and religious values. Although political liberals such as Rawls, Charles Larmore, and Bruce Ackerman fully intend their theories to address circumstances of social pluralism, the conceptions of rationality and reasonableness they invoke to demonstrate an "ideal consensus" on a particular conception of neutral justice tell a different story.

Second, the actual constraints that neutral liberals seek to impose on political deliberation reflect a distinction between public / political and private / social ideals and arrangements that many citizens of minority cultures and religions could not (and do not) accept. Most problematic in this regard are notions of neutral public dialogue, neutral public reason, and neutral justification and deliberation. The requirement that citizens bracket their identities and comprehensive views when deliberating on political norms and institutions is not only counterintuitive in some sense, but could also impose unfair burdens on citizens from historically disadvantaged cultural communities. Those who view their distinct identities and values as contributing legitimately to their political proposals and arguments may be thwarted by neutral, liberal norms of deliberation, which could act as exclusionary devices in democratic politics. Although neutral liberals seek to accommodate citizens' diverse and sometimes incommensurable individual views of the good, their neglect of citizens' cultural identities and cultural memberships may jeopardize the justice they claim to be able to deliver.

Neutrality and Toleration

A central claim of neutral liberalism is that the principle of neutrality provides the basis for liberal legitimacy in plural states by ensuring that citizens agree to the basic principles and procedures of political life. Neutral liberalism is in one sense an extension of seventeenth- and eighteenth-century contractarian liberal thinking insofar as it echoes the belief of social contract theorists that the consent of the governed underwrites the legitimacy of the state. Moreover, just as earlier liberals considered practices of limited tolerance crucial to the stability of the state, contemporary neutral liberals point to state neutrality and toleration as integral features of liberal justice. Rather than viewing the principle of neutrality as a radical departure from toleration, its contemporary defenders thus understand it as a kind of parallel strategy, one that is more systematic and demanding than toleration—especially in what is required of the state—and whose scope is more clearly defined. We might say, then, that neutrality takes up where toleration leaves off.

Neutral or political liberals, however, associate toleration-based liberal theories (e.g., the liberalism of earlier contractarians such as Locke) with a comprehensive liberal moral orientation that cannot meet the requirements of justice in culturally plural liberal states. In contrast to liberals who invoke determinate (and controversial) liberal goods and values as the basis for justice, political liberals purport to offer a conception of justice based on neutral and widely acceptable principles. The notion of a merely political liberalism does not imply that other liberal theories are uninterested in politics, but rather that they are not *strictly* political in their scope and ambition. Political liberals' reasons for asserting that liberalism should be delimited in this way are both philosophical and pragmatic. First, liberals such as Rawls and Larmore believe that there is no philosophically satisfactory way in which to establish an "objectively" superior conception of the good. Second, they suggest that it is not practically possible in large, socially plural societies to secure wide agreement on norms and principles that presuppose comprehensive moral ideals or conceptions of the good. Even comprehensive norms conventionally associated with liberalism—such as individual autonomy and individuality—may be socially contested and for this reason are not appropriate norms on which to base a conception of justice for plural states.[4] And third, political liberals suggest that in socially diverse democratic states, a political system founded on a comprehensive view of the good will unjustly favor conceptions of the good held by *some* citizens; consequently, it may also prevent some

---

4. Autonomy and individuality are the two norms from which political liberals specifically seek to distance their accounts of justice, citing these as representative of more "comprehensive" liberal conceptions, such as those of Kant and Mill. See, for instance, the discussion by Charles Larmore, "Political Liberalism," *Political Theory* 18, no. 3 (1990): 339–60, especially 342–46, and Rawls, *Political Liberalism*, especially 78 and 199–200.

citizens from pursuing their chosen ways of life and, in so doing, fail to deliver justice to all citizens.

Contemporary neutral liberals who argue that a conception of justice should meet with the acceptance of all citizens in a democratic polity set themselves a more difficult task than the one their early modern and modern predecessors undertook. Earlier liberals' proposals for limited political rights and toleration for certain religious minorities were predicated on the assumption that religious minorities would remain *passive* citizens. Unlike many contemporary liberals, who are concerned to argue for liberal *democracy* (albeit a thin form), early liberals did not attempt to justify liberalism by appealing to neutral principles. Rather, they shared the idea that political society should be founded on certain concrete values (including some Christian ones) and ideals that we view as characteristically liberal, such as toleration and liberty.

The reluctance of today's liberals to justify liberal principles and policies in ways endorsed by earlier thinkers creates new problems of justification for liberalism. Contemporary liberals cannot plausibly rest their defenses of neutral liberalism on appeals to epistemological skepticism or on prudential claims about the threat of anarchy, much less invoke the humanistic and theistic arguments of their seventeenth- and eighteenth-century predecessors. More importantly, neutral liberals believe that they cannot rest their arguments for a liberal theory of justice on appeals to comprehensive, and contested, norms and ideals. In part, this reflects a commitment on the part of contemporary liberals to the development of a more philosophically satisfactory justification of liberal principles. But equally, neutral liberals' reluctance to invoke comprehensive norms also suggests that they are concerned to accommodate a much wider range of citizens' social and ethical differences than pre-democratic seventeenth- and eighteenth-century liberals thought it necessary to consider.

The rejection of comprehensive liberalism is typically associated with the adoption of what is generally spoken of as a Kantian perspective in political ethics. Neutral or political liberals incorporate earlier liberals' emphasis on the idea of a social contract as the basis of liberal legitimacy, but they eschew the moral worldview of their predecessors in favor of what they take to be a Kantian approach to political philosophy. Kant's thought was the culmination of the early modern Natural Law tradition, and it was he who broke decisively with the practice of appealing to theological claims to justify moral principles and political action. Kant also rejected attempts to ground morality and justice on nonuniversal or local norms or even prudential reasons. Although few contemporary liberals maintain that moral principles are by definition univer-

salizable in Kant's strict sense, Kant's influence is reflected in the neutral liberal view—articulated most famously by Rawls—that a conception of justice must be based on political principles that are acceptable
to all reasonable persons in democratic states.[5]

The Kantian turn in liberal political thought in the last twenty-five
years has caused liberal arguments that presuppose or appeal to comprehensive values and ostensibly shared conceptions of the good to fall
from favor.[6] Both the rejection of teleological and perfectionist
justifications of liberalism and an emphasis on models of instrumental
rationality in much moral and political theory have contributed cen-
trally to the development of "neutral" conceptions of liberal justice.
Neutral liberals develop arguments in which they attempt to invoke
only minimal beliefs about the rationality and agency of persons.[7] Contractarian liberal theories in particular insist that in order for liberal
principles to reflect the aspirations of all citizens, they should reflect
universal principles of right. These principles are to be identified and
justified as the outcome of a hypothetical contract or agreement. Neutral liberals reject political principles and state actions that appeal
either to a particular account of the good or to ideals that are not
widely held, on the grounds that these would be incompatible with the
rational autonomy and agency of moral agents. Such principles could
not meet the test of ideal consent, nor secure the actual (assumed) consent of the persons who would be bound by them.[8]

---

5. Much self-styled Kantian writing fails to employ Kant's own conceptions of practical reason, universality, and judgment and instead relies on an instrumental account of
reasoning and an idealized conception of agents. For example, the specific conception of
rationality that today's liberals have in mind leads them to understand "universalizability"
differently than Kant did. It is therefore important to distinguish between contemporary
Kantians who assert liberal justice against the background of other Kantian principles and
conceptions (e.g., judgment) and those who argue solely for a liberal (though Kantian-
derived) conception of justice. It is the latter that will be the focus of my discussion.

6. More recently, some liberals have reintroduced arguments for a conspicuously
comprehensive liberalism. A good example is Joseph Raz, whose liberal perfectionist approach I take up in the next chapter. Communitarian and neo-Aristotelian thinkers readily appeal to concrete values, some of which are, surprisingly, liberal.

7. In practice (as I shall show in subsequent sections), many liberals violate this
requirement.

8. Some liberals assert that no liberal principles should appeal to a particular account of the good; for instance, Thomas Nagel argues that liberalism requires a higher-
order impartiality. See Nagel, "Moral Conflict and Political Legitimacy," in *Authority*, ed.
Joseph Raz (Oxford: Basil Blackwell, 1990). Others, such as Ackerman, are careful to
state that only normative beliefs *that are not widely shared* should be excluded from
justifications of principles and political action. See Ackerman, *Social Justice in the Liberal
State* (New Haven: Yale University Press, 1980).

Neutral or contractarian liberals have proposed not only that principles of justice should be neutral in the sense of being ones that all could accept, but also that the state should be neutral as concerns different conceptions of the good. This latter form of neutrality is thought necessary not merely for purposes of justification but also to secure wide agreement on the basic political framework of society. This agreement in turn provides the stability necessary for the accommodation of diverse religious, ethical, and cultural beliefs in "private" and "social" life.[9] These ideas are central to Rawls's *A Theory of Justice*, the first contemporary liberal text to take the fact of deep pluralism, or of competing and possibly incommensurable conceptions of the good, as the starting point for liberal justice. What was notable about Rawls's theory was not just its ambition—his attempt to set out the basic principles, political framework, and institutions that could guide liberal societies—but that he fully expected that the principles of justice he elaborated could meet rigorous standards of rationality and secure the wide agreement of citizens of culturally diverse liberal states. So sure was Rawls that his theory of justice captured citizens' intuitions about justice as fairness that he staked the legitimacy of the theory largely on this conviction, which he maintains even in his most recent work.

Political liberals such as Rawls hold that neutral liberal justice offers a better strategy for dealing with moral and social diversity than a liberalism based on toleration. Rawls, in particular, views toleration as a specific political virtue which (like respect) is one aspect of a political conception of liberal justice.[10] Neutrality is, however, the broader principle on which this conception of justice is based, and indeed, Rawls posits that neutrality requires practices of respect and toleration. Neutrality, however, also requires more of the state: whereas toleration may sometimes require state intervention (to stop religious harassment, for example), it frequently requires only that the state refrain from persecuting—but not, say, from marginalizing—citizens with minority beliefs. By contrast, a much wider range of state actions and institutional changes is required by a commitment to securing neutral forms of justification and deliberation in public life. For instance, the state likely must introduce constraints on political deliberation and develop mechanisms to ensure that no particular account of the good is favored in

---

9. Sometimes, as in the case of Rawls, welfarist principles are employed in order to ensure meaningful access to resources that enable individuals to pursue their preferred way of life.

10. Rawls, *Political Liberalism*, 122 and 194.

politics. Some conceptions of neutrality even require that the state ensure equality of opportunity for different ways of life through policies of
meticulous impartiality and the redistribution of wealth.[11]

Perhaps the most important reason why neutral liberals favor their
own approach over earlier, toleration-based liberalisms is that even the
most minimal account of neutrality requires that the liberal state not act
deliberately in favor of one conception of the good over others, one set of
beliefs over another, or one group's interests at the expense of the rest
of society. By contrast, practices of toleration are fully compatible with
(though they do not require) comprehensive, perfectionist forms of liberalism. Political neutrality entails a commitment to fairness and a kind
of deliberate, measured neutrality about ethical matters, the combination of which might best be described as impartiality.[12] Among other
things, the principle of neutrality requires that government representatives, judicial authorities, and citizens critically examine their reasons
for proposing particular judgments, decisions, and actions and that
they justify their positions "neutrally"—that is, in broad, universal terms
that all could accept, rather than appealing to their private interests. Of
course, permissible state action may, as it turns out, favor one position,
but even a minimal account of neutrality requires that this not be the
express intent of the state: partialist commitments on the part of the
state are deemed illegitimate. By contrast, proponents of a liberalism
based on toleration and liberty did object to state perfectionism but
merely sought to forbid the grave *consequences* of state action such as
persecution and sometimes the grave consequences of state inaction—
such as the failure to prevent persecution by organs of civil society (e.g.,
by the church). Nor did these earlier advocates intend toleration to provide the basis for an overarching conception of justice, as today's neutral liberals expect of the principle of neutrality.

Contested Conceptions of Neutrality

Any assessment of the merits of neutral liberalism will depend in part
on the conception of neutrality under examination. It is for this reason

11. This is neutrality of outcome or consequences, which I take up in the next section.

12. Whereas impartiality is generally understood as a moral principle and practice,
neutrality is increasingly considered by liberals as a distinctively political principle. This
has concrete implications for the kinds of institutions and forms of deliberation operative
in liberal states. Neutrality is best seen as more political in scope than impartiality, requiring a wider range of state action and with fewer implications for *individual action* (save for
our activity as citizens) than impartiality holds.

that I sketch out and offer a brief assessment of the main types of neutrality below.

Charles Larmore perhaps best captures the spirit of neutrality when he states that it is meant to secure *predictability* in politics—in particular, to provide reassurance that liberal governments will not act in undemocratic and unforeseen ways, mainly by favoring one conception of the good over another. Larmore incorporates this thought into his succinct and minimal account of the core idea behind neutrality: "Pluralism and reasonable disagreement have become for modern political thought ineliminable features of the idea of the good life.... The state should not seek to promote any particular conception of the good life because of its presumed *intrinsic* superiority—that is, because it is supposedly a *truer* conception."[13] The stipulation that liberal principles and liberal states should not favor a particular conception of the good is the defining feature common to all arguments for political neutrality.

The two main conceptions of neutrality that figure in contemporary liberal theory are neutrality of outcome or consequences and neutrality of justification (sometimes known as neutrality of process or procedure).[14] Neutrality of outcome or consequences did not emerge first in liberal discourse, but I examine it first because I do not intend to revisit it in later critical discussions. It is neutrality of justification which informs the arguments of John Rawls and Charles Larmore, examined later in the chapter.

Neutrality of Effect / Consequence

Procedures that aim to secure neutrality of consequences seek, in effect, to *equalize* the chances for success and flourishing of different ways of life and to ensure that none is eliminated by poverty or lack of oppor-

---

13. Larmore, *Patterns of Moral Complexity*, 43.

14. There are numerous variations on these terms describing types of neutrality. For instance, Andrew Mason distinguishes "neutrality of justification" from "neutrality of effect." See his "Autonomy, Liberalism, and State Neutrality," *Philosophical Quarterly* 40, no. 160 (1990): 433–52. Others refer to "strong" neutrality (neutrality of consequences) versus "weak" neutrality (neutrality of justification). See, for instance, Peter Jones, "Ideal of the Neutral State," in *Liberalism and Neutrality*, ed. Robert Goodin and Andrew Reeves (London: Routledge, 1989). Neutrality of justification is sometimes discussed as "neutrality of procedure" or even "neutrality of process." However, these latter two terms are somewhat misleading: the term "procedure" is too easily taken to imply that existing political institutions should simply observe neutral forms of argumentation and deliberation, whereas proponents of neutrality of justification want to convey, in addition to this, the requirement that legal and political institutions and practices should *themselves* be subjected to the test of neutrality.

in terms that all rational and/or reasonable agents either could or would accept. Principles are deemed neutral insofar as they meet the test of public reason—that is, if all reasonable persons would agree to be bound by them. Neutrality of justification further demands that those acting in a political role or capacity (potentially all those living in a given polity, whether acting as citizens, activists, legislators, or judicial officials) refrain from *justifying* proposals of public or political significance in terms of the intrinsic superiority of one way of life, or of one set of beliefs, over another. Not only are such partialist proposals unjustifiable in the view of neutral liberals, they are also less likely to be politically persuasive.[18]

Unlike neutrality of outcome, neutrality of justification does not regard the neutrality or "equality" of consequences as proof of the state's neutrality or of the neutrality of political principles. However, neutrality of justification, it seems, presupposes simultaneous commitments to several liberal ideals, specifically autonomy, equal respect, and norms of rationality. Whether these ideals (as interpreted by political liberals) are compatible with and conducive to respect and recognition for cultural minorities in liberal societies is my main concern and the focus of the present discussion. It is useful to begin by distinguishing between two different general strategies for justifying neutrality of justification, for these bear directly on the question of neutral liberalism's suitability for culturally plural societies.[19] Some liberals attempt to defend neutrality as a core liberal *value* that coheres with other liberal ideals, such as equality and personal autonomy. More often, liberals appeal to rationality and "objective" arguments in order to justify neutrality on normatively neutral grounds. Arguments of the first type invoke liberal values in asserting that norms of neutrality are widely accepted by citizens in democratic states. This is a somewhat different strategy from that of early modern liberals, whose appeals to liberty and toleration did not rest on claims that these norms were actually accepted, but rather that enlightened and rational persons *should* accept them.

By contrast, attempts to defend neutrality without relying on normatively substantive grounds turn either to a particular conception of ra-

18. It is important to distinguish between the requirement that political agents not justify their political proposals by reference to a distinctive conception of the good, which neutrality of justification requires, and the view that citizens should not invoke personal (religious and moral) beliefs in making political choices, which neutrality of justification *may not* require. On this issue, see Michael Perry, "Neutral Politics?" *Review of Politics* 51, no. 4 (1989): esp. 490.

19. To avoid repetition, henceforth where the form of neutrality is not specified, I refer to neutrality of justification.

tionality (as exemplified by Larmore's work) or to an ideal of reasonableness (as seen in Rawls's thought) in order to justify this principle. Proponents of this conception of liberalism employ the notion of an ideal consensus on shared, liberal political norms in an attempt to defend their conclusions. They also sometimes appeal to the normative fit or acceptance of the principle of neutrality in democratic states or to what I call the "assumed consensus" of citizens. There is both a theoretical and an empirical aspect to this claim. The theoretical aspect is reflected in liberal attempts to demonstrate both the rationality and reasonableness of a system of liberal justice founded on neutral principles and procedures. Some employ a notion of *ideal consensus* to defend their claim that it is rational for agents to endorse norms and procedures instantiating the principle of neutrality. The empirical justification of neutrality includes the assertion that neutral political principles and aspects of the political framework proposed by neutral liberals meet with the actual acceptance—what we might call the *"assumed consensus"*—of citizens in democratic states. More typically, political liberals combine both kinds of arguments in defending neutrality: they assert the wide acceptance of liberal ideals and principles alongside a rational model of ideal consensus on a neutral, liberal political conception of justice. Rawls's notions of reflective equilibrium and overlapping consensus, which I discuss below, present a good illustration of a combined (rational and normative) strategy of justification. Few liberal writers employ what I call "assumed consensus" alone.

Neutrality of Justification Defended as a Liberal Value

The claim that key liberal values—especially individual autonomy, freedom, and equality—can be supported by neutral arguments is one that is made by few thinkers and is usually part of a broader set of arguments. On this view, neutrality is a liberal value, indeed, *the* core liberal value. Few neutralist liberal thinkers employ this justificatory strategy alone, but many employ aspects of it alongside arguments about the justice and rationality of neutrality.[20] Bruce Ackerman, for example, who claims to defend a conception of justice in abstraction from any particular conception of the good, states that neutrality is a central liberal value and should be defended as such.[21] Likewise, political philosopher

20. I address arguments about the justice and rationality of neutrality in the following sections.

21. Bruce Ackerman, "Neutralities," in *Liberalism and the Good*, ed. G. Mara, B. Douglass, and H. Richardson (London and New York: Routledge, 1990), 29.

Jeremy Waldron wants to maintain the principle of neutrality while hailing liberalism as a moral, evaluative doctrine:

> Liberal neutrality is not and cannot be the doctrine that legislation should be neutral in relation to *all* moral values. It is certainly not the doctrine that legislation should be "value free," whatever that might mean. Those ideas are incoherent. Neutrality is itself a value: it is a normative position, a doctrine about what legislators and state officials ought to do. It is a doctrine that holds that it is wrong for certain considerations to enter the political arena; it is a doctrine which holds out neutrality in political activity as a right and good.[22]

The identification of neutrality as a distinctly liberal value that is widely accepted by citizens in democratic states might, if substantiated, constitute part of a credible justification for neutrality. However, the claim that neutrality is a liberal value that most citizens endorse is vulnerable to the charge that it assumes too much about the motivations and outlooks of socially diverse citizens. The defense of neutrality as a substantive and authoritative liberal norm also precariously presupposes that citizens accord greater value to the ideal of neutrality and to the liberal goods it is deemed to support (at least in the public realm) than to competing cultural values and attachments.[23] It also begs the question what is to become of citizens who do not embrace the norm of neutrality in political life or whose ways of life are in some sense incompatible with the principle of neutrality.

Values of Inclusion

As indicated at the outset of this chapter, my critical assessment of neutral liberalism in its various forms is shaped by my claim that many political institutions and practices in liberal states presently fail to include the voices and perspectives of numerous cultural minorities within those states. It might be asked whether proponents of neutral liberalism even intend for their approaches to accommodate citizens of diverse cultural communities at all. If so, should these liberals be held accountable for any burdens that might arise as a result of the constraints and

---

22. Waldron, "Legislation and Moral Neutrality," 156–57.

23. In connection with this point, see, for instance, Michael Sandel's criticism of liberalism's ideal of the self, which he claims posits "a subject whose identity is given independently of the things I have, independently, that is, of my interests and ends and my relations with others." See Sandel, *Liberalism and the Limits of Justice* (Cambridge: Cambridge University Press, 1982), 55.

demands entailed by liberal neutrality? Moreover, the neutral liberal theories under discussion also claim to be democratic theories fitting for culturally and socially plural societies. As such, it is not unreasonable to expect these writers to propose changes to political institutions and practices of deliberation and decision-making that could yield more inclusive and equitable relations between citizens of different social and cultural groups.

It is surely inaccurate to say that most minority ethnic and religious groups in liberal states are simply uninterested in democratic politics or that they would prefer, on balance, to limit their involvement to their local communities. Demands for greater inclusion in democratic politics—both in terms of political representation and direct political participation—figure prominently in the justice claims of many cultural minorities. In the United States, this is illustrated by attempts on the part of some Latino and African American national and local community lobbying groups to increase the number of racial and ethnic minority candidates both in local, state-wide, and federal party politics, as well as to get issues of key importance to their communities on the political agenda. Proposals for race-conscious electoral redistricting to secure seats for black candidates in majority African American voting districts, which have met with partial success, are yet another example of the demand for greater political involvement and representation by minorities.

Values of inclusion are equally invoked by cultural and religious minority groups that seek autonomy in the sense of having primary responsibility for and control over the affairs of their communities. Such groups may merely be asking to be incorporated differently into the broader polity or for a special set of arrangements to be worked out that helps them to maintain their distinctive social practices. In the United States an example of a community seeking special arrangements for the dual purposes of securing both local autonomy and integration into the broader polity is that of the Satmar Hasidic village of Kiryas Joel in upstate New York. By petitioning the state of New York to fund a special school district for their disabled children, this community expressed a desire to resist the integration of their children with non-Hasidic children. Yet equally, their actions reflect the expectation that relatively closed Hasidic communities might be able to work out asymmetrical arrangements with state and federal authorities that signal their inclusion (however marginal) within U.S. political culture. Although state courts have repeatedly struck down initiatives for government funding of the school district and the U.S. Supreme Court recently rejected a request to hear an appeal from Kiryas Joel, a new law passed in New York under

Governor George Pataki should make it possible for school districts to split off from larger districts and to receive state funding under special circumstances.[24] This might simply be an attempt on the part of state leaders to placate a powerful political community, but it is surely also an indication of the willingness of some state governments to integrate religious and cultural minority communities into political life—to enfranchise them—on special or asymmetrical terms.

It is often insisted that recent immigrant groups to North America and Europe have little or no interest in becoming actively engaged in the political affairs of their new host state. Yet there is little evidence beyond the anecdotal variety to suggest that this is the case. Even relatively recent immigrant communities—such as South Asians and West Indians in Britain—have demanded that attention be paid to the special needs and views of their communities, oftentimes directing these appeals at government institutions rather than lobbying specific political parties. In part, this could reflect the conviction on the part of some recent immigrant groups that traditional party politics remain closed to their direct participation and involvement. Of course, the openly bigoted and even racist attitudes of some members of traditionally conservative, anti-immigration parties such as the Tories in Britain have done much to reinforce this impression. Occasionally protests at the exclusion of immigrant communities' interests from party politics and government policy have taken dramatic forms, as in the case of the Brixton riots in Britain in 1981 and 1985.

Finally, although ethnic nationalist struggles stand as counter-examples to my claim that cultural minorities in liberal polities often demand greater *inclusion* in democratic political life, efforts by some national minorities to gain greater political autonomy and self-governance may follow years of frustrated attempts to gain access to real political power within the state. Nationalist movements in Wales and Scotland, for example, might arguably be understood in this light. And where religious, ethnic, and linguistic national minorities have successfully negotiated access to power—such as in the consociational democracies of the Netherlands and Belgium, for example—it has tended to diminish more radical nationalist aspirations. The more moderate elements of the independence movement in Québec, for example, seek a form of "sovereignty-association," or a kind of asymmetrical federalism that would allow the province to be included within broader federal politics but on different terms (and with different powers) vis-à-vis such issues as education, social policy, immigration, and constitutional reform.

24. Lisa Foderaro, "Hasidic Public School Loses Again Before U.S. Supreme Court, but Supporters Persist," *New York Times*, 13 October 1999, 5.

Calls for greater inclusion and accommodation in liberal democratic politics by minority groups frequently reflect not only demands for better political representation, but also the desire to help shape the broader political culture of society in which they live. This might include having a direct voice in determining which public values should prevail and whether and how certain political institutions should be reformed. The demand for greater inclusion may also be shorthand for the perceived need for more direct representation by members of one's group, as well as input into the issues that directly affect it, such as education, social policy, and legal and constitutional reform. Regardless of the specific demand, it is hard to avoid the conclusion that in order for marginalized cultural and ethnic minority groups to have opportunities to help shape the public norms and practices that bind them, they will need to be granted a greater role in mainstream political institutions. As suggested at the outset of this book, securing justice for cultural minorities in democratic states will require the reform of some political institutions so as to secure better representation and inclusion of cultural minorities and possibly permanent representation for long-standing and historically disadvantaged national minorities. A commitment to values of political inclusion, in the view argued here, requires that citizens not be made to bracket their culturally specific identities and normative worldviews when participating in democratic institutions, whether at the level of deliberation, decision-making, or merely voting. Democratic inclusion in the context of culturally plural societies requires that we recognize the potential political significance of group-based, essentially nonvoluntary, social differences. The more substantive and deeply democratic politics that I shall defend in chapters 5 and 6 emphasizes the importance of citizens' participation in public life and the need to foster political relationships and practices based on reciprocity, political equality, and mutual respect. All of these features, I argue, are crucial to meeting basic justice claims by national minorities and immigrants alike. A more inclusive and deliberative account of democracy that recognizes the importance of cultural identity and membership for many citizens is so far the most promising approach to the dilemma of how to meet the demands of cultural minorities for greater recognition and accommodation.

Larmore's *Modus Vivendi* Liberalism

Some liberal thinkers believe that the principle of neutrality requires reasoned, neutral justification. To this end, writers such as Charles Larmore and John Rawls employ conceptions of rationality and / or arguments about reasonableness to show that an ideal consensus on a neutral, political conception of justice is possible.[25] In so doing, these liberals eschew what they perceive as illegitimate attempts to defend neutrality as a liberal value or comprehensive ideal. Neutral standards of justification are taken by these proponents to be universal, rational standards. Their appeals to rationality are accompanied (especially in the case of Rawls) by the additional claim that the norm of neutrality accurately reflects the actual intuitions of citizens in democratic states— or that there already exists a consensus on much of the political framework of neutral liberalism. Both the justificatory and empirical aspects of these arguments by neutral liberals incorporate assumptions about ideal and actual agreement or consensus and about citizens' motivations and aspirations. As I shall argue, these assumptions present obstacles to their purported goal of securing justice for all citizens, especially cultural minorities.

Charles Larmore pitches his defense of neutrality at a higher level of abstraction than do those who, like Stephen Macedo, defend neutrality as a core liberal value. Larmore invokes Kantian (though not Kant's) conceptions of practical reason and universality to show that neutrality is the central articulating principle for a liberal society and that it is a norm which rational agents would endorse.[26] However, Larmore stresses that although for Kant, reasoning can justify certain principles, in his own *modus vivendi* conception of liberal justice the justification is both a strategic and a political one.[27] As Larmore writes:

> There are limits to what the bare idea of rationality can establish. Even if it constrains how a conversation should develop, it cannot alone justify that the conversation be undertaken. Thus, the reasons for continuing the conversation in the face of disagreement will have to embody more substantive commitments than just a commitment to reason.[28]

25. As I discuss below, Rawls's argument is by no means strictly about rationality: he also appeals to the normative fit of the principle of neutrality, that is, he asserts that reasonable, democratic citizens actually do accept the norms of public reason and neutrality.

26. This is not strictly a claim about what it is rational to agree to, however; as Alan Montefiore has noted (even before the emergence of neutral liberalism), the view that neutrality in politics is inherently rational is equally a claim about the inherent *ir*rationality of nonneutrality: "there is at least a certain practical incoherence in the position of anyone who, while claiming a universal status for his role, so understands it that he regards himself as committed thereby to actions whose most probable impact would be to destroy the very conditions on which its continued existence depends." See his "Neutrality, Indifference and Detachment," in *Neutrality and Impartiality*, ed. Montefiore (Cambridge: Cambridge University Press, 1975), 17.

27. Larmore, *Patterns of Moral Complexity*, 75–77.

28. Ibid., 61.

The best way to mediate citizens' conflicting conceptions of the good, in Larmore's view, is to determine which minimal principles best guide political deliberation in plural societies. Only a liberal model that incorporates norms of rationality and universality can meet the requirements of justice amid conditions of social diversity. Larmore's proposed solution, *modus vivendi* liberalism, is best defined as "a minimal moral conception by which people can escape the rule of force and live together in political association, despite their enduring disagreements about the nature of the good life."[29] Citizens will engage in rational political dialogue both because to do so is to express equal *respect* for persons and because the norms that bind us in dialogue (i.e., rationality and universality) embody correct precepts of rationality. By requiring our public institutions and public debates to reflect respect for others, we commit ourselves to a form of neutrality which demands that "political principles are to be 'neutral' with respect to controversial ideas of the good."[30] In our political arguments, we should thus appeal only to neutral, publicly acceptable reasons to justify proposals and principles. This is not merely a requirement for politicians and judges; rather, even citizens arguing in favor of specific legal and political decisions and actions must be seen to justify their positions in terms of neutral, public reasons.

Since Larmore appeals to the norms of rational dialogue and equal respect to justify the principle of neutrality, his argument cannot be dismissed as instantiating a merely instrumental form of rationality. This is important in view of Larmore's requirement that political liberalism meet the demands of socially diverse democratic states, made up of a plurality of different moral agents. Eschewing a simple model of instrumental rationality, Larmore emphasizes that it is primarily our "commitment to treating others with equal respect"—and not rationality alone—that motivates us to affirm the ideal of political neutrality.[31] Principles of equal respect and rationality / rational dialogue thus lie at the heart of Larmore's *modus vivendi* liberalism. Moreover, these norms help to determine the concrete constraints imposed on public dialogue and liberal institutions generally, which in effect "operationalize" the principle of neutrality.

Before examining Larmore's arguments from the vantage point of concerns about justice for cultural minorities, it is worth noting that Larmore does not view liberal neutrality as supporting a politics devoid

29. Charles Larmore, "The Limits of Aristotelian Ethics," *Nomos* 34, *Virtue*, ed. John W. Chapman and William A. Galston (New York: New York University Press, 1992), 194.

30. Charles Larmore, "Political Liberalism," 341.

31. Ibid., 347; and Larmore, *Patterns of Moral Complexity*, 67.

of substantive moral commitments. Nor does *modus vivendi* liberalism itself provide our moral framework; rather,

> Neutrality is simply a means of accommodation. It is a stance that we
> adopt in order to solve a specific problem to which our various commit-
> ments give rise, so it is not a stance that expresses our full understanding
> of our purpose. It establishes a modus vivendi between persons whose ul-
> timate ideals do not coincide.[32]

Similarly, although Larmore's reference to minimalism in moral and
political life may seem to echo libertarian positions, it is in fact quite different: Larmore defends minimal moral assumptions, not minimal state
institutions. Indeed, he views neutrality as fully compatible with social
welfare policies and economic redistribution, which libertarians uni-
formly reject.[33] This is because political liberalism does not preclude
substantive moral and normative commitments: "neutrality is a political
ideal," rather than a comprehensive moral view. Accordingly, "the principle of political neutrality still has a moral justification, but it is one intended to be far less controversial than the Kantian and Millian ideas of
autonomy and individuality."[34]

Although Larmore eschews what he understands as the comprehensive moralities of Kant and Mill, a closer examination of his conception
of neutrality reveals certain controversial substantive commitments.
Consequently, it is not clear that his theory is as inclusive of citizens' social, cultural, and moral differences as he claims. The main difficulty, I
suggest, lies with Larmore's requirement that political principles and
proposals be justified by appealing to neutral, public reasons. This demand and the constraints it imposes on citizens' reasoning and deliberation are especially problematic for citizens of certain minority cultural
and religious communities. Political institutions and public deliberation
structured according to what Larmore calls the "universal norm of rational dialogue" (i.e., the norm of neutral, public reason applied to dialogue) require that people who wish to keep discussing and deliberating on a set of issues agree to by-pass areas of moral disagreement and
continue to debate less controversial subjects, seeking more minimal
agreements. The procedural rules that bind citizens and legislators in
their deliberations are aimed at preventing them from appealing to illegitimate, partialist norms and reasons: "Political neutrality consists in a

32. Larmore, *Patterns of Moral Complexity*, 74.
33. Ibid.
34. Ibid., 45; and Larmore, "Political Liberalism," 345–46.

constraint on what factors can be invoked to justify a political decision. Such a decision can count as neutral only if it can be justified without appealing to the presumed intrinsic superiority of any particular conception of the good life."[35] In practice, however, this would prevent cultural groups who seek special recognition from appealing to the norm of cultural self-determination or invoking the distinctness of their language, history, and forms of community to justify political proposals for, say, cultural education, language policies, and special constitutional arrangements.

The requirements that citizens refrain from appealing to contested moral norms and social views and set aside areas of disagreement also lies at the heart of Bruce Ackerman's model of "Neutral Dialogue," which proposes certain conversational constraints on political deliberation derived from the norm of public reason.[36] Both Larmore and Ackerman view their respective constraints on public reasoning and debate as minimal and unlikely to meet with objections; as Larmore writes, "neutrality as a political ideal governs the *public* relations between persons and the state, and not the *private* relations between persons and other institutions."[37] However, Larmore seems to overlook the extent to which his proposed conversational constraints reflect and reinforce a distinction between public / political and social / private life that citizens are not free to challenge and oppose.[38] The requirement that we appeal to neutral, publicly justifiable reasons and norms to defend proposals will also surely prevent groups seeking cultural recognition from invoking their communities' traditional beliefs and distinct ways of life in the course of political deliberation. In instances where such appeals are actually necessary to convey the nature and importance of the cultural "good" at stake—and cannot merely be translated into "neutral reasons"—the justice claims of cultural minorities will not be met.

35. Larmore, *Patterns of Moral Complexity*, 44.

36. Strictly speaking, Ackerman's *defense* of neutrality is not neutral: although he does appeal to norms of rationality, he also invokes skepticism and the ideal of autonomy as reasons for adopting neutral principles and procedures in liberal states. I do not discuss Ackerman at length here because the notion of reasoning he invokes takes a more instrumental form than that of Larmore and is therefore easier to dismiss. Whereas for Larmore, engaging in the actual process of public reasoning according to neutral principles is itself a way of showing our respect for others, Ackerman views "Neutral Dialogue" as a necessary condition that enables citizens to pursue their own conceptions of the good. Ackerman, *Social Justice in the Liberal State*, 372 and 254.

37. Larmore, *Patterns of Moral Complexity*, 45.

38. Similarly, as Seyla Benhabib notes, Ackerman's conversational restrictions are neither to be publicly debated nor are they open to contestation. See her "Liberal Dialogue Versus a Critical Theory of Discursive Legitimation," in *Liberalism and the Moral Life*, ed. Nancy Rosenblum (Cambridge, Mass.: Harvard University Press, 1989), 145.

Larmore's assumption that citizens will adhere to the norm of public reason and moral bracketing procedures is held in place by conceptions of rational agency and of the appropriate division between public / political and private / social life, which he fails fully to defend. In diverse, culturally plural societies, it is by no means evident that citizens will agree that public norms of rationality, universality, and moral respect supersede private and / or community goods; yet Larmore's *modus vivendi* liberalism requires that agents "rank the norms of rational dialogue and equal respect above our other values."[39] Although Larmore concedes that not *all* citizens will act according to the rational precepts he sets out, his response to this problem further reinforces the criticism that he places too much faith in an idealized model of rational dialogue. Not only does Larmore suggest that a state's claim to be neutral does not require indifference vis-à-vis views that challenge the value of neutrality, but he also dismisses those who might reject the norm of rational dialogue on the tautological ground that they must therefore be irrational:[40] opponents of the norm of rational dialogue are likely opponents of civil peace and in any case, are mere "fanatics." Larmore offers only a glib response to the problem of what to do when faced with citizens who reject the universal norm of rational dialogue:

> Here, then, is a limit to the neutrality of my argument for political neutrality, but it is not, I think, a very grave one. Why must a political value be made justifiable to those who are scarcely interested in rational debate about justification anyway? A liberal political system need not feel obliged to reason with fanatics; it must simply take the necessary precautions to guard against them.[41]

Larmore intends for his minimal moral conception to presuppose little in the way of social requirements. However, he is mainly con-

---

39. Larmore, "Political Liberalism," 351. The stipulation that proposals and decisions must not appeal to the "presumed superiority of any particular conception of the good life" is of course not the same thing as requiring public respect for many different ways of life or distinct cultural communities. On Larmore's view, respect is due to persons in view of their rationality (narrowly defined) — it is not owed to communities or ways of life. *Patterns of Moral Complexity*, 44.

40. Larmore is not alone in making this move. Peter Jones, for instance, makes a similar assumption, without providing a satisfactory explanation. See Jones, "The Ideal of the Neutral State," 28.

41. Larmore, *Patterns of Moral Complexity*, 60. Even if we were to take seriously the challenges of those who reject the norm of rational dialogue, Larmore argues, they pose no threat to the moral coherence of *modus vivendi* liberalism. See also Larmore's "Political Liberalism," 353.

cerned that rational dialogue should not unwittingly invoke comprehensive norms other than rational dialogue and equal respect, which "are assumed to enjoy a general mutuality."[42] Rational persons, according to Larmore, will also agree to separate their roles as citizens from personal views and conceptions of the good or will "abstract from disputed views of the good life in order to devise principles for the political order."[43] From the vantage point of concerns about respect and inclusion for cultural minorities, the main problem with Larmore's requirements of rationality and rational dialogue is not merely that they idealize agents in unwarranted ways, but that when formulated as constraints on political deliberation they have the potential to operate as exclusionary devices. The actual constraints required by Larmore's conception of rational dialogue are ones that many persons, especially citizens with a strong sense of cultural, religious, or ethnic community identity, could not accept.

Larmore's model of neutral public debate relies on a further problematic assumption. In addition to supposing that citizens will endorse the style of deliberation presupposed by neutral, rational dialogue, Larmore assumes that they will have the necessary self-esteem, reasoning skills, and articulacy to participate in neutral liberal political deliberation.[44] Important requirements for participation are left unarticulated: in order to engage in Larmore's political conversation, or indeed, Ackerman's Neutral Dialogue, citizens would need leisure time, economic resources, education, and political confidence.[45] Where these

---

42. Although Larmore fully admits that the norm of rational conversation is not a morally neutral ideal, he strenuously rejects suggestions that his theory invokes respect and rational dialogue as *comprehensive* norms or that by requiring adherence to these norms political liberalism might exclude persons with morally significant positions. *Patterns of Moral Complexity*, 54.

43. Note that the stipulation that all agents must (or do) agree to the universal norm of rational dialogue is a much stronger requirement than the demand that all citizens refrain from the use of violent means to promote and pursue their own conception of the good. This latter requirement is easier to defend than the norm of rational dialogue.

44. These requirements are not, of course, unique to Larmore's political model. As Susan James has noted, citizenship in democratic states requires articulacy, self-esteem, and a form of emotional independence. See her essay "The Good Enough Citizen: Female Citizenship and Independence," in *Beyond Equality and Difference*, ed. S. James and G. Bock (London: Routledge, 1993).

45. The five necessary components of Neutral Dialogue or discourse, none of which Ackerman believes we should have trouble attaining, are: (a) that citizens do not dominate one another; (b) that all citizens receive a liberal education; (c) material equality for all; (d) the existence of a free exchange / transaction network; and (e) that we pass on liberal structures to the next generation. See Ackerman, *Social Justice in the Liberal State*, 28. Ackerman does not discuss the implications of these requirements for cultural minorities in democratic states.

features are not present or are present to a lesser degree than required, citizens' political deliberations may merely reflect prevailing social, cultural, and economic inequalities; as Seyla Benhabib reminds us, "public dialogue is not external to but constitutive of power relations."[46] However, because neither Larmore nor Ackerman addresses the ways in which our personal capacities and social relationships of power inevitably impact political debate and decision-making, they cannot account for the specific ways that neutral deliberative procedures and constraints might pose an unfair burden on cultural minorities. Such burdens could in turn prevent the inclusion of ethnic and religious groups in democratic politics.

In sum, Larmore's account of neutral, rational dialogue seems unlikely either to mediate entrenched conflicts between diverse citizens or to help meet the claims of cultural minorities for respect and recognition. These latter demands are frequently manifested as social and political conflicts, including disagreements about the procedures and institutions of political life. In response to these conflicts, it is not enough to assert (as does Larmore) the irrationality of noncompliant parties. Larmore's particular conception of neutrality presents a determinate and controversial picture of rationality and political deliberation, as well as of the proper relationship between public and private spheres, that many citizens could not accept. Moreover, he rules out serious consideration of the legitimate grievances of certain citizens and groups against aspects of liberal principles and political procedures. If those groups traditionally marginalized from liberal political life (such as historically disadvantaged national minorities and recent immigrants) are to have access to political debate and decision-making, they will need have to have a say in how deliberative procedures are to be conducted and regulated and what reforms may be required. This voice is likely precluded by Larmore's *modus vivendi* liberalism.

Rawls's Political Liberalism: Neutral or Selective Justice?

In his recent work, John Rawls attempts to defend neutrality on the grounds both that it is the principle that rational agents would ideally

46. Benhabib, "Liberal Dialogue," 155. There is also, as Benhabib notes, a logical problem with the idea of conversational constraints, at least as Ackerman understands these. Ackerman's Neutral Dialogue requires that parties bracket their moral disagreements in an attempt to keep the political conversation going; however, it is not clear that we can know how to classify issues and disagreements as *moral*, or even fully know our own views, in advance of dialogue and deliberation (p. 149).

choose and that it is a widely held norm in liberal states. The idea of "reflective equilibrium" is intended to capture this combination of rational and normative reasons for endorsing neutrality: "a political conception of justice, to be acceptable, must accord with our considered convictions, at all levels of generality, on due reflection."[47] Neutrality also makes possible what Rawls calls an "overlapping consensus," which refers to the search "for a consensus of reasonable (as opposed to unreasonable or irrational) comprehensive doctrines" and to the fact that "only a political conception of justice that all citizens might be reasonably expected to endorse can serve as a basis of public reason and justification."[48]

In assessing the conception of neutrality that lies at the heart of Rawls's ideal of justice as fairness, it is important to emphasize that he views appeals to ideal rationality as only one part of an adequate justification of neutrality. Rawls's distinction between the rational and the reasonable, both of which supply reasons for adopting neutrality, is pivotal here: neutrality is both the principle that *rational* agents would endorse (given the terms of the veil of ignorance) and the norm that *reasonable* citizens can willingly affirm and act on.[49] To highlight the difference between a justification of neutrality that appeals strictly to rationality and one that applies to both rationality and reasonableness, Rawls contrasts two conceptions of neutrality: neutrality of procedure and neutrality of aim. The former is defined "by reference to a procedure that can be legitimated, or justified, without appealing to any moral values at all," or, failing that, "justified by an appeal to neutral values, that is, to values such as impartiality, consistency in application of general principles to all reasonably related cases ... and equal opportunity for the contending parties to present their claims."[50] By contrast, Rawls believes that justice as fairness should embody the principle of neutrality of aim, which seeks to ensure that "institutions and policies are neutral in the sense that they can be endorsed by citizens generally as within the scope of a public political conception."[51] He distinguishes

47. Rawls, *Political Liberalism*, 8.

48. Ibid., 144 and 137.

49. See ibid., esp. 48–54. Rawls emphasizes that the reasonable is not derived from the rational, nor is the rational in any sense more fundamental than the reasonable.

50. Ibid., 191.

51. Rawls, "Priority of the Right," 262. Neutrality of procedure, in Rawls's view, allows no room for the substantive liberal values that are so central to his account of the overlapping consensus that (supposedly) prevails in liberal democracies. Thus, Rawls dismisses strictly procedural neutrality as yielding only the most superficial "procedural values"; he views "neutrality of procedure" as only one aspect of justificatory neutrality.

both of these from neutrality of effect or consequences, which he rejects as impracticable and conceptually flawed.

Rawls views the principle of neutrality in public life not as a means of securing a thin *modus vivendi*, in Larmore's sense, but rather as a way of discovering shared public norms and accommodating a plurality of "reasonable, comprehensive doctrines." In the "well-ordered society" that justice as fairness ensures, our basic political institutions satisfy neutral principles, and citizens affirm and willingly comply with these same norms of justice:[52]

> Justice as fairness aims at uncovering a public basis of justification on questions of political justice given the fact of reasonable pluralism. Since justification is addressed to others, it proceeds from what is, or can be, held in common; and so we begin from *shared fundamental ideas implicit in the public political culture* . . .[53]

Like Larmore, Rawls gives only scanty details of just what his "shared political culture" presupposes in terms of norms and beliefs. Broadly, it seems to assume that citizens endorse a conception of justice as fairness, at the heart of which lies the principle of neutrality.

Rawlsian neutrality, like Larmore's *modus vivendi* liberalism, requires that citizens and legislators adhere to the norm of public reason in debating political principles: "citizens' reasoning in the public forum about constitutional essentials and basic questions of justice ... is ... guided by a political conception the principles and values of which all citizens can endorse."[54] As for Larmore, so for Rawls, the norm of neutral, public reason entails certain practical constraints; in particular, views of a moral, religious, philosophical, or associational nature "are not, in general, to be introduced into political discussion of constitutional essentials and the basic questions of justice."[55] The reasons that citizens and legislators supply as justification for political principles, proposals, and decisions must be widely acceptable (i.e., meet the test of public reason), which in practice means that our justifications must be stripped of substantive moral content.

---

52. Rawls, *Political Liberalism*, 35.

53. Ibid., 100 (emphasis added). Here, as elsewhere, Rawls slides confusingly between "is," "could," and "would" in reference to citizens' beliefs and agreements. For a discussion of this problem, see Onora O'Neill, "Political Liberalism and Public Reason: A Critical Notice of John Rawls," *Philosophical Review* 106, no. 3 (1997): 411–28.

54. Rawls, *Political Liberalism*, 10.

55. Ibid., 15–16.

Rawls defends these deliberative constraints in part by asserting that they reflect norms that democratic citizens actually agree with. Whether or not the norm of neutral public reason and the sharp public / private division on which it rests enjoy wide acceptance in socially plural democracies is in some sense an empirical question. Although I cannot attempt to answer this issue definitively here, it is useful to suggest some reasons why Rawlsian neutrality may not be acceptable to—and probably is not accepted by—certain cultural minorities. First, Rawls's *ideal of reasonableness* marginalizes, even effaces, the perspectives of those who view their group identity and attendant comprehensive views as inextricably linked to their political convictions. Second, the *actual deliberative constraints* that Rawls (like Larmore) seeks to impose on political actors in public debate will make it difficult for certain cultural minorities to press their claims for recognition, and especially for special constitutional arrangements, because of the way that norms of neutrality prohibit them from appealing to "comprehensive" premises and arguments. And third, Rawls's proposed constraints may also tend to exclude from political life certain cultural minorities whose deliberative styles do not fit within the strictures set out by political liberalism and who may lack the articulacy and social standing to press their justice claims against the liberal state. I take up these three points below.

Reasonable Citizens

For Rawls, citizens who affirm a conception of justice as fairness are not simply rational in the sense of being self-interested and taking efficient means to secure their own ends; they are also reasonable in that they are "ready to propose principles and standards as fair terms of cooperation and to abide by them willingly, given the assurance that others will likewise do so." Reasonable persons thus "recognize the burdens of judgment ... and accept their consequences for the use of public reason": that is, they accept that the only just and fair principles are those that are also acceptable to all others. Citizens are "fully autonomous," on Rawls's view, "only if they comply with the "fair terms of social cooperation" as determined by the norm of public reason. Since they accept that "the burdens of judgment set limits on what can be reasonably justified to others," *reasonable citizens*, by definition, will refrain from making truth claims about their own private views and beliefs. By contrast, *unreasonable citizens* are those who assert that "their beliefs alone are true"; such claims are unreasonable because clearly they "cannot be made good by anyone to citizens generally."[56] Significantly, Rawls does not discuss the intermediate case of citizens whose political arguments invoke some comprehensive ideals but who do not insist on the exclusive veracity of their claims.

The notion of reasonableness that Rawls invokes is predicated on the assumption "that citizens have two views, a comprehensive and a political view."[57] Yet the requirement that we separate out these "views" in political life is both more strenuous and more controversial than might first appear.[58] Contra Rawls's view, it is entirely possible to imagine reasonable political dialogue in which citizens present the concerns of their particular communities in ways that invoke certain partialist beliefs and norms, rather than appealing strictly to widely acceptable political norms. A good example is provided by the case of Nunavut, the newly autonomous area of Canada's Eastern Arctic. When Inuit peoples demanded significant changes to their political arrangements and institutions—matters that would correspond to Rawls's "constitutional essentials"—they appealed *not* so much to political principles that all persons (including differently situated citizens) could accept but rather to their community's distinct history, ways of life, and special requirements for cultural survival. These contextualized arguments were important not only to obtain important constitutional changes, but also to justify their claims for land use rights for hunting and fishing and for Inuktitut to be adopted as the language of schooling and government. Negotiations on the future of Nunavut were carried out by representatives of the three parties with different interests—the government of the Northwest Territories, the federal government, and the main Inuit peoples' organization—each of which invoked the specific concerns of the body and / or communities they represented. These successful talks were based on a model of mutual decision-making and political bargaining and *not* on procedures requiring political bracketing of non-neutral claims.[59]

The accounts of reasonableness and public reason so central to Rawlsian liberalism stand in tension with some claims for cultural recogni-

---

56. Ibid., 49, 54, and 61.

57. Ibid., 140.

58. For a parallel critique of Rawls's deliberative constraints that focuses more on the contentiousness of Rawls's list of primary goods, see J. Donald Moon, *Constructing Community* (Princeton, N.J.: Princeton University Press, 1993), 56–57, and his "Practical Discourse and Communicative Ethics," in *The Cambridge Companion to Habermas*, ed. Stephen White (Cambridge: Cambridge University Press, 1995), esp. 158.

59. It may be possible to construe some of the claims of Inuit peoples in terms of neutral, public arguments, but I suggest that this would require a great deal of distortion.

tion. Although Rawls rarely addresses such claims directly, he does of course deal extensively with the problem of moral diversity. Like Larmore, his response to problems of judgment and moral disagreement in diverse societies is to place restrictions on agents' public reasoning so as to avoid political standoffs, foster agreement, and help secure justice. Ultimately, then, for Rawls reasonable citizens are those who will reach agreements or, failing that, "be able to explain disagreements in a certain way."[60] Yet his accounts of reasonableness and public reason effectively would prevent certain cultural minorities from discussing political norms and procedures on terms that are acceptable to them.

In contrast to Rawls's account of the requirements of public reason, a more discursive conception of public reason—in which citizens' disagreements, even those with moral content, are freely discussed—would require considerably fewer constraints.[61] Political deliberation based on a plural, discursive account of public reason might more readily permit communities to state their cases in ways that reflect their own deliberative and decision-making styles. I shall argue these points at greater length in chapters 5 and 6.

The Deliberative Constraints of Neutral Liberalism

The specific constraints that Rawls seeks to impose on political debate and decision-making, like those of Larmore, would pose specific obstacles to cultural minorities' claims for respect and recognition. Rawlsian constraints would affect not only legislators and jurists in their deliberations, but also citizens in their public, political discussions and in voting, for the norm of public reason "applies to citizens when they engage in political advocacy in the public forum" and should even bind them in political campaigns and when voting on "fundamental questions."[62]

Like Larmore's *modus vivendi* liberalism, Rawls's conception of justice as fairness requires citizens to set aside their comprehensive moral views in debating and justifying "constitutional essentials" (i.e., political norms and institutions) and to appeal only to principles that are acceptable to all. Legislators and citizens alike "should be ready to explain the

---

60. Rawls, *Political Liberalism*, 112.

61. Amy Gutmann and Dennis Thompson have recently developed an account of deliberative democracy that would allow much more moral disagreement in political deliberation than neutral liberals permit. See their "Moral Conflict and Political Consensus," *Ethics* 101 (1990): 64–88, and Gutmann and Thompson, *Democracy and Disagreement* (Cambridge, Mass.: Harvard University Press, 1996).

62. Rawls, *Political Liberalism*, 252.

basis of their actions to one another in terms each could reasonably expect that others might endorse."[63] But Rawls's emphasis on public reason-giving and neutral justification presupposes, probably counterfactually, that all citizens can and will agree to alter their reasons and explanations for proposals so as to meet prescribed standards of liberal neutrality.[64] Moreover, it is not clear how certain national and cultural minorities could press particular claims for special constitutional recognition and for greater control over matters that affect their communities directly—such as language policy and education—within the constraints imposed by neutrality.

This last point is worth emphasizing. To be clear: the problem is not that neutral public reason requires agents to dispense entirely with their distinct views or to take a fully skeptical stance toward their beliefs. As Nancy Rosenblum suggests, neutral and impartial reasoning may be understood as a minimal requirement that applies only to certain situations: "Standing back from your own opinions describes only one kind of agency; it is demanded of people only sometimes; and even then the capacity to set aside certain considerations deemed politically unjustifiable is achieved only with the greatest discipline."[65] Although the norm of neutral public reason does not require citizens to abandon their own comprehensive views, there are reasons to suspect that its attendant constraints will make it difficult for certain national minorities and cultural groups to make particular sorts of justice claims against the liberal state. In particular, cultural groups that seek special constitutional status would be prevented by neutral liberalism's deliberative constraints from appealing to their community's distinct traditions, language, history, and ways of life to justify their political claims and proposals. It is unlikely that the claims of minorities for cultural recognition can be articulated effectively in terms of neutral, public reasons.

63. Ibid., 218.

64. One example of culturally specific reasons that would fail Rawls's neutrality requirement is a principle to which some aboriginal peoples in Canada appeal, even in their negotiations with the federal Canadian government: the "seventh generation principle." This principle requires that proposals which will affect native communities and their physical environment be subjected to the test of seven generations (i.e., that the projected consequences for the next seven generations of their own community be taken into account in deciding whether a certain course of action should be taken). Although they invoke this principle in their own community deliberations and in considering government proposals, native people do not suggest that this principle should be adopted by all citizens.

65. Nancy Rosenblum, Introduction to *Liberalism and the Moral Life*, ed. Rosenblum, 16.

Political Inclusion and Exclusion: The Hindmarsh Affair

Justifications of neutrality that appeal primarily to idealized norms of reason and reasonableness are predicated on controversial ideals of political morality and rationality, as we have seen. Moreover, they presuppose a problematic dichotomy between private moral and social views on the one hand and political norms and issues on the other. One concrete implication of these features is that citizens who are more at ease with styles of public deliberation deemed impermissible by neutral norms of debate could face exclusion from aspects of political life. For instance, those citizens who approach policy issues against the background of comprehensive religious views will suffer certain disadvantages in Rawls's scheme of justice, for they will have to bracket their most deeply held beliefs in order to comply with the requirements of public reason. Rawls requires not simply that we be willing to justify our beliefs and actions to others but that we justify them in particular ways (observing norms and constraints of neutral justification). Yet cultural minorities may seek to participate in politics precisely because of a sense that their cultural identities are denigrated, or their membership disadvantages them in some way, and they may need to appeal to nonneutral reasons to justify certain demands. Yet it is difficult to see how these concerns could be articulated in terms of reasons that are sufficiently neutral. By requiring citizens to set aside their cultural identities, values, and beliefs in central political processes, the norm of neutral justification may thus systematically tend to benefit those without deeply held religious and culturally specific moral beliefs.[66] Agents who do not come to liberal rational dialogue fully willing to bracket off their moral and evaluative commitments when justifying political proposals would also be less likely to articulate and defend their proposals successfully under neutral liberalism and may be penalized if they refuse or are unable to do so.

Minority cultural groups whose traditional styles of public deliberation and decision-making incorporate historical narrative or descriptions of particular community problems and relationships might further be disadvantaged in neutral liberal dialogue. A good example of how Rawls's requirements of neutral reasoning and neutral justification might pose unfair burdens for certain cultural minority groups with different deliberative styles, goals, and expectations is suggested by the recent "Hindmarsh affair" in Australia. Beginning in late 1993, aboriginal

---

66. For a discussion of this problem, see Perry, "Neutral Politics?" 484.

women protested against the building of a bridge to Hindmarsh Island (in the lower River Murray area of southeastern South Australia) on the grounds that certain areas of the island were sacred to them. They refused to divulge in any detail the reasons for its sanctity, insisting that making the reasons public would violate their privacy as well as their community's norms of secrecy. It was however made plain that the island's significance was related to women's "business" or "knowledge" and that certain sites on the island were important to the fertility of Ngarrindjeri women. Only Ngarrindjeri women, so it was claimed, are permitted to know the history and mythology of the island; not even aboriginal men are privy to this information.[67]

The testimony of women protesting the planned construction of the Hindmarsh Island bridge and supporting arguments by a few academics retained to investigate the matter were met with considerable skepticism and ultimately led to the creation of a Royal Commission in 1995 to assess the matter.[68] Objections centered on the plausibility of claims to women's secret knowledge among the Ngarrindjeri, who were not previously thought to have gender segregated cultural knowledge, at least according to available anthropological studies.[69] Doubts about the sincerity or indeed legitimacy of the women's arguments were compounded by the refusal of many Ngarrindjeri women to participate in the hearings, which they said reflected a process that was offensive and condescending. Although it is of course possible that the "proponent women" (there were also women among the Ngarrindjeri who denied that such secret knowledge existed) were concerned that testifying before the Royal Commission could reveal inconsistencies in their claims, the sense of exclusion and alienation from the political process that they expressed is surely significant:

> We, as Ngarrindjeri women believe the women's business, the subject of the Royal Commission into Hindmarsh Island is true. We are deeply offended that a Government in this day and age has the audacity to order an inquiry into our secret, sacred, spiritual beliefs. Never before have any group of people had their spiritual beliefs scrutinised in this way.... We do not seek to be represented at this Royal Commission. We do not rec-

67. Marcia Langton, "The Hindmarsh Island Bridge Affair: How Aboriginal Women's Religion Became an Administerable Affair," *Australian Feminist Studies* 11, no. 24 (1996), 212.

68. Robert Tonkinson, "Anthropology and Aboriginal Tradition: The Hindmarsh Island Bridge Affair and the Politics of Interpretation," *Oceania* 68, no. 1 (1997): 1–26.

69. Ron Brunton, "The Hindmarsh Island Bridge and the Credibility of Australian Anthropology," *Anthropology Today* 12, no. 2 (1996): 1–7.

ognise the authority of this Royal Commission to debate and ultimately to conclude that women's business relating to Hindmarsh Island exists. We know women's business exists and is true.[70]

Whether or not Ngarrindjeri women's claims about the connection between Hindmarsh Island and their secret knowledge accurately represent their community's cultural traditions, it is instructive to reflect on the ways in which their deliberative styles contrast sharply with the norms and requirements of liberal institutions. The specific conflict between the norm of secrecy invoked by these aboriginal women and liberal requirements of neutral justification and universalizability is especially striking. In the Hindmarsh case, it appears that liberal norms of public reason and neutral justification failed to help mediate the conflict at hand. If anything, the government's expectation that the Ngarrindjeri women would present their arguments in an open and transparent way generated greater indignation and opposition. Moreover, aboriginal women were initially penalized for refusing to comply with these norms, as the initial ruling held that without presenting their reasons fully to the court, the development could not be stopped (though this decision was later overturned by the minister for aboriginal affairs). Although the Hindmarsh case may seem to present an extreme example of the inappropriateness of neutral liberal norms of public reason, it is just one instance of the sorts of problems that might arise if such norms were to be imposed in culturally plural, democratic states in the ways that Rawls proposes.

Social Consensus

Rawls's deliberative constraints might disadvantage certain cultural minorities in a further way: namely, by assuming the existence of a neutral liberal "social consensus." Rawls not only expects that reasonable citizens can and will endorse a political conception of justice as fairness, but that this conception will ultimately come to shape their *own* ideals and comprehensive views. On this view, citizens will affirm the conception of political justice from the standpoint of their own comprehensive views: that is, their individual moral views should connect up in some way with the political conception of justice.[71] However, Rawls seems to overlook the possibility that citizens with highly determinate religious and cultural identities are much less likely than are others to perceive their views as

70. Cited in Langton, "The Hindmarsh Island Bridge Affair," 214.
71. Rawls, *Political Liberalism*, 38.

cohering with the norm of neutrality. If citizens are to accept political liberalism as a "normative scheme" that we adopt and use to "express ourselves ... in our moral and political thought and action," surely citizens whose cultures do not cohere well with liberal ideals will find themselves at a distinct disadvantage and may not receive equal justice.[72]

Another aspect of the "social consensus" problem that relates less directly to issues of cultural diversity is the following. When applied to politics, the norm of public reason as envisaged by Rawls would lead us to deem certain principles and arrangements unsuitable topics for public deliberation. That is, some matters are simply taken as either settled or as illegitimate topics of political debate (usually because they violate the precepts of public reason in some way).[73] However, Rawls points only to easy cases such as slavery as examples of issues which can be "taken off the political agenda" because "they are no longer regarded as appropriate subjects for political decision by majority or other plurality voting." He stresses that this move is not intended to eliminate all controversial issues from politics but rather to secure basic liberties. Nonetheless, the scope of issues Rawls takes as "settled" seems to disregard the fact that many so-called basic liberties are highly contested: for example, even freedom of speech is contested, as debates about pornography and defamatory speech show.

As with Larmore's account of neutrality, so it is important to ask to what extent the ideals Rawls endorses are truly universal, particularly within culturally plural, liberal states. The principle of neutral justification in political life and the stark public versus private / social division that it presupposes may stand in tension not only with deeply held religious beliefs, but also with numerous moral and cultural views. Contra Rawls, not all of these views are manifestly unreasonable, much less malicious or dangerous, in the context of debates about political principles and institutions. Should a cultural minority group be marginalized from politics merely because its public practices and political styles do not cohere with the terms of neutral justification? Will members face exclusion from political deliberation because their conceptions of what is public and private, or moral and political, conflict with some liberal values—or because they order their evaluative commitments in different ways than neutralist liberals propose?[74]

---

72. Ibid., 88.
73. Ibid., 152, ff.
74. For an even more worried assessment of the negative impact that a political model of liberal neutrality would have on the claims of cultural minorities for recognition, see Derick van Heerden, "Liberal Neutrality and Cultural Pluralism," *South African Journal of Philosophy* 13, no. 2 (1994): 97–103. Van Heerden is particularly concerned that the ap-

Rawls recognizes that political liberalism might have the effect of marginalizing some perspectives and ways of life and inevitably of favoring others, but does not accord this problem much significance. His defense seems to consist mainly in his insistence that there is an important difference between neutral norms and practices merely having an *incidentally* advantageous effect on certain ways of life (which he freely admits) and "a political conception [being] arbitrarily biased against these views, or . . . unjust to the persons whose conceptions they are, or might be" (which he denies of neutral liberalism).[75] Equally, Rawls recognizes the limitations of public debate that systematically brackets questions of the good life; however, he remains convinced that a conception of justice that prioritizes and gives a neutralist justification for "the right" over "the good" best meets the needs of socially plural democracies.[76]

Although Rawls concedes some limitations and imperfections of neutral liberalism, he has not yet addressed the issue of neutral liberalism's exclusionary implications for certain cultural and ethnic minorities. As we have seen, Rawls does not seem to recognize the extent to which the norm of neutral justification and his proposed deliberative constraints depend on a problematic, sharp demarcation of public and political life from citizens' private and social needs and arrangements. Nor does he acknowledge that it is precisely this stark dichotomy that makes it difficult to address the concerns and needs of some cultural, religious, and ethnic minority groups. That certain ways of life will tend to flourish under a system of political liberalism does not, Rawls asserts, contradict the aims of a neutral conception of justice; nor does it suggest that key norms and practices of political neutrality are exclusionary in the ways discussed above. Indeed, Rawls is curiously nonplused and even fatalistic about the natural biases of neutral justice: "No society can include within itself all forms of life. We may indeed lament the limited space, as it were, of social worlds . . . and we may regret some of the inevitable effects of our culture and social structure."[77]

Still more perplexing for a theorist apparently concerned to secure justice for all citizens amid conditions of social diversity, Rawls further-

---

plication of liberal neutrality in deeply plural (and as yet not fully democratic) societies such as South Africa would require greater attention to securing the "neutrality of effect" of government policies. The consequence of this strategy, he argues, "is invariably a greater homogenization of culture," which "may cause conflict if cultural minorities resist these effects and demand recognition for and protection of their own cultures" (p. 97).

75. Rawls, "The Priority of the Right and Ideas of the Good," 265.

76. Ibid., 264.

77. Ibid., 265.

more suggests that if a way of life is *worth* preserving, it will somehow survive in the level playing field created by political liberalism.[78] Clearly, for theorists concerned with meeting the claims of cultural minorities for basic cultural survival as well as respect and recognition, Rawls's sanguine response to the likely loss of certain traditional communities is unsatisfactory.

Conclusion: Neutrality and the Politics of Cultural Diversity

The criticism that neutral liberalism necessarily presupposes norms and practices that are far from neutral has recently been taken up by Brian Barry, who defends a limited form of neutral liberalism that he calls "justice as impartiality."[79] Although Barry's arguments for neutrality and a certain conception of impartiality are primarily a response to Alasdair MacIntyre's dismissal of neutral liberalism as mere liberal individualism, his arguments are instructive for the present purposes. Barry denies that a commitment to the principle of neutrality in democratic politics necessarily favors a liberal individualistic view of the good life—though he readily concedes that some liberals endorse such a conception, citing Bruce Ackerman and Will Kymlicka as examples.[80] Even more so than Rawls, Barry insists that neutral liberalism must avoid favoring goods and goals simply because they have been chosen autonomously, as well as avoid endorsing the value of autonomy more generally. This is particularly critical within socially plural societies with deeply contested conceptions of the good life, for, as Barry writes:

> [A] conception of the good as autonomy does not imply that the pursuit of all substantive conceptions of the good is equally valuable. Only those conceptions that have the right origins—those that have come about in ways that meet the criteria for self-determined belief—can form a basis for activity that has value. It is therefore unlikely that the good as autonomy will be advanced by distributing resources in a way that takes no ac-

78. Rawls writes, "The principles of any reasonable political conception must impose restrictions on permissible comprehensive views, and the basic institutions those principles enjoin inevitably encourage some ways of life and discourage others, or even exclude them altogether.... Now, the encouraging or discouraging of comprehensive doctrines comes about in at least two ways: those doctrines may be in direct conflict with the principles of justice; or else they may be admissible but fail to gain adherents under the political and social conditions of a just constitutional regime.... Examples of the second case may be certain forms of religion." Ibid., 264–65.

79. Brian Barry, *Justice as Impartiality* (Oxford: Clarendon Press, 1995).

80. Ibid., 131.

count of the autonomous or non-autonomous origins of people's substantive conceptions of the good.[81]

In contrast to self-styled proponents of liberal neutrality that privilege a "conception of the good as autonomy," Barry conceives of neutrality as a more minimal constraint, one that corresponds to a higher or second-order impartiality. He insists that "there is ... nothing built into justice as impartiality that leads it to endorsing policy prescriptions derived from a conception of the good as autonomy."[82]

Justice as impartiality does not require that citizens bracket their moral comprehensive views when deliberating on important political matters, much less the specific conditions and circumstances in which they happen to find themselves (as Rawls's notions of an original position and veil of ignorance require). This is in part because Barry's ideal of justice does not demand the sort of first-order impartiality associated with the demand that agents be neutral vis-à-vis their own intuitions about the good life or their primary attachments and commitments. Instead, what is sought is "some mutually acceptable basis for the accommodation of different conceptions of the good," which ultimately requires that one "voluntarily accepts constraints on the pursuit of his own ends."[83] At least as Barry conceives of them, these constraints would not seem especially onerous for citizens of cultural minority communities.

Perhaps what is most important about the minimal constraints demanded by impartiality as conceived by Barry is that they do not extend to the sort of bracketing requirements and strong neutrality required by Rawls's and Larmore's conceptions of public reason and neutral justification. Instead of defending proposals by appealing to broad principles that citizens in liberal states supposedly could and would agree to, justice as impartiality asserts that "the criterion of just rules and institutions is that they should be fair, and the motive appealed to is the desire to behave fairly."[84] The criterion of fairness in turn ultimately requires that social arrangements encourage and permit "partisans of different conceptions of the good to share common social and political institutions."[85] Significantly, Barry acknowledges that power relations in socially stratified liberal democracies often prevent such fairness, reinforcing the political advantages of wealthy indi-

81. Ibid., 131–32.
82. Ibid., 132.
83. Ibid., 31.
84. Ibid., 51.
85. Ibid., 133.

viduals, lobbyists, and groups with access to political power.[86] One possible way to mitigate this tendency is to require widespread consultation on proposed policies and laws and to introduce political mechanisms and funding to make this possible. Indeed, Barry's suggestions of open consultations and hearings in which "concerned individuals and organizations are given enough time to formulate comments on proposals" could well foster the greater inclusion of views of cultural minority communities, for these mechanisms might allow citizens to gain access to public decision-making outside of the traditional party-politics channels. As Barry notes, "public commissions and committees of inquiry are settings in which alternative laws and policies can be subjected to public scrutiny."[87]

Barry's conception of justice recognizes in ways that Rawls's and Larmore's conceptions do not the need to allow citizens and groups to speak and deliberate on issues against the background of their moral conceptions and beliefs. This insight and the suggestions that Barry offers for the construction of a more equitable political landscape— funding for smaller political groups and nongovernmental associations and greater reliance on public hearings and commissions to solicit a wide array of citizens' views on issues—would seem to make his theory more appropriate for culturally plural democracies than the variants of neutral liberalism surveyed thus far. However, Barry proposes deliberative constraints which, if imposed, might prevent cultural minority citizens in particular from participating in political life on terms of their own choosing. Whereas Rawls and Larmore bracket identities in advance of deliberation, Barry proposes what he calls "the criterion of reasonable acceptability of principles."[88] This requirement essentially restricts the kinds of reasons which could reasonably be rejected—or which would count toward "reasonable rejectability," a notion he derives from Thomas Scanlon. Among these reasons, I suggest, are appeals to cultural group identity and membership. Many such claims are plainly illegitimate from the standpoint of liberal democratic values, of course: as Barry notes, those who assert that they deserve better treatment or more resources because of their race or ethnicity offer reasons that are easily rejected. But although it is hard if not impossible to imagine an instance in which such reasons could stand *alone* as normative justifications for proposals, it is a commonplace and perhaps inevitable feature of political deliberation in plural democracies that appeals to

86. Ibid., 108.
87. Ibid., 103 and 105.
88. Ibid., 8 and passim.

cultural group identity will figure in public debate. Oftentimes such appeals serve an important function, illuminating the demands at hand. For example, aboriginal peoples typically invoke their distinct traditions, cultures and languages in order to explain and justify their claims for special cultural recognition and forms of community autonomy. Barry's conception of justice as impartiality fails to take serious enough account of the importance in democratic political life of citizens' cultural identities and memberships and of the legitimacy of appeals to such attachments in the course of political deliberation and debate.

The requirements that our reasons be open to reasonable rejection and that they should not presuppose principles that could be reasonably rejected are not necessarily onerous constraints. However, I suggest that in some contexts these could be disadvantageous to members of minority communities whose justice claims resist reformulation into less contentious demands, impartially justified. Although Barry does not seek to exclude from political deliberation and debate cultural groups with pressing justice claims, he offers no account of how to compensate for the unfair burdens that the requirements of higher-order impartiality and reasonable rejectability may pose for minority citizens.

> [A] decision-making process is fair to the extent that all those concerned are well informed and have their interests and perspectives expressed with equal force and effectiveness. It is fair to the extent that what counts as a good argument does not depend on the social identity of the person making it. And it is fair to the extent that it aims at consensus where possible, and where consensus is not possible it treats everybody equally (e.g., by giving everybody one vote).[89]

Ultimately, Barry seems to retreat to something like a thinner version of Rawls's neutral liberalism when he describes the conflictual, less-than-ideal circumstances in which liberal justice can be expected to play out. Yet the norm of basic liberal political equality which he proposes as a minimal principle to serve us where no consensus is possible is very unlikely to help us address the entrenched disagreements at issue. Despite Barry's clarification of the demands of impartiality and neutrality, then, there remain a number of important ways in which neutral liberalism could pose disadvantages and burdens to citizens of cultural minority groups. Let me summarize my central objections here. I have tried to show that liberals such as Larmore and Rawls invoke numerous unwarranted assumptions in their defenses of neutrality, both in appeal-

---

89. Ibid., 110.

ing to the rationality of this principle and in claiming that citizens in democratic states could and / or do widely endorse the principle of neutral justification. Moreover, neutral liberal political bracketing procedures—and to a lesser extent Barry's criterion of reasonable rejectability—might make it difficult for cultural minorities to press for special recognition and arrangements to secure their group identities and ways of life.

Larmore's and Rawls's proposals for a conception of justice based on the principle of neutrality rely on an overly sharp demarcation of public and political arrangements from our social and personal lives. This division merely echoes the conventional division between public and private life common to liberal theories of justice, which liberals have so far failed satisfactorily to support. It is further predicated on the expectation that we can and should maintain a distinction between moral and political issues (or aspects of issues) in choosing public principles and in our public deliberations. Both Rawls's conception of justice as fairness and Larmore's *modus vivendi* liberalism aim to keep highly-charged and divisive moral issues off the political agenda so that we may identify political principles and terms of dialogue on which we can all agree. Not only is it far from clear whether all issues of public concern can conform to such a neat demarcation, but the insistence that we separate off moral and social issues from public and political ones may merely reinforce prevailing inequalities. In particular, it could further reinforce the marginalization of certain cultural minorities, who may not readily adhere (or be able to adhere) to norms of neutral public deliberation.

Contra the views of Rawls and Larmore, an adequate conception of justice should also reflect the fact that citizens of diverse communities come to politics through different routes and with very different expectations. Sometimes citizens may need to enter politics as representatives of their cultural, linguistic, racial, or gender groups rather than simply as individuals arguing for neutrally justified proposals. This is especially so if they are to counter the political marginalization that results, in the main, from their disadvantaged social and economic status. Such a strategy is disallowed by liberal politics committed to a strong form of neutrality.

The distinction between merely political norms and comprehensive moral ideals is one that comes back to haunt those liberals who, like Rawls, hold up neutrality as a central tenet of liberalism. Neutral liberals' insistence that neutrality is defensible as a political principle that all citizens can accept and whose procedural implications we endorse depends on their making good their claim that moral and political beliefs can and should be separated. It depends further on their showing that doing so will not jeopardize the goal of justice for all citizens. Not only are there too many issues of a public nature which incorporate both moral and political concerns for these to be so easily set aside, but the very expectation that they should be separated violates the beliefs and social norms of some citizens, particularly those members of cultural communities with a marked absence of liberal traditions.

In order to frame conflicts of values and principles in such a way so as not to exclude certain cultural groups, neutral liberals would need to rethink the way they draw the boundary between moral and political matters and beliefs. It may be possible and useful at times to distinguish moral and social aspects from political aspects of public issues, but not at the expense of polarizing these in incoherent ways. The very idea of bracketing deep disagreements in politics is also of questionable practical merit. As Amy Gutmann and Dennis Thompson have argued, there are good reasons for liberals to permit much more moral disagreement in politics than they currently allow; indeed, framing some political questions in terms of rival moral conceptions would often be more faithful to the actual sentiments of citizens.[90] They suggest that we shift our attention from principles of *preclusion* to principles and procedures of accommodation that would permit our political institutions to welcome a greater range of diverse viewpoints, political styles, and concerns. This in turn might allow for the inclusion in politics of a greater range of cultural communities whose belief systems resist neat demarcation into moral and political concerns.

Neither Rawls nor Larmore seeks explicitly to include cultural minority groups *per se* in political life, nor advocates a deliberative approach to determining which social and cultural differences should be accommodated in politics. Both of these features are important requirements of respect for cultural pluralism, as I suggested in chapter 1. Indeed, these

90. Gutmann and Thompson propose an alternative strategy for managing disagreement in public life, one that emphasizes the importance of developing and extending liberal "principles of accommodation." They hope this would allow us safely to take on board many more moral disagreements in politics than neutral liberals will permit. What they call "principles of preclusion" of the sort neutral liberals endorse merely aim to eliminate morally charged issues and perspectives from the political agenda. However, like the liberal norm of rational dialogue, Gutmann's and Thompson's idea of principles of accommodation does not necessarily address important questions of power—such as who steps forth to propose a policy, who listens, and who gets heard. Moreover, these authors rely problematically on an unspecified impartial standpoint from which to judge the practices and conduct of moral discourse. See their "Moral Conflict and Political Consensus," 64–65.

writers oftentimes seem to assume that the different beliefs and practices that neutral justice should seek to protect are largely *chosen* ones.[91]
Of paramount importance to neutral liberals is the freedom of individuals to pursue and revise their own conception of the good, and the political procedures and deliberative constraints they propose reflect this
priority. Rawls, for his part, understands self-respect in terms of agents'
capacities to form, revise, and pursue an account of the good: "our secure sense of our own value" derives from "the conviction that we can
carry out a worthwhile life plan."[92] He does not view self-respect as inte-
grally related to cultural group identity and membership.

Many forms of liberalism assign greater priority to individual, self-
chosen plans rather than to shared public / community goods or virtue-
oriented ideals and ways of life, and so protect and include these sorts of
differences preferentially.[93] From its genesis in early modern Europe onward, liberalism has greeted parochial ethnic and religious identities as
well as nationalist aspirations with a hermeneutics of suspicion. Although contemporary liberals are much more sensitive to the pull of cultural identities and attachments than their predecessors, there remains a
presumption against individuals that identify closely with a particular
community or group. As political theorist Stephen Macedo notes:

> The character that flourishes in a liberal, pluralistic social milieu, will
> have broad sympathies. The liberal citizen, capable of reasoning and act-
> ing from an impersonal standpoint in a pluralistic social milieu will also
> have a less exclusive or unreflective commitment to anything in particu-
> lar. That is, liberalism may temper or attenuate the devotion to one's own
> projects and allegiances, by encouraging persons to regard their own ways
> as open to criticism, choice, and change, or simply as not shared by many
> people whom one is otherwise encouraged to respect. If a liberal plural-
> istic society is also, as I have suggested, an experimental and dynamic
> society, then people may also be encouraged to regard their commit-
> ments and ideals as contingent and vulnerable, as apt to become out-
> moded or trivial in an unpredictably changing world.[94]

If neutral liberalism is well equipped mainly to accommodate those
differences that can be held up to public scrutiny, critically assessed, de-

---

91. George Sher, "Liberal Neutrality and the Value of Autonomy," *Social Philosophy and Policy* 12, no. 1 (1995): 136–59.

92. Rawls, *Political Liberalism*, 319.

93. See David Paris, "The Theoretical Mystique: Neutrality, Plurality, and the Defense of Liberalism," *American Journal of Political Science* 31, no. 4 (1987): 909–39.

94. Stephen Macedo, *Liberal Virtues* (Oxford: Clarendon Press, 1990), 267.

bated, and revised—such as individual beliefs and life-plans—this does not bode well for the suitability of this theory for culturally plural societies. Protecting individual differences in belief is not the same thing as according respect and recognition to vulnerable cultural communities. Significantly, the forms of diversity which most concern Rawls and Larmore tend to attach to the liberal citizen who is poised to formulate, revise, and pursue his or her notion of the good. Not coincidentally, neutral liberals sidestep more entrenched sources of difference and conflict that, as I have argued, may be irresolvable by neutral, rational dialogue—such as claims for cultural recognition.

Skeptics may argue that the exclusion of nonliberals does not pose a serious problem for neutral liberalism. In countering this claim, we need first to point out that political liberals themselves expect neutrality to be convincing to nonliberals. At a deeper level, however, the cavalier disregard some neutral liberals show for the exclusion of certain minority groups may reflect their view that culture and ethnicity can have no legitimate impact on politics and political morality. By refusing to recognize that cultural identities and mores are not confined to "private" or "social" spheres, neutral liberals fail to see several important sources of social and political inequality and overlook serious challenges to the legitimacy of liberal principles.

These difficulties, I suggest, recommend against the adoption of neutrality as an ideal and a guide for political practice. We would do better to turn our hands instead to the task of developing political norms, institutions, and practices that address basic social and economic inequalities and gross imbalances in power. This is unlikely to be accomplished by focusing on the selection of political "first principles," or by imposing "neutral" deliberative constraints and bracketing procedures on citizens and legislators. Nor is it helped along by falsely construing liberal ideals as widely held or by foisting onto such ideals the unrealistic expectation that they will help us to mediate entrenched moral and social conflicts. It may be that in order to negotiate such conflicts, we will need to displace some of neutral liberals' most cherished principles, including neutrality itself, from the center to the margin of our political thinking. A more contingent politics, in which principles as well as policies are negotiated continuously, may be the only answer.

A commitment to a continual process of reassessing and revising liberal democratic political institutions and practices the better to include diverse perspectives may make some aspects of political life in liberal states more unpredictable, but it would also require a more deeply democratic politics. As I argue at greater length in chapter 5, this is an appropriate price to pay for granting a political voice to all members of a political community, rather than a voice which is token or marginal. Only this more robust form of inclusion ensures equal access to deliberations on political arrangements and political institutions, as opposed to an intermittent voice at the level of piecemeal, interest-group politics.

My criticisms of neutrality by no means preclude the use of this principle in some aspects of political deliberation or in legal and administrative procedures. However, they suggest that neutrality must play a far more limited role in political life than some contemporary neutral liberals expect. Securing recognition and respect for cultural minorities will require liberal theorists to be better democrats, by looking beyond strategies of bracketing and minimal accommodation and toward more comprehensive forms of political inclusion.

FOUR

Cultural Pluralism from
Liberal Perfectionist Premises

S ome of the most robust recent arguments in favor of collective rights and protections for cultural minorities in democratic states have come from proponents of a curious hybrid position in political theory: perfectionist liberalism.[1] Rejecting the suggestion by political liberals that questions of the good can and should be bracketed from politics, liberal perfectionists attempt to develop an account of liberalism that is more sensitive to the ways in which people's attachments and memberships contribute to their well-being. Unlike many other kinds of liberals, liberal perfectionists suggest that a concern with questions about the good life and its requirements leads us to appreciate the importance of cultural identity and cultural membership and also to consider demands for certain forms of state protections for minority groups. There is of course something paradoxical about such a claim. Perfectionist theories are by definition directed toward a particular conception of the good life, truth, or moral excellence; how, then, can they

1. Here I adopt the political definition of state perfectionism suggested by Jeremy Waldron: "Perfectionism is simply the view that legislators and officials may consider what is good and valuable in life and what is ignoble and depraved when drafting the laws and setting the framework for social and personal relationships." See Waldron, "Autonomy and Perfectionism in Raz's *Morality of Freedom*," *Southern California Law Review* 62, no. 4 (1989): 1102. What I call weakly perfectionist liberalism is the combination of the account of perfectionism offered by Waldron and certain conceptions of liberal commitments to personal autonomy, equal respect, and toleration.

possibly point the way to greater respect for and inclusion of citizens' moral, cultural, and social *differences*? As liberals readily remind us, many perfectionist conceptions of the good are monistic in content and do not readily encourage (indeed, may refuse) respect for differing views of the good. Witness the wave of criticisms aimed at virtue ethicists and communitarians—leading proponents of perfectionist moral theory—for emphasizing shared virtues, traditions, and moral beliefs at the expense of respect for social and ethical diversity (or even of acknowledgment of its importance and ubiquity).[2]

Paradox notwithstanding, some recent liberal writers have attempted to extend the scope of perfectionist thinking by asking how cultural identity and cultural membership may contribute to human flourishing. In addressing this question and the related matter of which social and political arrangements best protect cultural communities, some liberal perfectionists claim to offer a better response than proponents of a "merely" political liberalism, agnostic on all questions of the good. This chapter assesses recent work by liberals who argue that the main value of cultural membership and identity derives from the role these features play in sustaining individual well-being. I address work by Joseph Raz, who explicitly endorses perfectionist liberalism, and Will Kymlicka, whose "comprehensive liberal" perspective (to use Rawls's term) reflects a concern with the cultural requirements and preconditions of personal agency and choice. Both committed liberals, these writers nonetheless defend limited protections for certain cultural minorities by citing perfectionist sorts of claims about the role of culture in people's well-being and flourishing. Far from raising liberal objections to their views, I suggest that both Raz and Kymlicka adopt an overly liberal account of the significance of cultural identity and group membership, which locates the value of these features in their autonomy-enhancing role. This in turn leads these authors to delimit unnecessarily the *scope* of respect and accommodation for cultural minorities and in particular to reject formal protections for what they view as illiberal cultural minorities, whose practices may not support or indeed may undercut members' personal autonomy. A more adequate argument in favor of cultural recognition, I shall argue, must begin from a broader (and *less liberal*)—conception of the value of religious, ethnic, and cultural identities and memberships to well-being.

2. Numerous such criticisms have been made, for instance, of Alasdair MacIntyre's discussion of shared goods and virtues in *After Virtue* and of shared ethical and normative traditions in *Whose Justice? Which Rationality?*

I begin from the provisional assumption that to articulate what is important about cultural membership and identity, if anything, we need to ask how these features contribute to people's well-being. Liberal perfectionist and comprehensive liberal approaches, like perfectionist perspectives more generally, inquire directly about the nature of the good and the requirements of human flourishing. In connection with issues of cultural pluralism, liberal perfectionists and comprehensive liberals may ask why a secure sense of cultural identity seems both emotionally and psychologically valuable for so many people and whether membership in a stable cultural community is a central component of a good life (and if so, why?). These are questions that many contemporary liberals, most notably proponents of neutral or political liberalism, tend to dismiss as inappropriate subjects for liberal justice. Rawls specifically eschews discussions of the good in setting out principles and procedures of justice, largely out of the conviction that in plural societies, no comprehensive agreement on the good life is possible.[3] Although this is surely true, I try to show that we can make a case for the importance of cultural group identity and membership to many people's well-being without requiring or presupposing consensus on substantive norms and ideals. In response to political liberals' insistence that the state should be neutral on all questions of value, I shall argue that this form of state neutrality is problematic in view of increasing demands on the part of ethnic and national minorities in liberal democratic states for more formal political recognition and accommodation.

Liberal Objections to Perfectionism

Contemporary contractarian liberals reject both moral and state perfectionism as exemplified by the diverse perfectionist doctrines of such thinkers as Aristotle, Aquinas, or on certain readings, Mill and Marx. Moral perfectionism—the idea that we should direct our lives toward the attainment of some determinate ideal of moral excellence or of the good—is thought to be incompatible with liberal commitments to value pluralism and toleration. To the extent that a state pursues or imposes ideals of excellence, it is believed to jeopardize the personal autonomy of its citizens or their freedom to form, revise, and pursue their own conceptions of the good. Liberals who insist that the state should refrain from influencing citizens' diverse views of the good or shaping

3. Rawls, *Political Liberalism*, 15–16.

life plans, whether through indirect or coercive means, usually argue in favor of some version of state neutrality. This neutral liberal model, as exemplified by Rawls's political liberalism and Charles Larmore's *modus vivendi* liberalism, requires that we work out principles and procedures of justice in abstraction from any comprehensive conception of the good.[4]

For political liberals, the idea that we can and should determine a single, objectively "best" conception of the good life—or that the state should direct our social, political, and economic institutions toward attaining this ideal—is fundamentally incompatible with liberalism's endorsement of value pluralism. The familiar debate between liberals and virtue ethicists (including communitarians) about the priority of the right versus the priority of the good is perhaps the main manifestation of this central dispute in normative political philosophy. Many variants of moral and state perfectionism indeed fail liberalism's basic demands for individual freedom and toleration of diverse views and ways of life. But *liberal* perfectionists—in contrast to, say, many Aristotelian, Platonic, or Thomist perfectionists—insist on specifically liberal ideals such as personal autonomy, ethical diversity, and toleration. Crucially, liberal proponents of perfectionism (unlike these other kinds of perfectionists) do not believe that the state should impose on its citizens a single, overarching account of the good. Rather, they are careful to affirm that there are many different but nonetheless valid conceptions of the good and that it is not within the proper purview of the state to impose any such conception (regardless of its content). Nonetheless, liberal perfectionists such as Raz part company with contemporary political liberals in suggesting both that the state should set constraints on *how* individuals pursue their own conceptions of the good and that it may legitimately invoke determinate moral principles in doing so.[5] As Raz puts it, "there is no fundamental principled inhibition on governments acting for any valid moral reason."[6] Liberal perfectionists, quite unlike political liberals, also see value in the cultivation of shared goods, moral be-

---

4. See especially Rawls, *Political Liberalism*, and Larmore, *Patterns of Moral Complexity.*

5. As Raz writes: "People's preferences should be freely pursued only within certain bounds. They should be free to engage in valuable activities, pursuits, and relationships within the limits set by consideration for the interests of others. They should be free to do so because activities, pursuits, and relationships contribute to their well-being. Thus the function of government, besides the provision of a minimal protective net guaranteeing the satisfaction of basic needs, is to demarcate the boundaries of such freedom of action so as to enhance, inasmuch as is in its power, the quality of the options it makes available to people." From "Liberalism, Scepticism, and Democracy," in his *Ethics in the Public Domain,* 108.

6. Raz, "Facing Up: A Reply," *Southern California Law Review* 62 (1989): 1230.

liefs, and virtues, and some go so far as to suggest that the state should encourage practices and ways of life it deems valuable and discourage worthless ones.

A number of features, then, distinguish liberal perfectionists from recent neutral or political liberals. Perhaps most obviously, liberal perfectionists do not accept that a conception of justice must be worked out in abstraction from all comprehensive ideals and goods. Moreover, although they readily accept the fact of ethical diversity, liberal perfectionists reject the assumption by some political liberals that citizens' moral and political ideals and values are most often incommensurable. Indeed, they hold out the hope that our plural moral conceptions can cohere in a more substantive way than is supposed by normatively "thin" strategies, such as Rawls's idea of an overlapping consensus. Moreover, liberal perfectionists normally endorse at least limited forms of state perfectionism that political liberals would reject as incompatible with respect for citizens' autonomy. For instance, for many liberal perfectionists the coordination and shaping of citizens' conceptions of the good is fully within the state's purview. Raz, for instance, asks why "I should apply my beliefs about the good life to the conduct of my own life, but not to public policies which affect the fortunes of others," and answers that people should apply them to both.[7]

An obvious liberal objection to even Raz's moderate liberal perfectionism—with its emphasis on the ideal of personal autonomy—is that it introduces illegitimate forms of state interference in the lives of citizens. This criticism is best articulated by Rawls, who argues in *A Theory of Justice* that perfectionism is plainly at odds with liberal justice in pluralistic societies. Rawls rejects strict, teleological perfectionism on the grounds that it invokes highly contestable conceptions of human excellence and of the good life and therefore poses a threat to the stability and legitimacy of liberal justice. Perfectionism also violates the precepts of rationality: rational choosers in Rawls's original position will reject perfectionist moral and political principles because they recognize that "they have (or may have) certain moral and religious interests and other cultural ends which they cannot put in jeopardy, ... [and] ... have no way of knowing that their claims may not fall before the higher social goal of maximizing perfection."[8] Rawls's view still leaves room for the thought that the desire to pursue their conception of moral excellence will be among *some* agents' highest order interests, but rejects the suggestion that it is (or should be) everyone's ideal.

7. Raz, "Liberalism, Scepticism, and Democracy," 103.
8. Rawls, *A Theory of Justice*, 327.

The claim that perfectionism is incompatible with neutral liberal justice is however more often expressed pointedly in terms of the irreconcilability of perfectionism and pluralism.[9] This is the view with which I am most concerned here. To respect citizens' diverse moral views and also to fulfill the requirements of justice, publicly binding principles must not incorporate any particular comprehensive accounts of the good.[10] But although liberal perfectionists agree that many variants of perfectionism do not accord respect to citizens' different ethical and social beliefs and values, they do not view it as a criticism to which their own theories are vulnerable. To demonstrate why, they employ three main (though not necessarily compatible) strategies, each of which is central to understanding how it is even possible to combine liberal and perfectionist perspectives. The first strategy is to claim that neutral liberals misunderstand what is entailed by perfectionism, as revealed by their readiness to impute coercive tendencies to the perfectionist state—even the liberal perfectionist state. Liberal perfectionists deny that coercion is a necessary feature of perfectionism; they attempt to play up the liberal aspects of their position while distancing it from stricter, more hierarchical and more coercive forms of perfectionism, such as those concerned with the pursuit of a single or particularly intolerant conception of human excellence and virtue.[11] A second, somewhat contradictory strategy is to offer "corrected" versions of some key liberal conceptions, particularly identity and autonomy, with the partial aim of falsifying the neutral liberal view that citizens' different moral comprehensive views cannot be integrated into political principles and institutions and so should be set aside.[12] William Galston, a liberal perfectionist, argues that liberals misperceive the nature and potential of liberal community and shared goods and that citizens in liberal states share much more in the way of public goals than neutral liberals typically admit: "Despite the pluralism of liberal societies, it is perfectly possible to identify a core of civic commitments and competencies the broad acceptance of which undergirds a well-ordered liberal polity. The state has a right to ensure that this core is generally and effectively dis-

---

9. See for instance Rawls, "The Priority of the Right and Ideas of the Good," *Philosophy and Public Affairs* 17, no. 4 (1988): esp. 269.

10. See Rawls, *Political Liberalism*, 38.

11. For an example of this strategy, see Raz, "Facing Up," 1231.

12. The tension lies in the fact that the first strategy is an attempt to show that liberal perfectionists can comply with such key liberal principles as respect for personal autonomy, while the second presents a case for reconceiving certain liberal goods, including autonomy.

seminated...."[13] A final strategy is to try to show that neutral liberals themselves covertly rely on a comprehensive conception of the good—that they do not succeed in securing a "value-free" or neutral account of justice.[14] In the view of liberal perfectionists, debates about whether ever to endorse ideals in political life are misguided, since political institutions and practices already reflect certain norms and ideas of the good.[15] Some versions of this thought assert that it is impossible to devise social, economic, and political institutions and practices that do not express ideas about what is valuable about human life or that do not indirectly favor certain ideals.[16] Instead of seeking ever more neutral premises, some argue that we should seek to establish in an open, democratic fashion the set of ideals and values we want to shape our social and political arrangements—particularly with respect to questions of social and economic distribution.[17]

13. William Galston, *Liberal Purposes: Goods, Virtues, and Diversity in the Liberal State* (Cambridge: Cambridge University Press, 1991), 255–56.

14. Contrary to the picture drawn by Raz and some other liberal perfectionists, liberals who reject perfectionist arguments do not necessarily rule out the introduction of moral ideals altogether; rather, they believe that these should be restricted to our social and individual activities, not introduced into public life. This is why Kymlicka views the opposition between perfectionism and neutral liberalism as mistaken: "the dispute should perhaps be seen as a choice, not between perfectionism and neutrality, but between social perfectionism and state perfectionism—for the flip side of state neutrality is support for the role of perfectionist ideals and arguments in civil society." Similarly, he writes, "Liberal neutrality does not restrict the scope of perfectionist ideals in the collective activities of individuals and groups." Kymlicka, "Liberal Individualism and Liberal Neutrality," 895 and 897.

15. For example, Donald Moon makes this point in *Constructing Community*, 70–71. Vinit Haksar argues that liberalism presupposes the presence of perfectionist views, especially about human nature and the intrinsic value of some forms of life (especially rational human lives) over other life forms, in his *Equality, Liberty and Perfectionism* (Oxford: Oxford University Press, 1979).

16. For instance, Michael Walzer asserts that "Unless we can identify a neutral starting point from which many different and possibly legitimate moral cultures might develop, we can't construct a proceduralist minimum. But there is no such starting point." Walzer, *Thick and Thin: Moral Argument at Home and Abroad* (Notre Dame, Ind.: University of Notre Dame Press, 1994), 14. Another way of expressing this point is suggested by George Sher, who argues that "no government can *avoid* either nonrationally shaping its citizens' preferences or providing them with incentives. Even if governments do not try to produce these effects, they are bound to occur as unintended consequences of many political arrangements." Sher, "Liberal Neutrality and the Value of Autonomy," *Social Philosophy and Policy* 12, no. 1 (1995): 154.

17. Martha Nussbaum's work provides an example of this position: she rejects the neutral liberal assertion that liberal governments are or can ever be neutral vis-à-vis conceptions of the human good and suggests that such conceptions already inform most decisions in political life. Since this is so, we would do better to think about what the

These three responses by liberal perfectionists to neutral liberals' criticisms of perfectionism form part of the backdrop to Raz's liberal perfectionist defense of rights and protections for cultural groups. To a lesser degree, they also inform Kymlicka's comprehensive liberal argument in favor of collective rights for national minorities and some ethnic minority groups.

Raz's Liberal Perfectionist Defense of Pluralism and Cultural Membership

In *Ethics in the Public Domain*, Raz argues that a liberal perfectionist conception of the good can fully account for the importance of cultural identity and membership in ways that neutral or political liberalism cannot. Before taking a closer look at Raz's claim, it is worth briefly reviewing his account of moral pluralism, which provides the basis for his arguments for state protection of cultural identity and membership. In an earlier book, *The Morality of Freedom*, Raz makes a strong case for the compatibility of a limited, liberal perfectionism and *moral pluralism*, which asserts "the existence of a multitude of incompatible but morally valuable forms of life." Unlike Rawls, however, Raz thinks moral pluralism is best secured not via state neutrality but rather through a form of liberal state perfectionism—"For it is the goal of all political action to enable individuals to pursue valid conceptions of the good and to discourage evil or empty ones."[18] This position invokes both Millian and Aristotelian ideas: like Aristotle and Mill, Raz believes that some social diversity is a requirement of human flourishing; following Mill, he suggests that the value of diversity derives primarily from the fact that it supplies agents with worthwhile "valid" options and choices, the value of which is determined according to whether they contribute to human excellence or good.

Much of Raz's argument for liberal perfectionism of course turns on the question of what constitutes a good life and whether people can come to agree on some of its basic components. If Raz were merely to assume that citizens shared goods and moral norms, this would of course signal a fatal weakness in his argument. But it would be a mis-

---

requirements of human flourishing are and to take steps to support these. Nussbaum, "Aristotelian Social Democracy," in *Liberalism and the Good*, ed. R. Bruce Douglass et al. (London: Routledge, 1990), 212.

18. Raz, *The Morality of Freedom*, 133.

take, at least at this stage, to foist this criticism on Raz. A brief comparison of his position with those of certain communitarians and virtue ethicists (such as Alasdair MacIntyre and Amitai Etzioni) demonstrates why. While the latter freely endorse determinate conceptions of moral truth or of the good life, Raz rejects the superiority of any single account of moral excellence or good and seeks to secure tolerance for a plurality of values and goods.[19] In his view, one of the most important ways in which social practices or arrangements can contribute to human excellence, and to good lives, is by fostering personal autonomy. So valuable is autonomy that Raz suggests we should devise public policies so as to secure for agents its necessary conditions. Its exercise furthermore requires the availability of a plurality of options—or diverse ways of life, goods, and opportunities from which to choose. Since many of these goods are public or collective in nature, they require the support of the state. It is this thought that forms the basis of Raz's arguments for moral pluralism, limited state perfectionism, and eventually, as we shall see, for cultural group rights.

What drives Raz's defense of moral diversity—and ultimately cultural membership rights—is his Millian view that personal autonomy is a central feature of a flourishing life.[20] There are three main components to autonomy as conceived by Raz: "appropriate mental abilities"; "independence"; and "an adequate range of options."[21] Each of these requirements is further supported in different ways by circumstances of social diversity and toleration. A context of diversity helps us to be reflective and aware of our choices and supplies us with the necessary options for exercising autonomy. For Raz, as for contemporary liberals generally, personal autonomy requires that we be free to form, revise, and pursue our own conception of the good; but unlike neutral liberals in particular, Raz also insists that such autonomy is not possible unless agents have an array of different goods and options from which to choose. Likewise, he emphasizes that the exercise of autonomy gives rise to a plurality of values, for familiar Millian reasons to do with the consequences of freedom of individual thought and opinion. All of

19. Similarly, whereas many communitarian and Aristotelian writers emphasize the "discovery" and preservation of common values, shared virtues, and traditions, Raz views these features not so much as pre-existing, but rather as goods that we cultivate through particular social and political arrangements and practices.

20. Raz employs the term autonomy in the sense of a capacity, one which "admits of various degrees"; he is not especially concerned here with moral autonomy, in the sense understood by Kant. See Raz, *The Morality of Freedom*, 6.

21. Ibid., 372.

these factors stand behind Raz's conclusion that "valuing autonomy leads to the endorsement of moral pluralism," and that "autonomy ... requires pluralism but not neutrality."[22]

In order to ensure that we all have the means to live self-directed lives, Raz argues that the state must help to ensure the availability of worthwhile options and goods. This claim comprises two thoughts. First, autonomy is *valuable* only insofar as it is directed toward *worthwhile* choices: "freedom consists in the pursuit of valuable forms of life."[23] Conversely, autonomy that is directed toward worthless pursuits has no place in a flourishing life. As we shall see, Raz's failure to problematize the question of how we determine what counts as valuable causes difficulties for his otherwise robust defense of cultural identity and membership rights. But for present purposes, suffice to say that Raz views his position as pluralist insofar as it acknowledges that morally "worthwhile choices" include a number of "different and incompatible *valuable* ways of life," and does not suggest that we should be limited by a single good.[24] This move distances Raz's approach from fully perfectionist theories—such as those propounded by virtue ethicists—which do not normally speak of plural conceptions of the good life but rather presuppose a more monistic account of the good.

The second aspect of Raz's argument for state support of "worthwhile goods" is his claim that because such goods are typically public, they cannot be sustained without the assistance of the state. Collective goods are not adequately secured by liberal neutrality or noninterference in social and political arrangements, but instead require public (e.g., social, legal, and economic) forms of assistance: "supporting valuable forms of life is a social rather than an individual matter."[25] Construed in a general way, it is the task of the state to create an "autonomy-supporting environment ... by providing individuals with the means by which they can develop, which enable them to choose and attempt to realize their own conception of the good."[26] More specifically, the state must help to secure the availability of *valuable* options.[27]

Raz has recently extended his thesis that worthwhile forms of personal autonomy require the support of the state to argue for the protection of cultural group rights. Here he posits that a sense of cultural

---

22. Ibid., 399, and Raz, "Liberalism, Autonomy, and the Politics of Neutral Concern," 324.

23. Raz, *The Morality of Freedom*, 395.

24. Raz, "Liberalism, Scepticism and Democracy," 103. Emphasis added.

25. Raz, *The Morality of Freedom*, 162.

26. Ibid., 133.

27. Ibid., 205.

identity and membership in a thriving cultural community are crucial to individual autonomy and to human flourishing more generally. These help to secure people's sense of dignity and self-respect, both of which are necessary if one is to form, revise, and pursue a conception of the good. Membership in a cultural group supports the development of our normative and decision-making capacities and furnishes us with the opportunities necessary for personal autonomy. By contrast,

> Those who belong to none [i.e., no group] are denied full access to the opportunities that are shaped in part by the group's culture. They are made to feel estranged, and their chances to have a rewarding life are seriously damaged. The same is true of people who grow up among members of a group so that they absorb its culture, but are then denied access to it because they are denied full membership of the group.[28]

Raz's view that membership in a cultural community supplies individuals with a normative context without which they could not even form a conception of the good has an affinity with recent arguments by Charles Taylor. Like Raz, Taylor suggests that a thicker form of liberalism should acknowledge the importance of cultural membership to human flourishing. Liberalism directed toward what Taylor calls the "politics of equal respect" is "grounded very much on judgments about what makes a good life—judgments in which the integrity of cultures has an important place."[29] For Raz, as for Taylor, "one's cultural membership determines the horizons of one's opportunities." Accordingly, this provides us with reasons to protect the collective good of cultural membership and so to heed basic demands for cultural respect and recognition within the broader political framework.[30] If, as Raz suggests, "individual freedom and prosperity depend on full and unimpeded membership in a respected and flourishing community," then liberal perfectionist principles demand that the state help to secure such membership by introducing forms of accommodation for some cultural minorities. These might range from subsidies for cultural community centers and funds for minority first-language education to special group rights for certain national (e.g., ethnic and linguistic) minorities who have established a moral right to self-determination.[31] Indeed, Raz's argument connecting cultural membership to autonomy and well-being yields two broad sorts

28. Joseph Raz and Avisahai Margalit, "National Self-Determination," in *Ethics in the Public Domain*, 115.
29. Taylor, "The Politics of Recognition," 61.
30. Raz, "Liberalism, Autonomy, and the Politics of Neutral Concern," 330.
31. Raz, "Multiculturalism," 159.

of policy positions: first, territorially concentrated cultural groups have a right (though not an absolute right) to self-determination; and second, in plural, liberal-democratic states, it is the duty of the state to introduce certain cultural rights and protections for viable but vulnerable cultural communities—in other words, to pursue a policy of multi-culturalism.[32] No doubt Raz's endorsement of polyethnic rights for certain cultural groups and a right of self-determination for national minorities goes a considerable distance toward suggesting ways to meet demands for cultural recognition.

Whether or not Raz can support these proposals depends in part on whether he can make good the claim that cultural membership and identity are valuable for the sorts of reasons he cites. The value of cultural identity, in his view, derives broadly from its role in fostering individual well-being, but it is especially critical to the development of self-respect—so much so that people's dignity and self-respect are "affected by the esteem in which these groups are held."[33] By contrast, however, Raz deems cultural membership in what he calls "encompassing groups" (cultural groups in which important areas of life are shared) valuable primarily because it provides members with access to social and economic goods and opportunities. As Raz writes, "membership in such groups is of great importance to individual well-being, for it greatly affects one's opportunities, one's ability to engage in the relationships and pursuits marked by the culture."[34] This is a similar but perhaps somewhat narrower account than that offered by some liberal perfectionists and many communitarians (such as Charles Taylor), who see cultural membership as valuable insofar as it provides a normative context within which agents acquire values and ideals, develop life goals, and form capacities for choice.[35] In any event, the case Raz presents for the importance of cultural membership and cultural identity reflects, as he readily admits, an "instrumentalist and pragmatic" approach: that is, the value of these features lies in their benefit to individual members of groups.[36] However, Raz insists that an instrumental approach to the value of culture in no way neglects or denies the beneficial "subjective aspects" of cultural identity and membership, such as the importance of one's feeling at home in a community.[37] This seems to be true of Raz's

32. Raz and Margalit, "National Self-Determination," 130, and Raz, "Multiculturalism," 171–72.

33. Raz and Margalit, "National Self-Determination," 119.

34. Ibid., 119.

35. Taylor, "The Politics of Recognition."

36. Raz and Margalit, "National Self-Determination," 120.

37. Ibid., 123.

account of the significance of cultural identity, but his discussion of cultural membership points to more narrowly liberal—and I suggest, contentious—reasons for valuing culture. In particular, Raz stresses the connection between cultural membership and *personal autonomy* (both opportunities and capacities for autonomy) in such a way as to make it difficult to appreciate these other aspects, especially those that may interfere with agents' independence. Raz emphasizes the role of culture in securing valuable forms of autonomy much more so than does Taylor, for instance, who wants to assign what he calls a presumption of equal moral worth to all cultures, even those for whom autonomy is not a cherished good.[38]

Raz's attempt to ground his argument for the value of cultural membership in an ideal of personal autonomy determines, to a large extent, the kinds of communities that he views as meriting the support of the liberal perfectionist state.[39] This is because his defense of policies to foster multiculturalism "emphasizes the role of cultures as a precondition for, and a factor which gives shape and content to, individual freedom."[40] Yet cultural communities may also need to restrict their members' horizons and choices: witness the Amish, who sought special dispensation from the U.S. Supreme Court to end compulsory education for their members at the age of 15 in order to ensure the survival of their community's ways of life.[41] Or we might consider the recent example of native Canadian groups, who in the early 1990s requested exemption from the Canadian Charter of Rights and Freedoms—which guarantees individual rights—on the grounds that it stands in tension with collective rights and sovereignty and might undercut the authority of aboriginal law. By linking the value of cultural identity and membership closely with the agents' capacities and opportunities for choice and freedom, Raz may overlook valuable aspects of cultural membership

38. As Lawrence Becker has pointed out to me, this criticism would not have the same force if Raz understood personal autonomy as acting from our deepest values and convictions, rather than as merely the capacity to make independent choices about one's life; however, I believe there is little evidence that Raz uses the word autonomy in the former, broader sense.

39. Raz might reject this reading of his work, but in my view he has no effective way out of this dilemma short of modifying his accounts of either autonomy or the value of culture. In an attempt to preempt just such a criticism, he writes, "Valuing autonomy and accepting moral pluralism does not ... entail that forms of life are good because they are chosen. On the contrary, they are chosen because they are thought to be good." Nonetheless, it seems undeniable that one consequence of Raz's understanding of autonomy is that those features and practices which can be *chosen* are much more likely to be deemed valuable. See Raz, "Liberalism, Autonomy, and the Politics of Neutral Concern," 348–49.

40. Raz, "Multiculturalism," 163.

41. *Wisconsin v. Yoder*, 406 U.S. 205 (1971).

which not only do not necessarily enhance individual autonomy, but also may actually stand in tension with it. An important consequence of this move is that Raz's "instrumentalist and pragmatic" approach delimits or restricts unnecessarily the range and kinds of social and cultural differences that liberals will have reason to recognize politically. In particular, cultural groups that are often referred to as nonliberal or illiberal are more likely to be dismissed as not meriting special accommodation or protections within the liberal state since they frequently do not contribute to their members' capacities and opportunities for autonomous agency. There are, of course, good reasons to deny many oppressive illiberal minorities exemption from prevailing liberal laws and to refuse demands for special forms of accommodation or rights. But membership in traditional cultural communities that are merely nonliberal in their belief system—and which effectively restrict the scope of individual choice in social and domestic arrangements—may well be valuable for reasons overlooked by liberals like Raz. Consider, for example, the sense of emotional security and well-being that can come from being a member of a collectivity with clearly defined norms and roles. Traditional cultural communities can be a source of comfort and refuge to members, providing direction and a sense of place, and delimiting social and personal options experienced by many as disorienting and burdensome. Some younger members of traditional immigrant groups in democratic states—for instance, South Asians in Britain and the United States—willingly opt for a life closely tied to their traditional community (by embracing religious customs, marrying within their culture, etc.). Restrictions on social arrangements and one's choice of marriage partner and career may well be a valuable *benefit* of cultural membership for some members of traditional cultures.

The instrumentalist case for the value of cultural membership asks what membership can provide for individuals and sets aside more evaluative questions about the specific kinds of goods and benefits such belonging provides. Yet without such a discussion, it is difficult to assess whether certain traditional, nonliberal cultural minorities merit formal accommodation and protection. What is valuable in Raz's view is not so much the *content* of particular cultural identities nor the specific beliefs and traditions they encompass—and for which cultural groups demand recognition and respect—but rather the role of cultures in supplying us with certain key requirements of a good life, conceived in more or less liberal terms. Our values, practices, and beliefs are thus in some sense instrumentally, but not intrinsically, valuable: "Freedom of religion, freedom of speech, freedom of association, of occupation, of movement, of marriage, and the like, are all important not because it is important that people should speak, should engage in religious worship, should marry or travel, etc., but because it is important that they should decide for themselves whether or not to do so."[42] Here my objection is not to Raz's presumption that cultural membership supports human flourishing nor indeed that such membership is instrumentally and not intrinsically valuable, but rather to the *aspects* of flourishing that he emphasizes. In locating the value of cultural membership in its autonomy-enhancing role, Raz tends to restrict the range of groups that can expect to receive positive support from the liberal perfectionist state to groups that do not challenge liberal sensibilities.[43] To be clear: Raz's position represents a considerable advance over liberal approaches that advocate cultural assimilation or mere tolerance; he goes so far as to say, for instance, that "there were, and there can be, non-repressive societies, and ones which enable people to spend their lives in worthwhile pursuits, even though their pursuits and the options open to them are not subject to individual choice."[44] Yet Raz tends to assume that such societies fall outside the boundaries of contemporary liberal states, as his reference to cultures that are "pernicious, based on the exploitation of people ... or on the denigration and persecution of other groups" seems to suggest.[45] Perhaps as a consequence, he neglects to discuss whether and why membership in such nonliberal groups might be valuable and what forms of institutional protection and support such groups might deserve.

In discussing the problem of illiberal (as opposed to merely nonliberal) cultural groups, Raz invokes several aspects of liberal perfectionist reasoning.[46] His rejection of such groups seems to entail the following steps. Illiberal communities, on his view, do not foster the autonomy of their members nor, consequently, contribute to their well-being or flourishing. The goods and options that these cultures secure are therefore morally worthless in the sense that they do not contribute to valuable forms of agency. Since the state is only bound to protect and support

42. Although it is not my intention to argue that cultural identity and membership must be viewed as intrinsically valuable—the very distinction between intrinsic and instrumental value being a thorny issue in philosophy—I suggest there is an inconsistency in Raz's attempt to ground an argument for what he claims is the *intrinsic* value of cultural membership by showing that it *instrumentally* supports other goods, especially autonomy. Raz, "Rights and Individual Well-Being," in *Ethics in the Public Domain*, 34.

43. Yael Tamir makes a similar criticism of Raz with regard to his emphasis on autonomy. See her *Liberal Nationalism*, 31.

44. Raz, "Facing Up," 1227.

45. Raz and Margalit, "National Self-Determination," 119.

46. For the most part, Raz does not distinguish between antiliberal and merely nonliberal cultures.

morally valuable options or ways of life, under no circumstances should the state accord positive forms of assistance to these illiberal minorities (though they may still merit tolerance). Raz makes the further assertion that liberalism, especially perfectionist liberalism, is not committed to tolerating all cultural differences—especially illiberal cultures—and that we therefore should not judge the justice and success of liberalism on whether or not it endlessly accommodates diverse ways of life.[47] These thoughts lead Raz to the conclusion that illiberal cultures do not merit the support or protection of the liberal state: "[A] difficulty arises for those *who believe the illiberal culture to be inferior to theirs.* Should they tolerate it? The perfectionist principles espoused in this book suggest that people are justified in taking action to assimilate the minority group, at the cost of letting its culture die or at least be considerably changed by absorption."[48] Significantly, Raz does not explain how we might determine which options and which cultures are valuable and which worthless (i.e., other than by appealing to the norm of autonomy). Taken in tandem with his perfectionist belief that there are determinate moral truths and goods and that a self-directed life is one of the most important of these, the limits of Razian pluralism come into clearer focus.[49]

My interest here is not to offer a blanket defense of cultural communities that impose restrictions on their members, illiberal or otherwise; surely there are limits to the sorts of practices that democratic states can countenance (as I discuss below). But Raz's account of the value of cultural membership and his liberal perfectionist view that only "worthwhile" cultural goods and options merit the protection of the liberal state beg numerous questions. In particular, Raz moves too rapidly from establishing a link between personal autonomy and the good of

47. Raz, "Liberalism, Scepticism and Democracy," 108.

48. Emphasis added. Raz goes on to say that this assimilation strategy applies primarily to those communities which are not self-sustaining and that in other cases toleration should be encouraged. *The Morality of Freedom,* 424.

49. Raz writes, "both in fostering a common culture and in providing access to its opportunities, one should act with discrimination to encourage the good and the valuable and to discourage the worthless and the bad." See "Liberalism, Scepticism and Democracy," 108. Raz's perfectionist agenda is all the more worrying given that he is also adamant that justice should, above all, be truth-directed (see "Facing Diversity," 55). Moreover, despite Raz's assurances that perfectionist liberalism merely sets constraints on how we each pursue our individual account of the good, he gives us no grounds for confidence that the state's evaluations of the good can be restricted to this more limited role. As Waldron has noted, the scope of permissible state action (for Raz's ostensibly limited perfectionism) extends beyond a seemingly innocuous account of the good life to a number of moral directives on personal and social relationships: this sets his perspective off from liberals like Rawls. See Waldron, "Autonomy and Perfectionism," 1133.

cultural membership to the claim that this relationship provides the best basis for a defense of multicultural policies and state support for cultural groups. He rightly reminds us that "the provision of many collective goods is constitutive of the very possibility of autonomy," and also that personal autonomy requires some form of cultural membership, broadly understood.[50] But it does not therefore follow that the sole or even primary value of culture is to be found in its capacity to enhance or secure individual choice and access to opportunities.

Raz's view of the benefits of cultural membership leads him inexorably to the conclusion that the liberal state should not extend positive support, nor under certain circumstances tolerance, to illiberal minorities. Although Raz thinks his defense of cultural membership is compatible with toleration of some nonliberal groups, he places the onus on them to demonstrate that they deserve this support: they must show that they preserve their members' well-being in ways that mesh with normative liberal commitments.[51] His position is problematic in a number of respects, not least because it represents an attempt to set the limits of tolerance and inclusion of diverse cultural groups without any attempt to engage these groups in political deliberation. Moreover, although it is not his explicit intention, it seems that Raz's argument is biased in favor of cultural groups that fit a liberal profile. His view that liberal democracies should on no account offer protections for illiberal minorities also obscures the extent to which modern, constitutional democracies can (and do) negotiate special arrangements for some cultural communities—such as the Amish—without necessarily jeopardizing core democratic principles or eroding individual rights and liberties.

Raz's perfectionist liberal account of why we should protect cultural membership might be contrasted with a more robust picture of the demands of cultural recognition, one that is neither strictly liberal nor strictly perfectionist. Cultural recognition, as I understand it, in no way requires that we accept or support any and all cultural beliefs and practices irrespective of their content. Nor does it entail the relativistic view that different ideas of the good and ways of life are of equal merit or value. Cultural membership is surely important for reasons irreducible to the role that cultures may play in fostering the personal autonomy of group members. Nor is it clear, *pace* Raz, why nonliberal cultural minor-

---

50. Raz, *The Morality of Freedom*, 207.

51. Raz writes, "The preservation of [a] culture is justified only in terms of its contribution to the well-being of people. This requires an adjustment of each of the cultural groups to the conditions of a relatively harmonious coexistence within one political society." From "Multiculturalism," 171–72.

ities should not be entitled to respect and recognition even if their ways of life stand in tension with liberal intuitions and certain core liberal beliefs. The assertion that equal concern and respect is owed to cultural groups is in large part a liberal insight and derives from the Kantian principle of respect for the dignity of all rational moral agents. Applied to the issue of cultural diversity, Charles Taylor's view of the presumption of the equal moral worth of cultures approximates this idea, as does James Tully's notion of intercultural respect.[52] Of course, the proposal that we accord basic respect to different cultural groups raises the problem of setting critical standards for supporting or condemning specific beliefs, arrangements, and practices. A broadly Kantian account of respect, however, involves reciprocal duties, including the duty not to hamper or impede another agent's dignity. This implies, for instance, that groups will not merit respect or support for their ways of life if they seek consistently to undercut the agency of their members or others. This includes not merely outright harm, but also hampering agents' abilities to refuse certain arrangements and practices.[53] Surely it is *this* criterion and not the fact that groups do or do not actively encourage their members to pursue their own account of the good, or to live fully autonomous lives, that should determine whether liberal states limit or restrict certain cultural practices. Although coercive cultures are probably also cultures that do not foster the independence of some of their members or afford them opportunities that liberals deem adequate, the converse is not necessarily true.

Although Raz recognizes some of the ways in which cultural membership and social diversity might be valuable, his theory cannot help us to grasp, much less meet, nonliberal cultural groups' claims for recognition and positive forms of support. The problem is not so much that Raz argues for a morally determinate view, but that the one he does put forth is so steeped in assumptions about the value of personal autonomy and the derivative or instrumental value of cultural membership that it is of limited use in precisely those societies Raz seeks to address—culturally diverse states. Nor can Raz's argument supply us with

---

52. Taylor, "The Politics of Recognition," and James Tully, *Strange Multiplicity*.

53. What I have in mind here is Onora O'Neill's suggestion that "principles of action that hinge on victimizing some, so on destroying, paralyzing, or undercutting their capacities for action for at least some time and in some ways, can be adopted by some but cannot be adopted as fundamental principles by any plurality." In "Justice, Gender, and International Boundaries," in *The Quality of Life*, eds. M. Nussbaum and A. Sen (Oxford: Clarendon Press, 1992), 315. Also see her "Constructivisms in Ethics," in *Constructions of Reason: Explorations of Kant's Practical Philosophy* (Cambridge: Cambridge University Press, 1989), and "Rights, Obligations, and Needs," *Logos* 6 (1985): 43–44.

adequate critical, conceptual tools with which to give serious consideration to the question of whether to accept or reject specific nonliberal cultural practices and ways of life.

Kymlicka's Comprehensive Liberal Justification of Cultural Rights

In his earliest discussions of cultural membership and cultural identity, Will Kymlicka argued that Rawls and other neutral liberals should concede that cultural membership is a primary good (in the Rawlsian sense) and so deserves the protection of the liberal state:

> Liberal values require both individual freedom of choice and a secure cultural context from which individuals can make their choices. Thus liberalism requires that we can identify, protect, and promote cultural membership, as a primary good.... It is the existence of a cultural community viewed as a context of choice that is a primary good, and a legitimate concern of liberals.[54]

By expanding Rawls's list of primary goods to include the good of cultural membership, Kymlicka tried to show that cultural minority rights can be justified within mainstream liberal theory. A pre-political-liberal conception of liberal justice that acknowledges the importance of personal autonomy to human flourishing will concede the significance of membership in one's own cultural group: "Cultural membership affects our very sense of personal identity and capacity," helps to provide "meaningful options for us," and fosters "our ability to judge for ourselves the value of our life plans."[55]

In more recent work, Kymlicka, like Raz, continues to emphasize the importance of cultural membership to the formation of agents' life plans and their capacities to evaluate and pursue their own conceptions of the good. But whereas Raz develops this point in a more explicitly liberal perfectionist direction—viewing the support of cultural groups as the responsibility of the perfectionist liberal state—Kymlicka defends a "comprehensive liberal" argument that foregrounds equality and autonomy. This view claims that if liberals are concerned to secure equal regard or consideration for citizens and to foster peoples' opportunities and capacities for choice to an equal degree, then they must support the introduction of special rights and arrangements for certain histori-

---

54. Kymlicka, *Liberalism, Community and Culture*, 169.
55. Ibid., pp. 175, 168, and 166.

cally disadvantaged cultural minorities in plural, democratic states. Kymlicka's defense of cultural minority rights thus combines some perfectionist liberal concerns with a strong liberal equality argument. In culturally plural polities, taking social equality seriously may require that the state distribute goods differently so as to equalize the chances of success of individuals from diverse cultural communities: "members of minority cultural communities may face particular kinds of disadvantages with respect to the good of cultural membership, disadvantages whose rectification requires and justifies the provision of minority rights."[56]

Like Raz, Kymlicka rests much of his case for greater accommodation and protection for cultural minorities in democratic states on the role that cultural membership plays in securing the circumstances and opportunities for individual freedom. This might seem a curious move for a writer with such clearly liberal sensibilities. However, Kymlicka does not treat autonomy as an idealized good so much as he considers it a structural requirement for living a life of one's own choosing, to the extent that this is possible. Although he agrees with political liberals that a conception of justice for pluralistic democracies should be in some basic sense neutral vis-à-vis conceptions of the good, Kymlicka denies that this requires that we bracket all substantive ideals from liberal political deliberation and liberal principles. Indeed, he criticizes Rawls's argument for a merely political liberalism on the grounds that it is both inadvisable and futile to try to restrict the ideal of autonomy to the political realm: liberals need (and, Kymlicka asserts, Rawls's theory covertly depends on) a conception of the autonomous person in both public and in private life.[57] Cultural membership supports independence by supplying individuals with the capacities and opportunities to pursue their own account of the good life: "Put simply, freedom involves making choices amongst various options, and our societal culture not only provides these options, but also makes them meaningful to us."[58]

Also like Raz, Kymlicka links the value of cultural identity and membership to the ideal of personal autonomy without sufficient warrant or

---

56. Ibid., 162. Kymlicka refers to his own position as a comprehensive liberal view. His response to Rawls's failure to supply strategies for meeting cultural minorities' justice claims is that liberals should "continue to defend comprehensive liberalism, but to recognize that there are limits to our ability to implement and impose liberal principles on groups that have not endorsed those principles." See his "Two Models of Pluralism and Tolerance," 54.

57. Kymlicka, "Two Models of Pluralism and Tolerance," and *Multicultural Citizenship*, 158–62.

58. Kymlicka, *Multicultural Citizenship*, 83.

justification. Although he stops short of endorsing an overarching liberal conception of the good, Kymlicka's liberalism remains firmly committed to an ideal of human flourishing that emphasizes individuals' capacities to form, revise, and pursue an independent conception of the good. His criticisms of Rawls, as well as his own proposals for group-differentiated cultural rights, reflect his belief that citizens cannot achieve the conditions for individual autonomy, nor the extensive equality demanded by comprehensive liberalism, unless they enjoy secure membership in one or another flourishing cultural community. But if, as Kymlicka claims, "people's capacity to make meaningful choices depends on access to a cultural structure," it is surely true that societal cultures may shape and constrict people's options and choices in significant ways.[59] Yet Kymlicka tends to dismiss those cultures that restrict their members' choices as "illiberal" and undeserving of the support of the liberal state, on the grounds that such groups violate core liberal principles and do not seek to improve the prospects of all of their members.

Since Kymlicka does not have a general theory of the good to underpin his proposals for cultural rights, the scope and content of his argument for cultural minority rights are directly shaped by the few liberal ideals that he *does* endorse. Whether Kymlicka's approach can help to secure substantive respect, recognition, and concrete rights and provisions for a wide range of cultural groups thus rests squarely on his interpretation and application of the norms of autonomy and equality.

Before turning to a discussion of the merits of Kymlicka's strategy, it is instructive first to consider his concrete political proposals and his views on perfectionism. He considers group-specific rights and "external protections" for otherwise viable ethnic and cultural minority communities as necessary to secure equal chances for minority citizens to pursue their own conceptions of the good and proposes a wide range of measures aimed at achieving social, political, and economic equality.[60] Indeed, Kymlicka derives a wider range of cultural rights from his comprehensive liberal view than does Raz, identifying three types of external protections that plural, democratic states might introduce: special group representation rights (e.g., within mainstream political institutions); self-government rights to transfer power to local units on such issues as language and culture; and "polyethnic rights" to

---

59. Ibid., 84.

60. Ibid., 36–37. In some respects, we might say that Kymlicka's position incorporates aspects of the "neutrality of effect / consequences" argument discussed briefly in chapter 3, insofar as he is eager to secure equal opportunities for citizens of cultural minorities to pursue their chosen ways of life.

protect religious and cultural practices, especially of immigrants (who, as recent rather than long-standing and / or founding communities, do not merit self-government rights). At the forefront of Kymlicka's mind is the example of Canada, which in recent years has seen the introduction of protective French-language laws, the granting of land titles (or the return of lands) to some aboriginal peoples, and calls for special representation rights for groups underrepresented in intergovernmental bodies.[61]

Despite the fact that Kymlicka justifies his extensive political proposals for "group-differentiated rights" by pointing to the role of cultural identity and membership in human flourishing, his argument is only weakly liberal perfectionist. He believes liberals should appeal freely to certain comprehensive goods, notably autonomy, to justify social and political arrangements which will give vulnerable cultural communities equal chances of survival.[62] However, unlike Raz, Kymlicka does not think the state's role should extend to encouraging worthwhile ways of life or discouraging worthless or repugnant ones (though, as we shall see, he draws the limits to liberal toleration in much the same place as Raz does). Rather, he sees perfectionism as fundamentally about the ranking of ideals and conceptions of the good and believes that since no acceptable procedures for ranking can be found, we should reject an overall strategy of state perfectionism. Instead, it is in virtue of the importance of culture for individuals' capacities for choice, and the principle of equal regard for citizens, that the state has positive duties to protect the conditions of choice for members of all cultures.[63]

Kymlicka shares Rawls's view that hierarchical forms of perfectionism are destructive of cultural diversity and individual liberty, but for pragmatic rather than for philosophical reasons. He is particularly concerned about the practical consequences that state perfectionism might

---

61. Ibid., 37–38. Kymlicka draws several kinds of distinctions here, with national minorities such as aboriginal groups at one end of the spectrum, deserving land concessions and self-government rights, and recent immigrants at the opposite end, deserving fewer protections. He also attaches the important proviso that to merit state protections and support, cultural groups must be deemed essentially viable but "unequal" or vulnerable due to past or present state actions.

62. As Thomas Hurka notes, Kymlicka's argument is an odd admixture of egalitarianism and indirect perfectionism: "Kymlicka is ... a philosophical perfectionist, believing that some lives are intrinsically higher or finer.... But he does not endorse state perfectionism; on the contrary, he defends state neutrality. Though the best state is the one that most promotes good lives, the state should not aim at this goal directly." See his "Indirect Perfectionism: Kymlicka on Liberal Neutrality," *Journal of Political Philosophy* 3, no. 1 (1995): 38.

63. Kymlicka, "Liberal Individualism," 902–3.

hold for cultural minorities, who are often less able to defend their particular conceptions of the good within mainstream institutions. Even a "democratic" perfectionism—which Kymlicka defines as "the public ranking of the value of different ways of life ... through the collective political deliberation of citizens, rather than through the secret or unilateral decisions of political élites"—poses unacceptable threats to equal justice. This is because it would require that those groups who wish to demand support or special recognition from the government first "publicly formulate and defend their conception of the good" according to liberal-defined standards and styles of political engagement and to convince others of the merits of their cases. Due to social, economic, and political marginalization, many cultural minorities may be particularly ill-equipped to do this. Kymlicka is worried that overt state perfectionism would unfairly discriminate against cultural minorities and so violate liberal principles of equal justice.[64] For these reasons, Kymlicka rejects monistic and hierarchical forms of perfectionism in favor of a more moderate, Millian perfectionist liberalism that foregrounds individual liberty. His thesis that special rights for cultural minorities are required so as to secure the circumstances for personal autonomy (and to make good on the promise of liberal equality) invokes the more specific and controversial ideal of autonomy. Like Raz, Kymlicka is faced with the challenge of providing a strong argument to defend the claim that cultural identity and membership are valuable primarily insofar as they support individual members' capacities and opportunities for independence and choice; and he must furthermore show why groups which do not help to secure members' independence forfeit the support and protection of the liberal state.

For reasons similar to those encountered by Raz, Kymlicka faces considerable difficulties at this juncture. Certainly, both writers are correct to suggest that membership in a secure cultural group fosters individual members' capacities for personal independence in a general sense, by educating and socializing them into adulthood. Kymlicka insists that "liberals should recognize the importance of people's membership in their own societal culture, because of the role it plays in enabling mean-

---

64. Specifically, Kymlicka is concerned that even "democratic perfectionism" would require that cultural groups operate like "interest groups," and that this in turn would require a more intensive form of promotion than minorities are necessarily capable of: "state perfectionism raises the prospect of a dictatorship of the articulate and would unavoidably penalize those who are inarticulate." More generally, he worries that "state perfectionism would in fact serve to distort the free evaluation of ways of life, to rigidify the dominant ways of life, whatever their intrinsic merits, and to unfairly exclude the values and aspirations of marginalized groups within the community." Ibid., 900.

ingful individual choice and in supporting self-identity."[65] But does his account of the value of cultural membership support this conclusion? And does it mesh with cultural groups' own accounts of why their cultural identities and forms of community are essential to their well-being? Rather than citing "meaningful individual choice" as the most important benefit of cultural membership, members of cultural minority groups might stress the ways in which membership provides a sense of place and belonging—a secure and stable context that provides emotional and psychological stability partly by *delimiting* the chaotic and confusing array of lifestyle choices in the modern world. Cultural membership may provide members with opportunities for living a self-directed life or for making independent life choices; equally, it may not. But cultural membership does far more than this: it instills members with a sense of collective identity and belonging and may also supply them with a social context and evaluative horizon that help to temper the emotional and psychological difficulties associated with making major life choices. This (admittedly partial) account of the value of membership is compatible with some aspects of Kymlicka's and Raz's liberal perfectionism, but it sits uneasily with the emphasis both writers place on the value of individual freedom and choice. Although there are good liberal grounds to reject many restrictions that traditional cultural communities may seek to impose on their members, it is far from clear (*pace* Raz and Kymlicka) that these restrictions are necessarily valueless and unjust.

There are at least two further reasons to resist Kymlicka's "autonomy argument" as shorthand for why cultural identity and membership are central to the well-being of many people. First, it is important that an account of the value of these features should resonate with the reasons that cultural minorities themselves would give. As I have suggested, members of minority groups (especially more traditional ones) by no means unanimously affirm the ideal of personal autonomy, nor do they necessarily accept it as the overriding reason for introducing special political arrangements to support their ways of life. More typically, such groups appeal to the identity and autonomy of their community as a whole and to the importance of preserving distinctive practices and traditions. They may offer these sorts of reasons, for example, in defending marriage within the group, distinctive conceptions of family and family laws, and other social arrangements. Second, we should reject aspects of Kymlicka's account of the value of cultural identity and membership because it leads to unjustified and very possibly unnecessary re-

---

65. Kymlicka, *Multicultural Citizenship*, 105.

strictions on the range of social differences liberals will have reason to recognize and support. Kymlicka's liberal perfectionist principles impose two limits on minority rights—limits that derive from the priority he assigns to personal autonomy: (1) these rights cannot include "internal restrictions" applied by minority group leaders that destroy certain members' abilities to make choices about their lives or which violate the basic civil and political liberties of their members; and (2) "external protections are legitimate only in so far as they promote equality between groups."[66] It may be essential to endorse these limits in many cases where groups impose serious internal restrictions on their members, of course. However, as with Raz, Kymlicka's argument cannot help us to distinguish between overtly antiliberal groups that restrict their members in coercive ways (which democrats cannot support) and merely nonliberal communities with more heteronomous ways of life (which democrats could potentially support). It is because Kymlicka identifies the securing of conditions for personal autonomy as the primary reason for introducing special arrangements and rights for minority groups that he must take a relatively narrow view of the range of cultures the state should support and a rather broad view of those which it must restrict.[67]

The limitations of Kymlicka's view come into clearer focus when we consider the recent case of demands in Britain for state support for sex-segregated Muslim schools (most Protestant, Catholic, and Jewish schools currently enjoy state funding). In important ways, this form of schooling might diminish students' personal autonomy as defined by Kymlicka, since children educated in a traditional Muslim religious environment are discouraged from taking up other lifestyles or mores that conflict with Islam. Restrictions on girls in such an educational environment may include a modified curriculum that limits their training in science and subjects perceived as leading to inappropriate careers for Muslim women. However, there are certainly other individual and collective benefits to be gained: a sense of place and belonging; reprieve from the constant sense of being culturally different (and perhaps from harassment by teachers and classmates); and in some instances, improved academic performance. Based on Kymlicka's account of the value of cultural membership and the central importance of members' personal autonomy, liberals would have to reject the demand for Muslim schools, if this form of schooling indeed hampers the development of students' independence. Indeed, this is just the position Kymlicka

---

66. Ibid., 152.
67. A laissez-faire approach is precluded by Kymlicka's welfarist commitments.

takes: he views Muslim schooling as a clear example of illiberal minority leaders seeking "the legal power to restrict the liberty of [their] own members, so as to preserve [their] traditional religious practices."[68] In rejecting state-supported Muslim schools out of hand, Kymlicka has thus ranked the ideal of personal autonomy over other possible goods—especially collective goods—without adequate defense.[69] Although there may be compelling reasons to consider rejecting proposals for state-maintained Muslim schools, it is surely wrong to view such requests as necessarily outside the scope of liberal justice.[70]

The difficulty with Kymlicka's liberal argument for the value of cultural membership is that it insists unreasonably on the priority of personal autonomy as a regulative ideal for diverse citizens and communities living within plural, democratic states.[71] A broader account of the value of cultural membership, incorporating some of the aspects discussed here, accepts that the value of membership does not reduce to the ways in which groups foster their members' personal independence. Indeed, the best account would not emphasize any *single* reason for valuing cultural identity and membership, for it would appreciate that reasons can differ across cultures. Nor need this approach imply a position of cultural relativism. Rather, my argument suggests that cultural groups that seek specific social and political rights and arrangements within democratic states must have a hand in articulating why it is that their cultural identities and memberships are important to them and deserving of protection. Similarly, much more emphasis needs to be put on *internal political criticism* in deciding whether to permit or restrict certain traditional practices that offend liberal sensibilities: in contrast to Kymlicka's cursory dismissal of Muslim schools, a more adequate approach to determining the acceptability of certain cultural arrange-

68. "Two Models of Pluralism and Tolerance," 39.

69. Margaret Moore also criticizes Kymlicka for failing to justify or defend his adoption of a conception of community that emphasizes individual choice over collective goods. She suggests that as a result, Kymlicka dismisses internal restrictions in cultural minority communities without adequate consideration. See her, "Liberalism and the Ideal of the Good Life," *Review of Politics* 53, no. 4 (1991): 685.

70. For a critique of Kymlicka's view, see Tariq Mohood, "Kymlicka on British Muslims," *Analyse & Kritik* 15 (1993): esp. 90.

71. At times, Kymlicka appears to concede that not all cultural minority groups can be expected to adhere to liberal norms. However, his concession amounts to the problematical view that liberals should allow the ideal of equality to be interpreted less strictly in cultural minority communities. In particular, Kymlicka views equality *between* the minority and majority groups as essential, but not necessarily *within* cultural communities. See *Multicultural Citizenship*, 113, 152, and 169.

ments would stress the importance of debate, discussion, and dissent within cultural communities.[72]

The Limits of Perfectionist Reasoning

My critical discussion of Raz and Kymlicka yields two conclusions. First, a defense of cultural rights that views cultural identity and membership as important mainly insofar as these support the development and exercise of individual autonomy fails to capture much of what is valuable about these features. Although cultural membership no doubt supplies members with rudimentary capacities for independence and choice, Kymlicka and Raz make the stronger—and I believe, undefended— claim that membership is not specifically *valuable* unless it fosters members' independence. There are good reasons to think that this view does not fully reflect communities' own views about why cultural membership and collective identity is important. Not only do cultural groups provide their members with social and economic opportunities—as Raz and Kymlicka suggest—but they may furnish them with a sense of collective identity and belonging and help them to negotiate their way through fractured social worlds. Just as members of a dominant culture may seek psychological and emotional security in their families or immediate communities, members of cultural minorities may look to their group's mores, traditions, and beliefs to achieve some sense of stability and normative grounding. They may well also reject the neutral liberal belief that a valuable life consists in forming, revising, and pursuing one's own conception of the good.

Second, by reducing the value of cultural identity and membership to the instrumental role that these may play in fostering individuals' autonomy and self-identity, both Kymlicka and Raz restrict the range of cultural groups that liberal societies have reason to recognize politically or to accord certain cultural rights and forms of constitutional recognition. Although communities that consistently jeopardize or restrict their members' capacities and opportunities to make any decisions about their own lives (and those of their immediate families) risk violating key democratic principles, many traditional religious and ethnic communi-

72. For a useful discussion of the issue of "internal criticism" see Martha Nussbaum and Amartya Sen, "Internal Criticism and Indian Rationalist Traditions," in *Relativism: Interpretation and Confrontation*, ed. Michael Krausz (Notre Dame, Ind.: University of Notre Dame Press, 1989).

ties that do not actively encourage or foster their members' capacities to form and pursue independent life plans may still deserve respect and protection. As the examples of Muslim schools and the Amish opting out of mainstream education show, there are reasons to support some traditional cultural structures that sit uneasily with liberal sensibilities. At the very least, there are no good grounds for rejecting such practices in advance of extensive public deliberation with the cultural groups concerned.

Kymlicka's and Raz's strategy for dealing with conflicts between individual rights and freedoms on the one hand and collective, cultural rights on the other is to suggest that where these clash, the former must trump the latter. Their justification for this move, however, reflects a normative ranking of ideals that some cultural minority communities could not accept (nor does it provide good reasons why they should). Although we need of course to consider carefully whether to discourage or restrict certain social practices—and to balance the rights and liberties of individuals against the collective rights of some cultural groups—an adequate approach to cultural diversity cannot simply apply conventional liberal norms and ideals. It may be that working out equitable arrangements that will enable cultural groups to preserve their identities, languages, and ways of life—and in the case of territorially concentrated national minorities, to enjoy some measure of political self-determination—cannot be accomplished without the direct participation and agreement of those groups.

Insofar as Kymlicka and Raz appeal to certain comprehensive and perfectionist liberal goods to determine where to draw the limits of liberal tolerance and inclusion of group differences, they encounter difficulties in justifying their positions. However, this criticism does not amount to the suggestion that these writers should substitute a thin conception of the good for a thick one. Both thin and thick conceptions may fail to capture some of the reasons that cultural membership and identity are vital to different communities and individuals and foreground other factors (such as the ideal of a self-directed life) that some groups could not readily endorse. In different ways, even the moderate perfectionist liberal approaches examined here presuppose widespread agreement on norms and goods without sufficient warrant. Appeals to a determinate conception of the good or human flourishing can too easily lead to restrictions on minority cultural practices that may deserve respect and assistance, as evidenced by Kymlicka's rejection of state-supported Muslim schooling. All liberal political theories that recognize the social and political importance of cultural identities and attachments face the serious difficulty of setting critical standards for the acceptance and protection of cultural beliefs and practices. Liberal perfectionists, however, face an additional set of difficulties by virtue of the fact that their moral conception may readily incorporate undefended ideals of excellence and flourishing. Raz and Kymlicka are surely right to suggest that we cannot begin to understand claims about the value of cultural identity and membership without reflecting on the requirements of well-being, but they need to ensure that at least some of these components are also ones with which cultural minority communities can identity. In overlooking the claims of nonliberal (as opposed to illiberal) minorities for respect and recognition, as well as the likely dissent of certain groups to ideals of personal autonomy and choice, liberal perfectionists fail to take account of the requirements of liberal principles of respect and consent.

FIVE

Deliberative Democracy:

A Theory of Pluralism and Inclusion?

I have argued that none of the three liberal approaches surveyed thus far—toleration, neutrality, and liberal perfectionism—supplies a vision of democracy for plural societies that would meet many of the justice claims of cultural minority citizens for greater recognition and inclusion. Liberal perspectives fail, however, for different sorts of reasons. Toleration-based theories set the threshold for justice for minorities too low, falling far short of demands for full respect and equal citizenship. Advocates of neutral liberalism propose restrictions and constraints on political deliberation and decision-making that would impose unfair burdens on members of many cultural minority groups—particularly those whose social and moral views are not easily separable from their normative and political convictions—such as aboriginal peoples, ethnic or linguistic groups with separatist aspirations, and some religious communities. Liberal perfectionists grasp the importance of cultural identity and group membership to individual well-being, but link the value of these features so closely to their role in securing personal autonomy that they preclude respect and accommodation for persons from nonliberal or traditional religious cultural communities (which may not accord much value to the ideal of independence).

One strand of contemporary democratic theory that purports to overcome some of these problematic and exclusionary aspects of liberalism is that of deliberative democracy. Unlike the liberal theories discussed so far, deliberative democracy starts from the thought that the legitimacy of democratic norms and institutions is secured through a process of actual moral argumentation among citizens. By shifting the locus of legitimacy from hypothetical, rational agreement to *actual* debate and dialogue, deliberative democracy incorporates a more radical ideal of democratic consent and agreement than most liberal theories propose. Proponents of a deliberative approach foreground the role of citizens in endorsing norms for deliberation more so than do liberals and stress the importance of their participation in political life more generally. For these and other reasons deliberative democracy theorists seem likely to conceive of institutions and practices that could meet minority citizens' demands for greater recognition and inclusion in democratic political life.

In the discussion that follows, I examine aspects of discourse ethics and theories of deliberative democracy which relate most directly to the justice claims of cultural minorities in democratic states. I ask whether deliberative democracy, as influenced in part by Jürgen Habermas's discourse ethics, can inform strategies for greater inclusion of diverse cultural groups and their perspectives in politics. In assessing the work of key proponents of deliberative democracy—and in presenting my own arguments for a thicker conception of democracy—I use as my conceptual yardstick the requirements of respect for cultural pluralism set out in chapter 1 and argued for in subsequent chapters. To focus specifically on the problem of justice for cultural minorities, it will be necessary to set aside some important aspects of deliberative democracy and discourse ethics (or communicative ethics) that relate less directly to the themes at hand. In particular, it is not my intention to address Habermas's writing exhaustively here, nor to examine the arguments of his numerous advocates and critics.

In the sections that follow, I suggest that a discursive ideal of *democratic legitimacy* may represent a significant step toward respect and recognition for minority cultures. I also argue that deliberative democracy offers a more realistic understanding of the relationship between public / political and social / private arrangements than does neutral liberalism. In contrast to the latter, deliberative democracy does not ask citizens to bracket their moral and cultural views from any aspect of political debate, least of all from discussion of constitutional essentials.

Despite its initial promise, however, there are aspects of deliberative democracy that present obstacles to the claims of cultural minorities for respect and recognition. It is not clear that the increased participation of citizens in public life envisioned by deliberative democrats could encourage better inclusion and representation of *cultural minorities* in political debate and decision-making. Additionally, there is a danger that some aspects of deliberative democracy might, like political liberalism, prevent citizens of cultural minorities from communicating their beliefs, needs, and interests.

I further argue that some of the most serious difficulties are imported from discourse ethics. For example, many proponents of discourse ethics are committed to an ideal of consensus or consensual agreement as the proper outcome of discourse; yet not unlike Rawls's conception of an overlapping (assumed) consensus, discourse ethicists' ideal of rational consensus fails to take seriously the implication of citizens' deep disagreements on questions of moral value in pluralistic societies. Although I do not advocate jettisoning reasoned argumentation or the attempt to reach agreements, I suggest that as an ideal for deliberation in pluralistic societies, strong consensus is simply impracticable. Moreover, it may be unjust. Theorists of deliberative democracy should instead devote more of their attention to the problem of how we might secure reasonable agreement or compromise on *procedures* for deliberation, which is still a difficult task. Moreover, no agreement on procedures for deliberation is adequate, let alone complete, without a realistic understanding of the practical conditions for, and constraints on, citizens' political deliberations and agreements—which proponents of deliberative democracy have on the whole neglected.

In response to the problem of how to ensure that diverse citizens' voices—particularly the voices of cultural and ethnic minorities—are heard in deliberation, some theorists of deliberative democracy have proposed that we radically rethink the very idea of universal citizenship. I take up one such argument: the proposal for a differentiated conception of citizenship by which citizens are viewed first and foremost as members of cultural and social collectivities rather than as individual citizens. Although this idea is not integral to deliberative democracy *per se*, some proponents of deliberative democracy argue that we need a differentiated conception of citizenship if we are to ensure the actual participation of diverse groups of citizens in public deliberation. I suggest that the justifications offered for such a conception are inadequate and problematic and that proposals are too far-reaching. However, a more limited and better defended conception of differentiated citizenship is an indispensable feature of respect for cultural pluralism in democratic states.

Why do deliberative democrats claim that their normative approach can meet the demands of cultural pluralism more readily than can other positions? One important reason is that they believe this model of democracy does not presuppose "pre-deliberative" norms or values— values which could exclude citizens who do not adhere to mainstream social and moral views. I argue that contra this claim, the institutions and practices of deliberative democracy (at least in some versions) depend on several determinate and by no means uncontroversial norms, such as those of respect, reciprocity, reasonable dialogue, and a certain ideal of impartiality. Proponents of deliberative democracy who purport to offer a model of unconstrained public discourse free from supposed norms simply cannot support this claim. On the whole, they also fail to account for the role that power and coercion inevitably play in most forms of public deliberation (to a greater or lesser degree).[1] Rather than dismissing deliberative democracy as inconsistent and untenable, however, a modified account of this political paradigm invokes norms that are both essential and defensible in the context of culturally plural, democratic states. A suitably reconceived model of deliberative democracy underpinned by the liberal principles of respect and consent— what I propose to call "deliberative liberalism"—could take us a long way toward the goal of securing justice for *all* citizens in culturally plural, democratic states.[2]

Deliberative Democracy and the Critique of Liberal Justice

The term deliberative democracy denotes an approach to democratic theory in which norms and institutions are open to challenge and debate and derive their legitimacy from the actual agreement of citizens. Joshua Cohen provides a concise definition along these lines:

> The notion of deliberative democracy is rooted in the intuitive ideal of a democratic association in which the justification of the terms and conditions of association proceeds through public argumentation and reasoning among equal citizens. Citizens in such an order share a commitment to the resolution of problems of collective choice through public reasoning, and regard their basic institutions as legitimate in so far as they establish the framework for free public deliberation.[3]

Contemporary discussions of deliberative democracy draw on diverse conceptual resources. Some proponents are influenced by classical

---

1. One proponent of deliberative democracy who does attend to issues of power and coercion in political deliberation is Jane Mansbridge. See her "Using Power / Fighting Power," *Constellations* 1, no. 1 (1994): 53–73.

2. I outline this model in greater detail in chapter 6.

3. Joshua Cohen, "Deliberative and Democratic Legitimacy," in *The Good Polity*, ed. A. Hamlin and P. Pettit (Oxford: Basil Blackwell, 1989), 21.

Greek and Renaissance Italian republican ideals of participatory citizenship; others take their cue from Hannah Arendt's writings on action, thought, and judgment in the public sphere.[4] The accounts of deliberative democracy I discuss in this chapter derive much of their inspiration from Jürgen Habermas's idea of discourse ethics. Neither my own proposals nor other discussions by proponents of deliberative democracy endorse all aspects of Habermas's ethical project. However, two important features of discourse ethics that all accounts of deliberative democracy adopt, mine included, are (1) a discursive account of democratic legitimacy, by which norms and institutions are legitimated in practical discourse by agents deliberating freely;[5] and (2) the idea that political deliberation should be *informed* by (though not mirror in any absolute way) a particular ideal of discourse. This ideal envisions that practical discourse must be open and democratic, permitting any agent to take part in discourse; that any participant may challenge assertions and convey their views, thoughts, beliefs, needs, and interests; and that no participant may force closure on dialogue.[6] However, as the ensuing discussion will make clear, even these idealized aspects of discourse require that certain amendments be made and other aspects be abandoned if features of a deliberative conception of democracy are to contribute usefully to the goal of securing respect and recognition for cultural minorities.

There are several broad reasons why a deliberative conception of democracy, informed by certain features of discourse ethics, might poten-

4. Contemporary democratic theorists who draw heavily on Arendt's work—especially on *The Human Condition* (Chicago: University of Chicago Press, 1958)—are better known as proponents of an "agonistic" account of democracy than deliberative democracy *per se*. The agonistic model of democracy incorporates some of the same features as deliberative democracy, such as an emphasis on a revitalized public sphere and greater participation by citizens in public deliberation. However, like Arendt—and unlike many proponents of deliberative democracy—agonistic democrats mistrust the idea that public debate should be directed toward consensus. Examples of arguments for an agonistic account of democracy include Bonnie Honig, *Political Theory and the Displacement of Politics* (Ithaca, N.Y.: Cornell University Press, 1993), and Honig, "The Politics of Agonism," *Political Theory* 21, no. 3 (1993): 528–33; and John Gray, "Agonistic Liberalism," *Social Philosophy and Policy* 12, no. 1 (1995): 111–35.

5. As Fred Dallmayr notes, the principle of democratic legitimacy at the center of discourse (or communicative) ethics has its roots in Kant's "categorical ethics" and "the contractarian model of modern natural law." Dallmayr, "Introduction," in *The Communicative Ethics Controversy*, ed. Seyla Benhabib and Fred Dallmayr (Cambridge, Mass.: MIT Press, 1990), 17.

6. Jürgen Habermas, *Moral Consciousness and Communicative Action* (Cambridge, Mass: MIT Press, 1993), 89. Habermas reiterates here the specific conditions of discourse as developed by Robert Alexy (which Habermas agrees reflect his ideal of moral argumentation).

tially form part of an adequate response to demands by cultural minorities for equal justice.[7] One of the most important of these reasons concerns the way discourse ethics interprets political legitimacy. If we follow Habermas in locating democratic legitimacy in actual, not hypothetical, argumentation and dialogue, then we should understand norms and institutions as open to contestation and challenge by the people who are to be bound by them. In his reformulation of Kant's Categorical Imperative, Habermas incorporates the principle of universalizability into what he calls the principle of discourse ethics: "Only those norms can claim to be valid that meet (or could meet) with the approval of all affected in their capacity as participants in a practical discourse."[8] Although Habermas unhelpfully runs together actual and possible consent here—and elsewhere equivocates between the two—some proponents have tried to reformulate his accounts of democratic legitimacy and practical dialogue to meet the needs of a deliberative theory of democracy. In so doing, they have shifted the emphasis toward the requirements of actual dialogue and agreement, away from hypothetical models of consent. This step is perhaps the most critical amendment of discourse ethics, in my view, for it seems likely that procedures based on a commitment to securing actual agreement will take seriously the need to solicit and include the voices and perspectives of cultural minorities.

Deliberative democracy, when disambiguated from Habermas's more idealized discourse ethics, proposes that legitimate political norms are those that actually meet with the wide acceptance of citizens. This acceptance or agreement is not adequately secured by mere majoritarian voting practices, such as those that characterize contemporary liberal representative democracies. Rather, agreement and consent is reflected either in citizens' actual expression of support for a specific principle, a policy that embodies this principle, and / or the institutions or practices it informs. Agreement may also be inferred from the absence of objections to a norm under circumstances of open, democratic deliberation. All political norms, on this view, are subject to democratic contestation,

---

7. The relationship between discourse ethics (as elaborated primarily by Habermas) and deliberative democracy is difficult to define with any precision. The deliberative theory of democracy, as conceived by such writers as Joshua Cohen, Seyla Benhabib, and Simone Chambers, is essentially a political conception or model that draws heavily on key aspects of communicative ethics (discourse ethics). Although Habermas himself sometimes uses the term "deliberative democracy" as though it were the natural political corollary of discourse ethics, it is possible to hold to central tenets of communicative ethics without necessarily endorsing a full program of deliberative democracy.

8. Habermas, *Moral Consciousness and Communicative Action*, 93.

negotiation, and amendment; we cannot justly impose principles (such as the norm of neutral justification) as appropriate constraints on political deliberation unless they are endorsed in the course of public debate. Habermas's suggestion for the procedure to deal with a contested norm is to "suspend" the legitimacy of the norm in question pending extensive public deliberation. Endorsing this move, I would add that such debate should include not merely discussion of the principle in question, but also of the contested issues, procedures or institutions that first brought the disputed norm into relief.

This brief sketch of some key features of deliberative democracy is broadly supported by Habermas's discourse-ethical conception of legitimacy. The central intuition of this notion of legitimacy is that deliberative and decision-making procedures and political norms are legitimate insofar as citizens actually perceive these as fair, democratic, and open to challenge. The requirement that procedures be seen to be fair will normally require that institutions and processes afford opportunities for citizens and groups to present their views, needs, and interests, as well as to challenge any unreasonable aspects of deliberation and decision-making procedures. From this broad description, it is not difficult to see how Habermas's account of democratic legitimacy could help to further the inclusion of cultural minorities in political life. Many demands for cultural recognition and respect reflect the desire of members of minority groups not merely for a say on practical issues, but also for a voice in the development and amendment of political procedures and even institutions. Consider for instance the 1997 Scottish referendum on devolution of power, in which a majority of Scots voted for greater political independence from Britain. This referendum vote has recently yielded the creation of a separate national assembly, with its own political leadership and system of governance. In voting for greater political self-rule, Scots decided that it was not enough to have their own educational system and criminal justice system (which had been in place for years). What made it possible to choose a more extensive form of independence, however, was the way in which questions of governance, political autonomy, and national identity were rendered open to contestation and debate in the period preceding the referendum and in the formulation of the actual referendum questions.

Calls for open deliberative procedures, greater access to political decision-making and opportunities to challenge the legitimacy of contested political norms are also much in evidence among Canada's aboriginal communities. The main native organizations, the Assembly of First Nations and the Native Council of Canada, have lobbied strenuously from the early 1980s onward to be included in any federal-level discussions of constitutional change in Canada—not merely as an interest group, but as central participants in the constitutional reform process. Moreover, they have contested the assumption that all Canadians, native peoples included, should necessarily be bound by the Canadian Charter of Rights and Freedoms. The Charter's normative focus on individual rights and freedoms, many native groups have argued, may pose tensions with the importance of collective freedoms and even native people's aspirations for collective self-government. This suspicion of the Charter, with its emphasis on norms and values that privilege the individual over the group, has since been met with resistance on the part of some native women (including the Native Women's Association of Canada) on the grounds that women's gender equality rights might not be adequately protected by collective aboriginal rights. Nonetheless, this example illustrates an instance in which it was essential to have opportunities to contest the legitimacy of particular norms, such as individual rights and liberties, and to debate both the morality and practicability of alternative norms, such as those instantiated by collective rights and freedoms.

The discourse-ethical conception of legitimacy elaborated by theorists of deliberative democracy lends particular support, I suggest, to claims by such national minority groups as the Scots and aboriginal peoples that the legitimacy of public norms and institutions is partly dependent on their consent. Although proponents of discourse ethics and deliberative democracy offer few practical proposals for how to foster the inclusion of national ethnic minorities in political debate and decision-making, their view of democratic legitimacy implies in principle that the state should introduce mechanisms to foster minority citizens' access to politics. Making it possible for different cultural communities to present their concerns and needs to government and to participate in decision-making—particularly on issues that directly affect their communities—might be facilitated by the introduction of special consultative bodies that ensure more than a token voice for minority groups. The inclusion of national minorities in deliberation on matters of constitutional significance is especially important, as the examples of aboriginal peoples in Canada demonstrates. The allocation of reserved seats in national assemblies and on inter-governmental bodies for certain minorities has proven an effective step in respecting the demands of cultural communities for a direct say on matters of urgent importance for them, such as legal reform and educational policy. One example from American politics, albeit contested, that has met with limited success is the re-districting of U.S. electoral districts that are heavily populated by African Americans so as to ensure more direct political representation for this group. Another example is the (much belated) mandatory inclusion of Canada's aboriginal leaders in federal-level constitutional talks. In European states that are deeply divided between two or three major cultural and/or linguistic groups of comparable size, such as Switzerland and Belgium, a consociational model of democracy has afforded representation for national minorities. Finally, limited political autonomy of the sort gained by Scotland in 1997 is an example of how a territorially concentrated national minority that is unsatisfied by prevailing arrangements can gain greater control through fully democratic, peaceful means over the legal, political, and social institutions that most directly affect their community.

Deliberation and Marginalized Cultures

I would like to shift the discussion to a more pointed inquiry into the potential importance of a deliberative conception of democracy for meeting the specific claims of those cultural minorities seeking a greater political voice. At least two questions come immediately to mind. First, does the increased participation of citizens in public life advocated by deliberative democrats necessarily translate into increased inclusion and representation of *cultural minorities* in political debate and decision-making? And second, is practical discourse (as depicted by proponents of discourse ethics) the best ideal on which to model deliberative procedures that permit citizens of cultural minorities and their representatives to convey their beliefs, needs, and interests?

A deliberative conception of democracy requires that citizens, wherever possible, present their own concerns and needs in the course of political deliberation. This requirement helps to secure the legitimacy of deliberative procedures and institutions by encouraging citizens to assess the fairness of procedures (and of the norms these express) and, where necessary, to recommend reforms. By creating opportunities for individuals to communicate their distinctive perspectives in political forums, deliberative democracy also affirms the importance of those perspectives and so may help to foster respect and recognition for social and cultural minorities. More generally, the inclusion of diverse citizens in political dialogue and debate helps bring to light the information and perspectives that citizens and legislators alike require in order to make fair decisions.[9] Since our preferences and interests are

---

9. See for instance the discussion by Seyla Benhabib, "Deliberative Rationality and Models of Democratic Legitimacy," *Constellations* 1, no. 1 (1994), especially 32–33.

partly formed through dialogue, they may also change as we listen to fellow citizens present their views, grievances, needs, and aspirations—possibly (though of course not necessarily) in ways that are conducive to securing agreement. For instance, during Canada's Meech Lake constitutional negotiations in 1990 and again in the talks leading up to the 1992 Charlottetown Accord, publicly voiced concerns of women's groups and aboriginal Canadians to the effect that their needs and interests would be disregarded by proposed constitutional amendments were widely credited with persuading large numbers of voters to reject the constitutional amendments as unjust.[10]

Can deliberative democracy afford greater opportunities for cultural *groups* to communicate their needs and interests in deliberation? Deliberative democracy, at least the version taken up here, rejects the idea that fair principles and procedures—much less just outcomes—can be determined merely by appealing to a single, rational moral viewpoint. Rather, since the legitimacy of norms depends on their being endorsed by citizens in practical dialogue, all persons competent to do so should be permitted to take part in discourse. That is, all citizens should be allowed to propose and question contested norms and assertions within practical dialogue.[11] This seems a promising move in light of concerns about the political inclusion of cultural minorities. However, it is significant that although deliberative democrats insist on much greater levels of participation by citizens in public debate generally, most tend to conceive of deliberation in terms of the participation of citizens as *individual* interlocutors, not as members of particular communities.[12] This obviously poses problems from the vantage point of cultural minorities, many of whom seek to be heard as distinct *groups* in political life. Writers such as Jack Knight and James Johnson recognize the need to "include mechanisms to actively encourage or solicit previously ex-

10. In Canada, a number of briefs and position papers prepared by native and women's groups served to underline these groups' different objections to the proposed constitutional amendments and the non-consultative manner in which federal ministers conducted negotiations. Public arguments by the Native Women's Association of Canada to the effect that certain constitutional proposals would undermine the gender equality rights of native women were instrumental in persuading many citizens to vote against the subsequent 1992 constitutional amendments. For a discussion of this case, see my "Conflicting Equalities? Cultural Group Rights and Sex Equality."

11. Habermas, *Moral Consciousness and Communicative Action*, 89.

12. For instance, Dryzek writes, "A discursive design is a social institution around which the expectations of a number of actors converge.... *Individuals should participate as citizens, not as representatives* of the state or any corporate and hierarchical body." Dryzek, *Discursive Democracy: Politics, Policy, and Political Science* (Cambridge: Cambridge University Press, 1994), 43. Emphasis added.

cluded constituencies,"[13] but on the whole they have not said enough about what political changes may be needed if cultural minorities are to be better included in political deliberation and decision-making.

A few proponents of deliberative democracy have proposed specific strategies to grapple with the problem of how better to include national and ethnic minorities in political deliberation. One approach, examined below, is to introduce a differentiated conception of citizenship such that citizens deliberate as members and representatives of particular social and cultural constituencies. This proposal has been made by Iris Young, among others.[14] A different strategy, one that lends evidence to my concern that a discursive, deliberative ideal of democracy may not encourage adequate representation of (and participation by) cultural minorities, has recently been suggested by Habermas. In response to the issue of how discourse ethics should address dilemmas of social and cultural diversity specifically in Europe, and also to the worry that immigration and emergent nationalisms could jeopardize universal citizenship and human rights, Habermas proposes a pan-European democratic political culture and pan-European citizenship under the legal and political auspices of the European Union. To underscore his mistrust of a politics founded on national identity, Habermas draws attention to the perils of republican approaches to cultural diversity; contra these perspectives, he suggests that we need to develop and identify the legal and political principles and norms of citizenship required for democratic pluralism:

> Examples of multicultural societies like Switzerland and the United States demonstrate that a political culture in the seedbed of which constitutional principles are rooted by no means has to be based on all citizens sharing the same language or the same ethnic and cultural origins. Rather, the political culture must serve as the common denominator for a constitutional patriotism which simultaneously sharpens an awareness of the multiplicity and integrity of the different forms of life which coexist in a multicultural society. In a future Federal Republic of European States, the same legal principles would also have to be interpreted from the vantage point of different national traditions and histories. One's own national tradition will, in each case, have to be appropriated in such a manner that it is related to and relativized by the vantage points of the other national cultures. It must be connected with the overlapping con-

13. Jack Knight and James Johnson, "Aggregation and Deliberation: On the Possibility of Democratic Deliberation," *Political Theory* 22, no. 2 (1994): 289.

14. Young, *Justice and the Politics of Difference.*

sensus of a common, supranationally shared political culture of the European Community.[15]

Despite the appeal of aspects of his proposal for democratic pluralism, Habermas fails to show how these can meet specific claims for cultural recognition from minorities within European states. His vision of a pan-European citizenship and political culture recognizes the basic citizenship rights of minorities and new immigrants—as any liberal position would also do—but leaves untouched the problem of how to meet their specific demands for greater respect and recognition. Habermas's suspicion of group-based rights and his endorsement of a pan-national European political culture may reflect his belief that only the latter arrangements support the development of "an inclusive public sphere" which is "open for and sensitive to the influx of issues, value orientations, contributions and programs originating from their informal environments."[16] Yet the idea of pan-European citizenship seems to require that participants deliberate as free, individual interlocutors or citizens—a feature which would not satisfy the desire of some cultural groups to be heard as distinct communities. Although not all cultural groups seek greater inclusion in political life, many claims for cultural recognition and respect emanate from groups' sense that they have little or no collective access to political power. This claim is reflected, for instance, in the movement for devolution of power to Scotland, in calls for greater political inclusion and representation of African Americans, and in demands for sovereignty by many Québécois.

At the heart of Habermas's proposal for a pan-European model of citizenship lies the assumption of certain shared norms and practices of universal citizenship. By contrast, a democratic model of citizenship that endorses some forms of group-based representation and deliberation need not necessarily presuppose extensive shared norms of citizenship. I shall say more about such a model in the next chapter. Of course, a group-based politics is not without its difficulties. An important objection raised by deliberative democracy theorists is that a group-based politics might erode participants' orientation to the common good (or to discovering generalizable goals) and so diminish the solidarity among citizens that deliberative democracy strives to foster.[17] The view that deliberation should be directed toward the common good is

15. Jürgen Habermas, "Citizenship and National Identity: Some Reflections on the Future of Europe," 7.

16. Ibid., 11.

17. This concern is also expressed by Joshua Cohen and Joel Rogers, who suggest that "group particularism" is a problem for deliberative democracy because it tends to prevent

closely tied to the goal of normative consensus, which features prominently in some accounts of deliberative democracy (but which is by no
means a necessary goal, as I shall argue). Absent this false requirement
of consensus, as I discuss below, there is no reason why practical dialogue could not also include representatives of cultural groups who aim
to convey the concerns, interests, and needs of their communities. Just
as a deliberative model of democracy may present opportunities for citizens to communicate their own diverse views in practical deliberation
through the creation of new local political bodies or the transformation
of existing ones, it could encourage cultural communities to bring their
concerns to bear on regional and national politics.

Consensus and Inequality: Obstacles to Justice?

Partly as a consequence of the emphasis that discussions of deliberative
democracy place on political inclusion and on "open" terms of discourse, the discursive ideal of deliberation appears to resemble a recipe
for endless conflict and bargaining. But most deliberative theorists do
not view the goal of deliberation as *modus vivendi*-style politics, wherein
agents pursue their own strategic interests and negotiate compromises.
Rather, they view practical discourse as aiming at attaining a higher degree of *consensus* than simple majoritarian, liberal politics can achieve,
in the sense of securing citizens' virtually unanimous agreement on a
contested norm or principle. This aspiration is potentially problematic
for a number of reasons, not least because it may reflect a tendency to
ignore the depth of citizens' normative differences. The objection that
a strong ideal of consensus is an inappropriate goal for politics in pluralistic societies is by now a familiar one in criticisms of discourse ethics
and to a lesser extent in critiques of theories of deliberative democracy.[18] As I discuss below, consensus is an especially problematic ideal
for politics in deeply culturally plural democratic states. But the notion
that moral argumentation should yield consensus is not necessarily an

---

citizens from working toward some common good. Joshua Cohen and Joel Rogers, "Associations and Democracy," *Journal of Social Philosophy and Policy* 10, no. 2 (1993): 282–312.
    18. See especially, Maeve Cooke, "Habermas and Consensus," *European Journal of Phi-
losophy* 1, no. 3 (1993): 247–67; James Bohman, "Public Reason and Cultural Pluralism,"
Political Theory 23, no. 2 (1995): 253–79, esp. 264–68; Donald J. Moon, "Practical Discourse and Communicative Ethics," in *The Cambridge Companion to Habermas*, ed. Stephen
K. White (Cambridge: Cambridge University Press, 1995), esp. 150–55; Benhabib, "Introduction," *Situating the Self* (New York: Routledge, 1992), esp. 9; and Knight and Johnson,
"Aggregation and Deliberation."

indelible feature of deliberative democracy. Securing wider agreement on procedures for political deliberation and debate is perhaps a more practicable goal.

Before discussing the ways in which the ideal of consensus might pose obstacles to the greater political inclusion of cultural minorities, it is worth looking at the genesis of this notion in Habermas's ideal of discourse. As is well known, Habermas views consensus-formation as both the goal and the logical outcome of practical discourse;[19] consensus does not issue from just *any* form of discussion. Habermas's distinction between strategic and communicative action is meant to illustrate this point: although both models of action assume that "actors ... have the ability to act purposively and an interest in carrying out their plans," only communicative action is "oriented towards reaching understanding [and] ... agreement. The extent to which agreement is necessary for communication to be adjudged successful is not clear, but Habermas typically speaks of the importance "of arriving at a shared interpretation of the situation or more generally, of reaching consensus."[20] Nor is Habermas alone in endorsing the goal of consensus: Joshua Cohen, for instance, claims that "ideal deliberation aims to arrive at a rationally motivated consensus—to find reasons that are persuasive to all who are committed to acting on the results of a free and reasoned assessment of alternatives by equals."[21] This account of politics would seem to throw us back onto political liberalism, with its emphasis on the need for neutral, public reason.

From the vantage point of concerns about justice for cultural minorities, linking deliberation too closely to the goal of consensus presents at least two related problems. First, the ideal of consensus presupposes that agents will come to agree on norms and proposals in part because their differences—in terms of divergent views and interests—are not so great that they cannot be resolved by good, publicly accessible arguments.[22] This supposition introduces unexamined (and possibly unjust) limits to the form and degree of pluralism that can be accepted in de-

19. Habermas's own understanding of what consensus entails, how often we can expect to attain it, and what to do when consensus does not follow from deliberation has changed over the years. I do not propose to take up his successive formulations of the idea of consensus here or the voluminous writings by his critics on this subject.

20. Habermas, *Moral Consciousness and Communicative Action*, 134–35.

21. Cohen, "Deliberative and Democratic Legitimacy," 23.

22. For instance, Habermas writes that communicative action characterizes situations in which "actors are prepared to harmonize their plans of action through internal means, committing themselves to pursuing their goals only on the condition of an agreement— one that already exists or one to be negotiated—about definitions of the situation and prospective outcomes." *Moral Consciousness and Communicative Action*, 134.

liberative democratic politics. And second, some theorists of discourse ethics and deliberative democracy link the ideal of consensus to the view that citizens' deliberations should always be oriented toward the common good; in so doing, they fail to take full account of the citizens' social differences.

The view that participants in dialogue are likely to be persuaded by the same public reasons relies in part on a distorted view—which Habermas has done much to promote—about the main sources of political agreement and disagreement in culturally plural societies. As Thomas McCarthy has argued, one of the reasons why Habermas has held so tenaciously to the ideal of consensus is that he tends to conceive of disagreement in terms of conflicting *interests*—which may be more readily resolved through practical discourse—rather than in terms of "disagreements rooted in social, cultural, and ideological diversity."[23] Although conflicting economic and political interests are indeed oftentimes bound up with (if not responsible for) citizens' apparent moral and political disputes, surely the latter cannot be said to reduce to the former. If we acknowledge that many social disputes in culturally plural democratic states frequently derive from group-based differences in our ethical and cultural frameworks, then the ideal of consensus as an outcome of discourse not only strains credibility, but may itself represent a failure to respect citizens' differences.

The assumption that strong consensus is the ultimate goal of public deliberation reflects a lack of respect for citizens' social, cultural, and ethical differences in one additional way. The ideal of consensus is linked, at least for some theorists of deliberative democracy, to the belief that deliberation should in general further the common good, which by definition excludes citizens whose comprehensive views are at odds with the public culture.[24] Interestingly, the requirement that deliberation be directed toward securing the common good would seem to introduce a covert form of perfectionism into what is purportedly an anti-perfectionist conception of political life. Just what such deliberation might mean as a practical condition of discourse is not entirely clear; however, enough writers have wisely rejected the notion that a strong orientation toward the common good is a requirement of deliberative democracy to make it unnecessary to take this point up at length here.[25]

23. Thomas McCarthy, "Legitimacy and Diversity: Dialectical Reflections on Analytical Distinctions," *Protosoziologie* 6 (1994): 199.

24. For example, Joshua Cohen writes, "Deliberation ... focuses debate on the common good." In Cohen, "Deliberative and Democratic Legitimacy," 25. This view is reiterated in Cohen and Rogers, "Associations and Democracy," 286.

25. Some proponents of deliberative democracy argue that although deliberation should be directed toward solving common problems, appeals to some "shared good"

Even a more attenuated appeal to the general good as the goal of political deliberation might reflect inappropriate assumptions about shared norms and goals. For example, the presumption that citizens are naturally ready, willing, and able to engage in discourse and to endeavor to reach workable solutions to collective problems may cause us to overlook the issue of trust between citizens and communities and in particular of how to develop greater trust. It may further direct our attention away from thinking about citizens' different capacities and opportunities for deliberation. For example, Chambers's discussion of deliberative democracy assumes without sufficient warrant that citizens are in fact "willing to reevaluate their political opinions in the light of argument, and make an effort to look at public questions *from an impartial point of view,*" and that they "are interested in genuine deliberation and authentic agreement, that is, that *citizens are motivated to find consensual solutions.*"[26] Yet without a better account of the reasons for such optimism, it is all too easy to overlook social and cultural cleavages that make it difficult for citizens to reach agreement, as well as to ignore the ways in which social and economic inequalities may undercut citizens' capacities to deliberate and agree freely.

A commitment to a strong ideal of consensus (and to a particular conception of public reason-giving) thus may not be acceptable from the vantage point of concerns about justice for social and cultural minorities. The inappropriateness of the goal of consensus for deliberation in plural societies is underscored by deliberative theorists' proposals for what to do when consensus breaks down in deliberative politics: faced with the prospect that deliberation might not always result in consensus, some proponents of deliberative democracy simply cite majoritarian voting as the default solution to seemingly irresolvable conflicts.[27] Entrenched disagreements often concern culturally contested norms and practices, and these in turn may reflect differences in interests and in power; consequently, a simple retreat to the majoritarian principle may serve only to further marginalize the voices of members of cultural minorities. Abandoning a strong ideal of consensus for deliberative democracy need not amount to the capitulation to endless dis-

---

should not structure public debate. Iris Young suggests that the problem with appeals to shared goods and understandings is that they invariably operate to the disadvantage of less privileged groups. Young, "Communication and the Other: Beyond Deliberative Democracy," in *Intersecting Voices: Dilemmas of Gender, Political Philosophy, and Policy* (Princeton, N.J.: Princeton University Press, 1997), esp. 66.

26. Simone Chambers, *Reasonable Democracy: Jürgen Habermas and the Politics of Discourse* (Ithaca, N.Y.: Cornell University Press, 1996), 197 and 190. Emphasis added.

27. This proposal is made, for instance, by Cohen, "Deliberative and Democratic Legitimacy," 23.

putes, however. In some cases, a legitimate agreement may consist of an agreement to disagree—hopefully reflecting a deeper understanding of the basis of the dispute than existed before deliberation—and a provisional account of how to proceed from this dissonance.

The supposition that moral argumentation will normally issue in consensus is partly predicated on the fallacious assumption that people are similarly situated in practical dialogue and so are readily persuaded by the same "good" arguments.[28] Discourse ethicists do not believe that actual social inequalities can be wished away, but following Habermas, some propose that in elaborating an ideal of practical discourse we simply bracket citizens' inequalities of power. This move begs the question of whether deliberative procedures modeled on the notion of ideal speech can take sufficient account of citizens' differences in power, as well as their differential capacities and opportunities to deliberate in political life. Nancy Fraser, for instance, writes:

> We should question whether it is possible even in principle for interlocutors to deliberate as if they were social peers in specially designated discursive arenas when these discursive arenas are situated in a larger societal context that is pervaded by structural relations of dominance and subordination.[29]

Many proponents of deliberative democracy have rejected this idealized view of discourse. Even some writers who align their projects closely with Habermas's discourse ethics, such as Chambers, think it makes little sense to bracket real-world inequalities in designing discursive procedures.[30] However, few writers have offered suggestions for how we might go about constructing open and democratic deliberative procedures that take adequate account of issues of power and inequality.[31]

Differentiated Citizenship

Some theorists of deliberative democracy, as we have seen, suggest that there is a need to shift from hypothetical moral reasoning and liberal

28. Versions of this criticism are also made by Bohman, "Public Reason and Cultural Pluralism"; Moon, "Practical Discourse and Communicative Ethics"; and Benhabib, "The Generalized and the Concrete Other," in *Situating the Self* (New York: Routledge, 1992).

29. Fraser, "Rethinking the Public Sphere: A Contribution to the Critique of Actually Existing Democracy," in *Habermas and the Public Sphere*, ed. Craig Calhoun (Cambridge, Mass.: MIT Press, 1993), 120.

30. Chambers, *Reasonable Democracy*, 206.

31. Again, one exception here is Mansbridge, "Using Power / Fighting Power."

models of conversational constraint (such as those proffered by Larmore and Ackerman) to actual debate and dialogue. A few, such as Iris Young, have even argued that in order to foster a culture of public deliberation we must view citizens first and foremost as embedded in particular social contexts, rather than as individual citizens. In this view, the only way to ensure the inclusion of diverse perspectives in public debate is if citizens are understood first as members of communities and *collectivities*—as people who belong to particular social or cultural groups. This in turn entails a rethinking of the very notion of universal citizenship.[32]

Iris Young's discussion of the norm of universal citizenship is an influential example of a critique of universal citizenship from the perspective of deliberative democracy. Like the liberal perfectionists discussed earlier, Young believes that conventional liberal accounts of universal citizenship have thus far failed to capture the importance of group memberships and collective identities. These features, she suggests, are central to the social and political self-understandings of many under-represented citizens. Both recent neutral liberals and some republican thinkers propose ideals of universal citizenship that do not take sufficient account of citizens' diverse constitutive attachments and beliefs or their concrete needs and circumstances. One of the main reasons for this omission, Young contends, is that these thinkers are committed to a particular, idealized notion of impartiality. The ideal of impartiality leaves no room for the actual moral reasoning and deliberative practices of many agents, especially those citizens who view their private, social, and public goods and beliefs as overlapping. In this way, the norm of universal citizenship that many liberals and republicans endorse may merely reflect the identities, agency, and outlook of those liberal individuals *already* dominant in the public sphere.[33]

Young moves rapidly from a critique of false impartiality to the suggestion that we should take collectivities, rather than individuals, as the primary "units" of moral and political life—the essence of her proposal for group-differentiated citizenship. The illusory equality offered by a politics of individual liberal rights, Young asserts, ignores the fact that social stratification and social differences are group-based, not random and individualized. In order to take serious account of citizens' particularities, we must therefore move to a group-based view of citizenship. The difference between universal citizenship and differentiated citizen-

---

32. This position is *not* taken by the more liberal proponents of deliberative democracy, such as Joshua Cohen, or for the most part, discourse theorists influenced by the work of Jürgen Habermas, notably Seyla Benhabib.

33. Young, *Justice and the Politics of Difference*, 116–17.

ship reflects "the difference between an assimilationist and a culturally pluralist ideal":[34]

> The assimilationalist ideal assumes that equal social status for all persons requires treating everyone according to the same principles, rules, and standards. A politics of difference argues, on the other hand, that equality as the participation and inclusion of all groups sometimes requires different treatment for oppressed or disadvantaged groups. To promote social justice ... social policy should sometimes accord special treatment to groups.... (and include) representation for oppressed groups in democratic decision-making bodies.[35]

Young's conception of differentiated citizenship does not seek to dispense altogether with individual rights, but rather aims to balance these with collective rights for disadvantaged groups, including mechanisms for their "self-representation" in politics. On her view, "a democratic cultural pluralism thus requires a dual system of rights: a general system of rights which are the same for all, and a more specific system of group-conscious policies and rights."[36] However, a number of problematic assumptions attend Young's critique of citizenship. For her version of a dual system of rights—"differentiated citizenship"—to work, the groups in question would need to be highly determinate and bounded, with a stable membership over time. This condition is not easily met: the composition of cultural groups is ever-shifting—for example, via intermarriage, exit from one's community, and immigration—and *overlapping* and *multiple* identities and loyalties seem to be a permanent feature of pluralistic liberal democracies. Young's view belies the extent to which citizens' allegiances and attachments overlap and inform one another. Not surprisingly, she has also come under criticism for attempting to reduce all social group differences to the model of the ethnic or cultural group and in the process conflating cultural and economic forms of oppression.[37] Ironically, where Young tries to accommodate the fluidity of social and cultural group membership, she ends up

34. Ibid., 180.

35. Ibid., 158.

36. Ibid., 174.

37. Nancy Fraser, "Recognition or Redistribution? A Critical Reading of Iris Young's *Justice and the Politics of Difference,*" *Journal of Political Philosophy* 3, no. 2 (1995): 171–73. Fraser also criticizes Young for offering an overly romantic treatment of identity and community and ignoring the importance of "exit" rights from what are often overly restrictive traditional groups. Ibid., 162–63; and Moon, *Constructing Community*, 182–85.

defining collectivities by such loose standards of membership that by her definition, few if any citizens could ever speak from any single constituency:

> A social group is a collective of people who have affinity with one another because of a set of practices or way of life; they differentiate themselves from or are differentiated by at least one other group according to these cultural forms.[38]

Perhaps Young's biggest mistake is that she does not grant the ways that liberal accounts of universal citizenship can be stretched to cover group rights, as writers such as Kymlicka have suggested.[39] Instead, Young's reasoning leads her to conclude rather hastily that those citizens unable to conform to the individualistic and falsely impartial strictures of liberal politics will necessarily find that their "private" identities and attachments present formidable barriers to full citizenship.[40] Although there is no doubt some truth to this claim, Young's belief that universal citizenship necessarily negates citizens' particular social and cultural identities is based at least in part on a misunderstanding of the notion of impartiality. A series of dichotomies, Young contends, are entailed by the ideal of impartiality: reason versus feeling, self versus 'other,' or more generally, the dichotomy between the "general will" and "particular interests."[41] Yet here Young's analysis fails in a number of ways. Liberal proponents of impartiality do not seek entirely to eliminate partial interests, beliefs, and preferences, but rather seek to place constraints on their imposition in moral and (sometimes) political reasoning. This move may well be contestable and impracticable, as I argued in chapter 3; but Young is wrong to dismiss the very notion of impartiality as incoherent.[42] The right question is not whether impartiality is coherent or ever fully possible, but under what circumstances—and in which moral and political processes—impartiality is useful and legitimate and in which it is cumbersome and unjust.

38. Young, *Justice and the Politics of Difference*, 186.

39. See, for example, Will Kymlicka, "Review: Justice and the Politics of Difference and Throwing Like a Girl," *Canadian Philosophical Reviews* 11, no. 6 (1991): 444–45, and Kymlicka, *Multicultural Citizenship*, passim.

40. Young, *Justice and the Politics of Difference*, 117.

41. Ibid., 103.

42. Young's discussion of impartiality has been cited by others as a weakness of her argument. See for instance, Kymlicka, "Review: Justice and the Politics of Difference and Throwing Like a Girl," 444–45.

Young's assertion that a commitment to impartiality suppresses difference thus relies at least in part on a caricature of impartiality.[43] She col-
lapses impartiality with universality, which she wrongly understands as
the requirement of uniformity.[44] Yet impartiality, as distinct from universality, is best understood not as an objective or general point of view
but rather as a constraint that agents can choose to impose on moral
and political reasoning and/or debate to serve specific ends. As
Marilyn Friedman writes, "impartiality ... is a requirement only of the
principles, practices or institutions which justify certain actions," and
not a permanent state of mind that agents are urged to take up.[45] Contrary to Young's claim that the requirement of impartiality *necessarily* op-
poses emotion to reason and suppresses particularity and difference—
indeed, her suggestion at times seems to be that impartiality is designed
to do *just* this—this principle need not necessarily require that we treat
moral agents as "unsituated" persons stripped of all attachments and
particularities.[46] In any event, it is inadvisable to preclude any possible
role for a critical account of impartiality in public deliberation.

Perhaps what we should take from Young's discussion is not her criticisms of impartiality and universal citizenship *per se*—many of which
seem hasty and ill-founded—but instead two aspects of her critique:
first, the intuition that we need to re-think the theory and practice of
public reason; and second, her claim that justice for all citizens in plural
democracies will require that we introduce differential rights for some
citizens. On the first count, Young is right to argue that the moral and
political reasoning that neutral liberals take as paradigmatic of justice
manages to eliminate *too much* in the way of different perspectives in an
attempt to hasten determinate solutions. Other proponents of deliberative democracy, such Benhabib, Williams, Chambers, and Bohman,
have argued along with Young that the idea of a single, rational stand-

43. Young takes a cursory look at what she takes to be the more sophisticated render-
ing of impartiality offered by Susan Okin, who attempts to refashion Rawls's original position to fit feminist and egalitarian ends. Young concludes that even Okin's account of impartiality fails because it assumes we can empathize with the feelings of all other
differently situated persons, regardless of differences of race, class, and gender. See
Young, *Justice and the Politics of Difference*, 105.

44. Ibid., 19.

45. Marilyn Friedman, "The Practice of Partiality," *Ethics* 101 (1991): 833. For a helpful discussion of the role that a more limited and "realistic" account of impartiality might
play in moral reasoning and political judgment, see a different version of Friedman's essay (under the same title) and also her "The Impracticality of Impartiality," both in *What
Are Friends For? Feminist Perspectives on Personal Relationships and Moral Theory* (Ithaca, N.Y.:
Cornell University Press, 1993).

46. See, for instance, discussions by Friedman (ibid.) and Barbara Herman, "Agency,
Attachment, and Difference," *Ethics* 101 (1991): 775–97.

point in moral reasoning flies in the face of ethical and cultural pluralism. However, these authors are careful not to dispense altogether with
impartiality, but rather reconceive it as a constraint on certain forms of
moral and political discourse.[47] In so doing, they direct their criticisms
at a particular liberal formulation of public reason and attempt to offer
a viable alternative conception.[48]

The second aspect of Young's discussion that I propose we adopt, albeit in a much modified form, is her view that justice in plural democracies will require some form of differentiated citizenship rights. Although Young is much too ambitious in her view of who should be
accorded special rights in liberal democracies—treating socially disadvantaged groups and cultural minorities with the same brush
strokes—her suggestions represent a useful counterpoint to the narrower view of citizenship endorsed by recent neutral liberals. Although
many of the arguments Young uses to defend differentiated citizenship
are flawed—especially those against impartiality—this should not
cause us to reject the need for a differentiated account of citizens'
rights (and responsibilities) in plural, liberal states.[49] As I have argued,
respect and recognition for cultural minorities in socially plural, liberal
states will require that certain groups (particularly national and territorially concentrated minorities) be accorded some collective, cultural
rights. These rights and arrangements will necessarily change aspects of
the theory and practice of democratic universal citizenship.

As these problems with Young's justification for a differentiated conception of citizenship make clear, we need to assess some of the claims
that attend this proposal. Perhaps the most important of these is the
claim that political life in liberal, democratic states should be based primarily on group self-representation and *collectivities*.[50] It is a weakness of

47. Melissa Williams agrees that Young's pronouncement that impartiality is impossible is premature and suggests instead that we think, along with John Locke, in terms of "a
spirit of impartiality, a will to prefer her just obligations over her narrow self-interest."
Melissa Williams, "Justice towards Groups: Political Not Juridical," *Political Theory* 23, no. 1
(1995): 85.

48. This alternative is a dialogical or communicative model of public reasoning, which
I discuss briefly below. A fuller account of this idea is, however, beyond the scope of this
chapter.

49. Other political theorists, notably Bhikhu Parekh, have also endorsed an ideal of
differentiated citizenship. Parekh writes, "We need a more differentiated theory of rights
and obligations that *both* safeguards the dignity and basic interests of all, be they full citizens or fresh immigrants, yet acknowledges their differential status and claims on society."
See his "The Rushdie Affair: Research Agenda for Political Philosophy," *Political Studies*
38, no. 4 (1990): 702.

50. Not all proponents of deliberative and discursive democracy endorse this idea. For
instance, Seyla Benhabib continues to argue that the "concrete other" (as opposed to

Young's discussion, and of arguments by other proponents of differentiated democracy (such as Melissa Williams), that they neglect to discuss
either the philosophical or the practical policy implications of the principle of *self-representation*. It may well be true, as Williams asserts, that
"increasing the political representation of marginalized groups has the
potential to build the kind of trust that makes ... deliberation
possible,"[51] but before endorsing differentiated citizenship we need to
know more about the dynamics of group self-representation and how to
combine group rights with a commitment to individual rights. Young
suggests that the principle of group representation "calls for specific
representation only of oppressed or disadvantaged groups" in government institutions and civil society more generally (e.g., in associations
and other politically active groups).[52] But as a number of critics have
noted, her account of oppression is so broad that it could encompass
well over half of the population of democratic states.[53]

Although there are good reasons to believe that limited group representation of cultural minorities should be an essential feature of justice in plural, liberal states, proponents of deliberative democracy do
not offer the best defense of this claim. Instead of grounding their proposals for group self-representation in arguments about respect and
recognition, some writers rely on problematic epistemological assertions and claims about the nature of identity. For instance, Melissa
Williams, like Young, cites as one such reason the *impossibility* that an individual can ever represent faithfully the views of a group of which they
are not a member:

> Because any representation of the perspectives of ... groups by individ-
> uals who are not members in them is likely to present their views through
> a distorted lens, this means that the critique of impartiality leads inexora-
> bly to an argument for the specific *self-representation* of groups whose
> voices have been excluded from deliberation about justice.[54]

Justifications of the principle of self-representation such as those offered by Young and Williams imply rather spuriously that oppressed
persons necessarily have sole access to epistemologically adequate anal-

---

"generalized other") should be the subject of moral discourse, a concept she interprets in
terms of individuals. See her "The Generalized and the Concrete Other."

51. Williams, 87.

52. Young, 186–87.

53. This point has been made, for example, by Kymlicka, in his "Review: Justice and
the Politics of Difference and Throwing Like a Girl."

54. Williams, 79.

yses of their condition. Certainly, in many circumstances minority groups themselves are best placed—even uniquely placed—to convey their interests and views in democratic deliberation. Yet we must also acknowledge that calls for self-representation may set off struggles within a particular group for the right to speak authoritatively on the community's behalf, possibly leading to the misrepresentation of some members of the community and to suppression of minority views and the reinforcement of prevailing hierarchies.[55] The defense of self-representation and group rights by such theorists as Young and Williams thus appears unsatisfactory and even politically naive because it is not accompanied by an analysis of the internal power relations that may structure particular groups and communities.

To raise questions about the justification of differentiated citizenship is not to condemn collective rights *per se*—far from it—but rather to caution against relying on misleading claims about the nature of representation and overly simple accounts of the nature of identity to justify these rights.[56] It is also to draw attention to some of the dangers associated with grounding citizenship rights in national and cultural identities. Young and certain other theorists of differentiated citizenship pay little attention to the distinctions between types of social and cultural groups and the different merits of their claims for special rights and arrangements. Yet as argued earlier, these distinctions are crucial. For instance, the case for assigning cultural and legal rights to *territorial* minorities in plural, democratic states is more easily made—barring complicated issues surrounding competing territorial and justice claims—because the claims of identity and community are much clearer here. To justify their demands for special rights, native peoples,

55. Some examples include the struggle within the British Muslim community for the right to speak on behalf of all members on the "Rushdie affair" (despite, or perhaps precisely because of, disagreements); and the attempt by the Assembly of First Nations (representing status Indians in Canada) to prevent their women members from organizing separately and advocating different constitutional proposals in the 1980s and 1990s. These examples illustrate that we need to attend to the dynamics of *intragroup* relations, some of which may lead even more readily to the silencing of members' voices through traditional mores and rigid social hierarchies.

56. For instance, Anne Phillips eschews strong "mirror representation" for cultural minorities on the grounds that it is both impracticable and incorporates too many essentialist assumptions about identity, but is keen to endorse the principle of self-representation. Yet as with Young, Phillips's *justification* for such measures is inadequate and leads her to propose rather inexplicably and inconsistently that only those mechanisms intended to secure *equal representation for women*—but *not* for cultural or ethnic minorities—are defensible. She suggests a limited system of "safe seat" strategies that might help increase the political representation of minorities. See her *The Politics of Presence* (Oxford: Oxford University Press, 1995).

for example, can point to both the "endurance" and distinctness of their identities and ways of life amid a real threat of assimilation and annihilation as a people. By contrast, recent immigrants to cosmopolitan cities in Western Europe and North America have both different claims and different bases for their demands.

A better strategy is one that endorses cultural membership rights and special rights of representation for some cultural groups within the broader context of democratic, universal citizenship rights, but rejects a fully differentiated conception of citizenship for all disadvantaged social and cultural groups, such as that proposed by Young. Young's view tends to presuppose that our social and cultural identities are singular and stable; although she recognizes the fact of overlapping memberships and the possibilities of coalition-building and alliances, her conception of differentiated citizenship, such as proposals for self-representation offered by Melissa Williams, belies this recognition. The view that disadvantaged social groups which are not territorially based cultural minorities deserve special group rights requires a rather different defense than is needed in the case of territorial minorities. Neither Young nor Williams provides such a defense, yet both endorse such rights in the same breath as they endorse rights for national (territorial) minorities. Surely the recognition of cultural differences and social disadvantages merit diverse political, legal, and institutional responses.[57] We gain little in running together very different forms of oppression: arrangements that will help to alleviate the subordination (and support the aspirations) of territorially concentrated national minorities, such as aboriginal peoples, are likely inappropriate ones for addressing the social problems facing some territorially dispersed cultural groups who make no sovereignty claims, such as Hispanic Americans.

Politics without Foundations?

The claim that deliberative democracy could secure greater respect for social diversity seems to rest on the assumption that this model of democracy eliminates unwarranted appeals to contestable, presupposed

---

57. This point is also made by Fraser, "Recognition or Redistribution?" 180, and Kymlicka, *Multicultural Citizenship*, passim. Fraser suggests "a differentiated view of difference" which "would help us to identify, and defend, only those versions of the politics of difference that coherently synergize with the politics of redistribution." Kymlicka urges liberals to distinguish between claims for self-government rights and claims for representation rights; he distinguishes further between the claims of territorial minorities, territorially dispersed minorities, immigrants and refugees, and others.

moral and political norms. As such, proponents believe, deliberative democracy will not tend to privilege dominant perspectives or suppress minority views. I would like to suggest that this is only partly true: when we look more closely at the underpinnings of proposals for practical discourse and a revitalized public sphere, we see that a plausible account of deliberative democracy, far from suspending all presupposed norms, depends on several determinate norms and institutions. In particular, a feasible account of deliberative democracy relies on principles of reasonable dialogue and a certain conception of impartiality and presupposes stable state and political boundaries. Far from being the outcome of unconstrained deliberation, these norms and features must in some sense already be in place for deliberative democracy to offer a coherent alternative to standard majoritarian politics. However, if taken up critically and in an amended form, some of these norms are defensible principles for political deliberation in culturally plural, liberal democracies.

The claim by deliberative democracy theorists that their account of politics does not invoke *pre-deliberative* norms and procedures derives from a contrast between deliberative and non-deliberative models of democracy. As we saw earlier, discourse theorists criticize Rawlsian-style conceptions of public reasoning for supposing that reason can unify and subsume diverse ethical perspectives. In its place, proponents of deliberative and discursive democracy suggest that we think of public reason as plural and communicative—as a process of communication in which consensus on public proposals is achieved through actual dialogue and deliberation. This process may require the self-representation of certain groups—especially national minorities—since in many circumstances only members can faithfully represent or convey the needs and beliefs of specially situated communities. Deliberative theorists envisage that citizens will speak out from the many local associations, movements, and groups of civil society as well as in formal deliberation.

Unlike neutral and *modus vivendi* liberals, deliberative theorists do not worry that unconstrained deliberation on topics with contested moral content will necessarily lead to political instability. Rather, they believe citizens will come to modify their views in the course of listening to and deliberating with others and that agreement is reached in this way. It is of course in the interest of citizens and legislators to present proposals that appeal to as wide a constituency as possible, as the term "public reason-giving" suggests.[58] Accordingly, proponents of deliberative democracy hope that public dialogue, taking place against a background of increased political trust and cooperation, will be directed to-

---

58. See for instance, Cohen, "Deliberative and Democratic Legitimacy," 22.

ward finding solutions to common problems. But although it may look like these writers are making a move strikingly similar to that of political liberals—that is, attempting to find an overlapping consensus among diverse citizens—there is an important difference. Deliberative democracy's claim to legitimacy is based not on the view that it reflects the basic political intuitions of all citizens,[59] or even that it represents a procedurally just and stable system; rather, it is based on the more minimal claim that deliberative democracy *expresses an ideal about how collective decisions should be reached*: through public dialogue and deliberation.[60]

Even this more moderate definition of the aims of deliberative democracy, I suggest, involves appeals to determinate norms. Most proponents of deliberative democracy maintain that norms are only valid if agreed to by all persons bound by them in a process of unconstrained dialogue and deliberation.[61] The procedures and institutions of deliberative democracy they set out, however, would seem to depend on norms that are not so much the outcome of deliberation as they are preconditions for the very possibility of public dialogue. Minimally, democratic deliberation requires both fair procedures and at least some minimal commitment to reasoned argument.[62] Public debate on the fairness of terms for dialogue and decision-making is essential, as I have argued, but provisional norms must be in place for these discussions to take place. Practices of toleration and an atmosphere of political trust are similarly indispensable, particularly if citizens who were previously excluded are to participate in public debate and dialogue. In an important sense, democratic deliberation also requires the absence of gross inequalities.[63]

As this brief sketch shows, public dialogue according to deliberative principles of democracy requires a commitment to principles of respect, consent, reciprocity, equality, and a certain ideal of impartiality (though not the impartiality caricatured by Young).[64] I suggest these

---

59. For example, Gutmann and Thompson are careful to note that their version of deliberative democracy does "not begin with a common morality, a substantive set of principles or values that we assume we share, and then apply it to decisions and policies." *Democracy and Disagreement*, 26.

60. Cohen, "Deliberative and Democratic Legitimacy," 20.

61. Benhabib, "Deliberative Rationality," 31.

62. This point is also made by Knight and Johnson, "Aggregation and Deliberation," 285–86.

63. Cohen has argued that both formal and substantial equality (in terms of "existing distribution of power and resources") are essential conditions for the success of democratic, deliberative procedures. See Cohen, "Deliberative and Democratic Legitimacy," 22–23.

64. Perhaps most obvious of all, deliberative democracy requires a "closed," modern state with fixed geographical and political boundaries. Cultural differences within a given

are defensible liberal norms for our times. As I shall suggest in the next chapter, they are critical components of a thicker account of liberal democracy, one that is more deeply democratic than conventional forms of representative liberal democracy. Respect and reciprocity are in some sense preconditions for citizens' mutual trust and their confidence in public deliberation more generally.[65] Mutual respect may also be reinforced through dialogue (as may be trust), but it is clear that no fully open and democratic dialogue is possible without some underlying commitment to equal respect. Similarly, as Chambers notes, we will not get very far in dialogue in pluralistic states unless citizens accept the need for impartiality at some levels of political debate: "putting oneself in the position of the other and trying to see the situation from her perspective"[66] is a necessary condition of both democratic debate and intercultural dialogue. Finally, without a serious political commitment to social and economic equality, deliberation may merely reflect the unequal relationships of power in citizens' social lives.

---

state are partly sustained by a range of social, cultural, and legal boundaries (oftentimes unjustly so, as with systems of ethnic and racial apartheid); see, for instance, the discussion by Jeff Spinner-Halev, "Difference and Diversity in an Egalitarian Democracy," *Journal of Political Philosophy* 3, no. 3 (1995): 268; and Walzer, *Spheres of Justice* (New York: Basic Books, 1983), 39.

65. See Seyla Benhabib, "Liberal Dialogue," 152. For a comprehensive discussion of the norm of reciprocity and the role it plays in a theory of deliberative democracy, see Gutmann and Thompson, *Democracy and Disagreement*, esp. chap. 2.

66. Chambers, *Reasonable Democracy*, 100.

SIX

Toward a Deliberative Liberalism?

Deliberation in Culturally Diverse Societies

One of the most striking features of deliberative democracy is the extent to which some of its most fundamental features pull in opposite directions. Theorists of deliberative democracy assert that few if any norms should be presupposed prior to deliberation, yet this position stands in tension with their endorsement of the discursive goal of moral and political consensus. The idealized model of deliberation they propose further depends on the wide acceptance of norms of mutual respect, consent, reciprocity, equality, and impartiality. In this chapter, I argue that proponents of deliberative democracy can and should abandon their claim that their perspective does not presuppose norms. Moreover, I seek to offer a better account of how a commitment to realizing liberal principles of respect and consent might help us to deepen our democratic practices. I will argue that by modifying these and other aspects of deliberative accounts of democracy, we can begin to elaborate institutions and practices that reflect a more adequate approach to cultural pluralism than is currently expressed by this approach. In particular, I suggest that by seeking to secure citizens' actual agreement on procedures for debate and decision-making, and even on procedures to manage *disagreements*,[1] we might better ensure the inclusion and consent of diverse groups in plural, democratic states.

---

1. A similar view is articulated by John Dryzek, who suggests that even when citizens cannot agree on a concrete proposal, "participants can still reach consensus based on rea-

Before proposing specific amendments and modifications to the theory of deliberative democracy, it is worth summarizing which features might contribute significantly to our attempts to understand and negotiate dilemmas of cultural diversity. Proponents of deliberative democracy offer some good criticisms of liberal theory's separation of public and private life and suggest a possible reconceptualization of the relationship between these spheres. They also demonstrate that citizens' senses of identity and community can have a legitimate place in politics, contrary to the views of their neutral liberal counterparts. Many, such as Iris Young, go so far as to offer a positive appreciation of cultural differences, notably absent in mainstream liberal and liberal perfectionist approaches to diversity and pluralism. Whereas liberals tend to treat social and cultural differences as possible obstructions to justice best dealt with by strategies of assimilation, exemption, or at best, limited group rights, theorists such as Young highlight the positive value of cultural identity and membership for individuals and the ways in which these differences can enrich public life.[2] In doing so, some of these writers help us to see that there are reasons to value social and cultural *diversity*. By contrast, even the best available liberal discussions of cultural pluralism, such as that offered by Kymlicka, reject appeals to the wider social benefits of cultural diversity on the grounds that it obscures or is even incompatible with the more fundamental reasons—related to autonomy and justice—why liberals should support limited group rights.[3] Finally, theorists of deliberative democracy also offer us a preliminary sketch of a more complex and satisfactory account of the public sphere, in which political deliberation is not reducible to legal procedures and majoritarian politics but rather is based on citizens' communicative practices.[4]

Despite these insights, the proposals of deliberative democrats remain vulnerable to a range of criticisms from the vantage point of respect for cultural pluralism. As I argued in chapter 5, attempts by delib-

---

soned disagreement, while striving to understand the cultural tradition and / or conceptual framework of the other participants." John Dryzek, *Discursive Democracy*, 42.

2. Young offers a good account of the positive contribution that social and cultural differences can make to politics; however, she moves too quickly from this point to the claim that the "assertion of positive differences" necessarily leads to group-based politics. See Young, *Justice and the Politics of Difference*, 165–66.

3. Kymlicka, *Multicultural Citizenship*, 121–22.

4. These writers have also shown that informal associations in civil society—or "secondary group" activity—may provide channels for increased political participation for diverse citizens, particularly those marginalized within mainstream electoral politics. Such activity may help to instantiate democratic norms. For a discussion of these themes, see Cohen and Rogers, "Associations and Democracy," esp. 283.

erative democracy theorists to reconceive citizenship beg more questions than they answer. Proposals for fully differentiated citizenship and
calls for wide-reaching rights for the self-representation of all social
groups—i.e., not just for territorially concentrated cultural minorities,
but for all socially marginalized constituencies—might offer limited
short-term solutions, but much is at stake in such a rethinking of citizenship. We need to distinguish between different sorts of claims for
collective rights and to listen to dissenting voices within cultural communities on the subject of special cultural rights.[5] Strategies such as
"mirror representation"—or fully proportionate representation of social and cultural groups—by no means guarantee that the interests of
groups will be represented fairly or accurately. In the first place, as
Kymlicka has noted, representation does not necessarily imply political
accountability.[6] The identity-based form of representation that Young
and Williams appear to endorse could also make it difficult at times to
hold in view our common responsibilities and at worst could disinte-
grate into a politics of private preferences or interest-group pluralism.

In addition to rejecting a solely identity-based politics and attending
more closely to the different kinds of collective rights and arrangements that cultural groups may merit, I propose three further important modifications to deliberative democracy. These modifications are
essential, I suggest, if this model of politics is to make good on its promise of including all citizens in democratic political life. They require
that we: (1) abandon the norm of strong consensus as a goal of public
deliberation; (2) rethink the terms and expectations of citizens' practices of public reason-giving; and (3) shift our focus to citizens' actual
capacities and opportunities to participate in political life, including for
citizens of cultural minorities.

Giving Up the Norm of Strong Consensus

In the modified account of deliberative democracy which I propose to
defend—which I call deliberative liberalism—it is not necessary to secure the unanimous consent of all participants in dialogue. Instead,
what is crucial is that open, democratic procedures of debate be fol-

5. For example, native women in Canada demand that they continue to enjoy the protection of their individual rights under the Canadian Charter of Rights and Freedoms. This
view contradicts the position of the mostly male leadership of the Assembly of First Nations, which argues that the Charter conflicts with native aspirations for self-determination
and collective rights.

6. Kymlicka, *Multicultural Citizenship*, 147–49.

lowed, that all participants have the opportunity to present their concerns, and that these views are listened to and debated. It is better that political procedures should afford opportunities for citizens and their representatives to present their opposing views than that legislators retreat to elitist and exclusionary models of decision-making (even if these occasionally yield prompt solutions). If negotiated settlements and compromises cannot be reached on specific, entrenched issues, it is of course always possible to fall back onto majoritarian principles. However, if those citizens and groups who disagree regularly with majority decisions and whose positions are set aside are also those who face serious social and economic disadvantages—or threats to their cultural group survival—then the legitimacy of the adopted deliberative procedures is in doubt. This is because legitimate democratic norms and procedures cannot simply be those that meet with the agreement of a majority of powerful citizens, but must rather be accepted by all those who are to be bound by them (or as near as possible to "all" as is practicable). In cases where citizens of minority groups consistently dissent on specific issues, three sorts of strategies may be pursued. First, we can increase the representation (on appointed committees) of dissenting groups whose perspectives have been marginalized. Second, we can introduce bargaining techniques to settle issues that do not require consensus on underlying, contested norms, but which focus instead on strategic compromises. Finally, it is possible that on some issues—especially those pertaining to constitutional reform and matters of concern to national minorities—it may be necessary to introduce a *stronger* requirement of consensus so that majority views do not automatically hold sway in decision-making or come to dominate dissenting views.

The idea of a thicker, more deliberative form of democracy is coherent without any normative commitment to the goal of strong consensus. Provided that issues of power, agency, and inequality are addressed, securing wide agreement on many of the *procedures* (as opposed to the entire outcome) of deliberation is a reasonable, if still difficult, goal. Decisions reached in the course of public dialogue—both on specific issues and on norms and procedures of debate—are contingent ones, open to subsequent renegotiation. But coming to provisional agreements on the shape that public discussion and political debate should take—the rules for presenting and debating proposals, at what point decisions need to be made, and how these decisions might be reassessed if the need arises—could help to establish ground rules that permit citizens to deliberate even when they strongly disagree. The importance of debating fair procedures for political deliberation and decision-making is typically overlooked by thinner conceptions of democracy, such as those associated with politics in liberal representative democracies. This may reflect a failure to take seriously certain core liberal norms, for striving to reach agreements (however temporary) on important features of deliberative procedures helps us to realize principles of political consent and respect for persons. At the same time, deliberation and agreement on procedures brings us closer to the goal of meeting the claims of cultural minorities for genuine political inclusion, respect, and recognition.

Rethinking Public Reason-Giving

Recall that one of the key merits of deliberative democracy (insofar as the greater accommodation and inclusion of cultural minorities is concerned) is that it does not propose to restrict the range of issues that citizens may address in political deliberation nor the views they may call on to support their proposals. The procedural rules that may emerge in deliberative democracy, and which allow for some group-based participation, differ significantly from the sorts of strong conversational constraints that proponents of *modus vivendi* and neutral models of liberalism seek to impose on citizens' deliberations. Discourse ethics in general rejects the imposition of conversational constraints on public deliberation, as well as the strict separation of normative questions pertaining to justice, from discussions of the good.[7] By contrast, as we have seen, liberals who endorse a "conversational constraints" model of liberalism, such as Ackerman and Larmore, hope to keep morally charged and divisive issues off the political agenda. Even Rawls's more moderate conception of political liberalism confines citizens' morally comprehensive views to a marginal status, in part by drawing a sharp distinction between public reason and what he calls "non-public reasons," which pertain to the "background culture" of social life rather than to the "public political culture." The norm of public reason and the burdens of judgment further require that "in discussing constitutional essentials and matters of basic justice we are not to appeal to comprehensive religious

---

7. As Brian Walker notes, Habermas's opposition to conversational restraints may be partly motivated by his belief that some questions of the good can be formulated in a generalizable way: see his "Habermas and Pluralist Political Theory," *Philosophy and Social Criticism* 18, no. 1 (1992): 91. For deliberative democracy theorist Seyla Benhabib, the liberal requirement that citizens bracket off their moral views from areas of political deliberation is problematic mainly insofar as it might tend to reinforce social and political power inequalities: see her "Liberal Dialogue Versus a Critical Theory of Discursive Legitimation," in *Liberalism and the Moral Life*, ed. Nancy Rosenblum (Cambridge, Mass.: Harvard University Press, 1989), 154.

and philosophical doctrines—and to what we as individuals or members of associations see as the whole truth."[8] This move effectively prevents citizens from introducing certain kinds of arguments or considerations in political deliberation, especially those that depend on specific moral, religious, and cultural norms.

Proponents of deliberative democracy do not seek to delimit the range of issues that citizens can raise, the moral views to which they can refer, or the kinds of reasons they can give for objecting to a given norm or procedure in constitutional or political discussions.[9] However, some versions of deliberative democracy incorporate a requirement of public reason-giving that is not unlike that proposed by neutral liberals. As argued earlier, the requirement of public reason-giving poses burdens to cultural minority citizens who are unable or unwilling to abide by the specific terms of this political practice. Why? On the face of it, public reason-giving simply encourages citizens to foreground reasons why the broader community might want to endorse their proposals and to offer justifications that others could accept. As Joshua Cohen notes, Participants "are required to state their reasons for advancing proposals, supporting them or criticizing them.... Reasons are offered with the aim of bringing others to accept the proposal, given their disparate ends."[10] However, this account overlooks the fact that not all social and cultural groups are equally well-adapted to—or would endorse—this form of politics. Some will reject the very idea of a politics founded on public reason-giving, as well as the ostensibly shared norms and practices it seems to presuppose. Indeed, the notion of public reason-giving, at least as conceived by such liberals as Rawls and Larmore, does not take adequate account of the different deliberative styles of citizens and ignores questions of power, inequality, and coercion in debate and decision-making.[11] As I attempted to show in my discussion of the Hind-

8. Rawls, *Political Liberalism,* 220 and 224–25.

9. That citizens are permitted to make public assertions based on their comprehensive views does not mean, of course, that local cultural norms can easily claim universal status. See Habermas's discussion of cultural values in *Moral Consciousness and Communicative Action,* 101.

10. Cohen, "Deliberative and Democratic Legitimacy," 22. A similar account of the role of public reason in deliberative democracy is that of Gutmann and Thompson: "Deliberative democracy asks citizens and officials to justify public policy by giving reasons that can be accepted by those who are bound by it. This disposition to seek mutually justifiable reasons expresses the core of the process of deliberation." See their *Democracy and Disagreement,* 52.

11. Iris Young's critique of aspects of deliberative democracy parallels my own in this regard, especially her suggestion that public deliberation runs the risk of reinforcing unacknowledged social and cultural biases toward models of communication that serve some citizens' interests better than others. Young, "Communication and the Other."

marsh case in South Australia in chapter 3, the requirement that participants in dialogue present arguments that can be seen as reasonable
from the perspectives of *all* citizens and legislators may make it difficult
for certain cultural minorities to receive justice. There are of course no
easy answers to such dilemmas, but deliberative theorists would do well
to remember that the norm of publicity and the expectation of full dis-
closure of reasons may clash with the fundamental beliefs of some cultural communities. This may signal the need to take steps to ensure that
the forms of debate and decision-making that deliberative democrats
propose do not exclude or disadvantage cultural minorities.

Since deliberative democracy does not require nor indeed encourage
participants to bracket their moral views and beliefs from political dialogue, not even when discussing public norms, it is all the more important that deliberative procedures be structured so as to ensure that a
few citizens or powerful groups do not monopolize public debate. No
arguments in favor of the institutionalized dominance of a few participants could meet with the free agreement of most citizens. In addition,
deliberative democracy also places a high premium on *listening* by requiring that all participants hear and grasp at least the rudiments of
other citizens' divergent views or positions.[12] This is no easy requirement, much less one to which citizens of diverse social and cultural
groups will readily adhere (consider, for example, cultures that set a low
value on listening, especially listening to outsiders). Nonetheless, it is
crucial to the success of deliberative democracy that debate not be
mere expression, but rather actual communication. Members of marginalized national and cultural minority groups stand to benefit from a
deliberative political model that emphasizes the communication of concrete needs, interests, and differences in belief.

The communication of differences by no means guarantees, of
course, that minority views will successfully displace the contested
norms or procedures. Nor should it. The call by some British Muslims
starting in 1989 for a ban on future printings of Salman Rushdie's *Sa-
tanic Verses*, for instance, could not justly be expected to yield in the displacement of broader, existing commitments to toleration and free
speech. The justice claims of religious and cultural minorities would
also require critical public debate, ideally of a more respectful and in-
formative type than is currently the case (where bias and misunderstanding frequently distort and polarize the positions at stake). Yet by
creating discursive procedures and institutions for citizens to protest

12. See for instance, Susan Bickford, *The Dissonance of Democracy: Listening, Conflict, and Citizenship* (Ithaca, N.Y.: Cornell University Press, 1997).

what they perceive as offenses and injustice and to debate these issues with other citizens (including dissenting members of their own communities), we might go some distance toward meeting British Muslims' demands for respect and cultural recognition. A thicker, more deliberative conception of democracy defends this sort of strategy for resolving citizens' moral disputes.

Citizens' Actual Capacities and Opportunities for Political Participation

Abandoning the requirement of strong consensus and the notion of public reason (narrowly conceived) also requires that we let go of the assumption that citizens are similarly situated in discourse and have comparable capacities and opportunities for deliberation. We need to develop much more specific and realistic understandings of what citizens require in order to reflect, deliberate, and make cooperative decisions. Similarly, we could think harder about how to design discursive procedures so as to offset the effects of social and economic disadvantages (all the while trying to change these inequalities). It might also be possible to incorporate the styles of deliberation and decision-making of certain cultural communities into broader political institutions or, at the very least to give political weight to some communities' autonomous decision-making within certain spheres. In short, if deliberative democracy is to make good its claim to provide reasons for including the broadest possible spectrum of diverse citizens in active deliberation, its proponents must seriously investigate the requirements and impediments to participation in public life in culturally differentiated societies. Here the solution cannot be merely to call for the right of group self-representation, though some such rights are surely indispensable in pluralistic democracies. Nor can we blithely assume, as some proponents of deliberative democracy do, that increased popular dialogue and participation necessarily support the inclusion and accommodation of minority citizens.[13]

If an account of deliberative democracy is to be at all applicable to socially plural societies, it will clearly have to acknowledge and find ways to mitigate the impact of social and economic inequalities and unjust power relations on citizens' capacities and opportunities for participation in public deliberation. Donald Moon has recently tried to address this problem more directly than most. Moon draws on Onora

13. For a good discussion of the social power dynamics of local democratic deliberation, see Jane Mansbridge, *Beyond Adversary Democracy* (New York: Basic Books, 1980).

O'Neill's discussion of the issue of practical constraints on citizens' agency and consent in defending the view that both discursive procedures and "the outcomes of discourse must respect the agency of participants."[14] Importantly, Moon discusses how to determine whether citizens have real access to discourse and just what the necessary capacities for deliberation are. Like O'Neill, he also suggests that we need to attend to the question of whether circumstances permit genuine consent (as opposed to coerced "agreement") to norms and deliberative procedures. Yet the fact of cultural diversity renders the issues of citizens' agency and consent even more complex than Moon suggests: for instance, membership in certain cultural groups may have a bearing on the discursive styles and deliberative procedures their members endorse as the Hindmarsh case illustrates. Moreover, membership in groups that do not respect some of their members' agency could seriously affect access of those members to deliberation and decision-making both inside and outside their communities.

Although proponents of deliberative democracy have not managed thus far to supply adequate answers to the problems sketched above, Moon's suggestion that we must attend to citizens' "agency rights" in designing discursive procedures perhaps comes closest to meeting this demand.[15] But the idea of agency rights will require considerably more thought and specification than even Moon supposes: his proposals are confined to suggestions that citizens' agency in the context of deliberative democracy might require welfare rights as well as a "basic set of rights protecting the privacy and integrity of individuals, and rights to speak and communicate."[16] Yet there is a significant difference between merely affirming citizens' rights to deliberate—and providing some basic social welfare rights to facilitate their political participation—and ensuring that citizens are actually *able* to deliberate effectively. The latter requires that citizens have opportunities to develop capacities for reflection, deliberation, argumentation, and the opportunities to deliberate publicly—and without detriment or fear of reprisals.[17]

If deliberative theorists take seriously the goal of including diverse citizens in political life, they must offer a more comprehensive analysis of the enabling and inhibiting factors of political participation, as well as of the dynamics of disagreement. Deliberation and public reason-giving require articulate, well-informed citizens who can, to at least

---

14. Moon, *Constructing Community*, 110.
15. Ibid., 110–12.
16. Moon, "Practical Discourse and Communicative Ethics," 160.
17. Moon, *Constructing Community*, 108–12.

some degree, think and reason publicly. But not only may the expectation of publicity disadvantage minority groups whose ideals and practices are more private and "internal," as the Hindmarsh case showed, but aspects of public deliberation may merely reinforce existing intergroup and intragroup relations of domination. If we concede that democratic politics require, ideally, the development of open practices of public debate—as I argue we should—we will need to pay much more attention to the social power relations that both foster and inhibit public dialogue. One way of accomplishing this is to ask not just about the tangible opportunities for political engagement—and to propose, as does Moon, certain "agency rights"—but also to attend to the capacities of agents to think, reason, debate, and decide publicly. It is not enough to invoke an idealized conception of the deliberative citizen engaged in unconstrained discourse, nor to assume that citizens participate freely in public dialogue in the absence of clear evidence of coercion.[18] In pluralistic societies, cultural cleavages frequently mirror socioeconomic disparities, so there is even more reason for theorists concerned with the political inclusion of diverse citizens to take seriously the implications for political agency of social disadvantages and disempowerment.

Issues of socioeconomic justice and the politics of public deliberation are deeply interwoven, but the latter are not reducible to the former. Numerous cultural minority communities in liberal societies face barriers to participation in political life that transcend economic and social disadvantage. To address the circumstances that enable and foster agents' capacities to form opinions, choose options, argue for proposals, and deliberate, we must therefore also consider the significance of different cultural practices and traditions of public debate and decision-making. Decision-making styles of minority groups frequently conflict with dominant liberal models of deliberation; demands for respect and political inclusion may require that some of these differences be accommodated.

Deepening Democratic Politics

The real merits of deliberative democracy lie not in the illusory goal of social consensus, nor in the ideal of unconstrained dialogue that it bor-

---

18. As Onora O'Neill notes, "noncoercion and nondeception do not have unique interpretations, [so] their application must deploy deliberation that takes account of actual conditions of action." See her "Ethical Reasoning and Ideological Pluralism," *Ethics* 98, (1988): 720.

rows (albeit in a modified form) from discourse ethics, but rather in the capacity of this model to deepen democratic practices in liberal states. It is only by striving to develop a thicker form of democracy, filtered through to the micro-level of political institutions, that citizens' cultural identities and memberships can come to be taken seriously in political life. In a broad sense, then, more robust democratic practices—linked to liberal principles of respect, consent, and reciprocity—help to foster recognition and accommodation of citizens' differences in political life. A commitment to these latter goals depends on certain determinate liberal democratic norms. In particular, the principles of respect and consent are necessary (but not sufficient) conditions for any meaningful agreement on democratic norms and deliberative procedures, not to mention practical political issues. Even where agreement does not prove possible, a more deliberative political framework has the benefit of helping to enfranchise previously excluded minority groups and encouraging more open debate about the sources of citizens' normative differences.

The potential contribution of a deliberative model of democracy to an account of justice for cultural minorities thus lies mainly in the discourse-ethical premise that democratic norms and institutions should be open to contestation and revision and in the kinds of deliberative practices the model envisages. Because the legitimacy of political institutions and norms is to be established through actual processes of public dialogue and deliberation—rather than by hypothetical suppositions about the outcome of rational and reasonable procedures—all citizens, including cultural minorities, could at least in principle present concerns about the fairness of political processes.[19] Although these objections—which would then need to be discussed and debated— might finally be rejected, good reasons for doing so would have to be of-

19. My argument presupposes that citizens want greater inclusion in democratic political life. Of course, this is not always the case. Certain religious minorities, such as the Amish and some Mormon sects, do not seek greater inclusion in liberal political life. However, at some stage even these groups must make public claims for the specific concessions they are seeking (e.g., dispensation to remove their children from public education). The deliberative norms and procedures I enumerate here (and which some theorists of deliberative democracy defend) may help to facilitate dialogue between these closed communities and liberal political society. A more difficult challenge is posed by groups whose sole goal is that of political secession or sovereignty. But even here, extensive deliberation and negotiations will be required in order to determine the form that secession or separation will take (at least in democratic states). Principles of deliberation and decision-making that require wide public consultation and debate, in addition to requiring the participation and agreement of key parties in constitutional talks, would be preferable to the more selective and elitist models of political bargaining that tend to prevail in liberal representative democracies. (Canada's recent constitutional negotiations are a case in point.)

fered: that is, a simple majoritarian vote, without extensive deliberation, would not be deemed acceptable. Moreover, since deliberative democracy considers proposals issuing from unconstrained public dialogue to be the most reasonable and legitimate solutions to given problems, it would require that we take seriously objections by minority communities to particular norms and proposals.

Although deliberation is of course an important feature of politics in liberal representative democracies, it is often confined to a few political institutions (and accordingly, to debates among a few legislators and interest groups). Federal or national politics in liberal democracies often consist of deliberation oriented toward short-term political goals and rarely aim at facilitating greater understanding of the different positions involved: in important respects, the positions of key political parties are decided in advance of debate and discussion in legislative assemblies. In addition, mere majoritarian principles do not mandate that legislators listen to or debate the views of minority groups (though, of course, prudence sometimes does).

Discourse ethics and deliberative accounts of democracy reject the notion that moral reasoning should be conducted by reference to the supposed standards of *hypothetical* rational agents and ethical dilemmas.[20] On the limited conception of deliberative democracy for which I am arguing, reasoning and deliberation are conceived in terms of the actual *communication* of agents' positions and beliefs, thus shifting the attention to actual processes of moral argumentation. Because this account of democracy links justice to the establishment of normative validity and legitimacy through public deliberation, it must seek to include as many citizens as is practicably possible. It is this deeper form of political inclusion that may better meet liberal requirements of respect and consent—central aspects of both a thicker form of liberal democracy and respect for cultural pluralism.

A deliberative liberal model of politics, in the view argued here, does not merely satisfy requirements of macro-level democracy—that is, supply formal political equality through universal franchise and basic individual rights—but also seeks to introduce and secure democracy at the micro-level of political life. The emphasis that deliberative democracy places on the increased participation of citizens in public life, in both political and civil society, suggests ways in which the perspectives of

20. Several critics of Rawls have tried to show that his conception of public reason is both insufficiently deliberative and simply brackets off too much in the way of moral and social views. See, for instance, James Bohman, "Public Reason and Cultural Pluralism," *Political Theory* 23, no. 2 (1995): 253–79, and previously cited works by Benhabib.

diverse citizens can come to be included in political debate. A few examples of the sorts of proposals that could significantly increase respect and recognition for cultural minority groups include the following: genuinely representative citizens' consultative bodies; the allocation of seats for cultural minorities on special councils and decision-making bodies; the guarantee of a say in debates on constitutional amendments and changes to political procedures and institutions; and mandatory representation of national minorities in legislative assemblies.

The modified account of deliberative legitimacy I defend does not require that *all* or even most citizens actively participate in public deliberation and decision-making. Not only is such a requirement impracticable in large states, but many citizens simply do not seek this degree of participation. The view that all citizens necessarily must partake in public debate may further presuppose that individuals and communities cannot trust those whom they choose to represent their views at certain levels of political discussion and decision-making. This is a particularly problematic assumption from the vantage point of cultural minorities, whose political interests and concerns are typically group-based, and so may require group-based forms of representation. For these and other reasons, I distance my own proposals from those of certain recent advocates of participatory democracy and from more idealized discussions of deliberative democracy.[21] I do not mean to imply that I am uninterested in the question of what constitutes adequately representative institutions and procedures of political deliberation and decision-making. Although this matter must itself be the focus of extensive public debate and discussion, I suggest the following as a rough guideline. To determine whether or not deliberation and deliberative institutions are sufficiently representative, we must ask: (1) whether political debate (especially, but not exclusively, in formal, representative institutions) includes a broad cross-section of citizens who can discuss issues involving contested norms and issues; and (2) whether national and cultural minority groups are guaranteed a central role in debates, talks, and negotiations on matters that affect their communities—from constitutional changes down to education and local planning issues.

The potential contribution of a deliberative democratic ideal to a thicker form of democracy—one in which political institutions reflect regard for liberal principles of respect and consent—thus lies in the

---

21. For example, my proposals differ significantly from those of Benjamin Barber, who argues against all representative forms of democracy. Unlike Barber, I do not advocate Rousseauian-style direct democracy or radical forms of participatory democracy, viewing these as implausible solutions for large, complex modern states. See Barber, *Strong Democracy: Participatory Politics for a New Age* (Berkeley: University of California Press, 1984).

way it conceives political legitimacy and practices of public deliberation. Deliberative accounts of democracy offer reasons why it is important that all citizens should have opportunities to shape the public and political culture of the societies in which they live. However, as I have argued, a conception of deliberative democracy would need to be modified in several respects if it is to contribute usefully to strategies for the accommodation of cultural minorities. In particular, it would need to recognize the importance of *group* representation for those minority cultural communities who so seek it, so as to recognize the importance of citizens' cultural identities and memberships to political life. This and other changes could make deliberative democracy a sound basis from which to develop political institutions and practices based on norms of political trust, mutual respect, and reciprocity—all necessary features of a just, democratic political system.

The Dilemma of Cultural Diversity
in Political Thought

To be rooted is perhaps the most important and least recognized need of the human soul. It is one of the hardest to define. A human being has roots by virtue of his real, active and natural participation in the life of a community which preserves in living shape certain particular treasures of the past and certain particular expectations for the future.... Every human being needs to have multiple roots.

—SIMONE WEIL, *The Need for Roots*

Toward an Account of Respect for Cultural Pluralism

I have argued that approaches based on appeals to toleration, neutrality, and liberal perfectionism fail in different ways to meet the claims for respect and recognition of cultural minorities in democratic states. Each of these liberal strategies presupposes a thin form of democracy, one which does little to expand on prevailing political practices in liberal representative and majoritarian democracies. This thin view of democracy neither aims nor purports to secure substantial political inclusion, respect, and recognition of the sort which certain cultural minorities demand and for which I have argued.

Against these approaches, I have attempted to defend a thicker account of democracy, one that takes fuller account of liberal norms of respect and consent. Central to this thicker conception of liberal democratic politics is my claim that macro-level democracy alone—that is to say, liberal representative and majoritarian forms of democracy and the basic political rights these supply—cannot secure adequate respect and recognition for cultural minorities. Rather, justice for these latter groups will require that citizens' cultural identities and memberships be accorded greater regard in political life. This is not possible unless members of minority cultural groups enjoy real political inclusion in liberal institutions and a voice in shaping the political and public cultures of their societies. It requires, in short, that democracy be filtered down to the micro-level of society. It is for this reason that I have suggested that a more robust form of democracy will need to incorporate several insights from deliberative democracy theory, albeit in a modified form. In particular, the account of normative legitimacy at the heart of deliberative conceptions of democracy and accompanying proposals for inclusive forms of political deliberation are indispensable to the development of a democratic politics that offers respect and recognition to cultural minority citizens.

Why should adequate respect and accommodation for cultural minorities be so difficult to attain within the framework of "thin" theories of liberal democracy? As discussed in chapters 2 and 3, toleration-based liberalism and recent neutral or political liberal theories fail to take serious enough account of the importance of cultural identities and group memberships in political life. Further, these liberalisms mandate constraints either on the sorts of proposals that citizens can introduce within liberal political life—such as demands for asymmetrical forms of political accommodation for cultural minorities—or on the kinds of reasons that citizens may give in justifying political proposals, or both. The failure of thin theories of liberal democracy to offer more adequate forms of accommodation for cultural minorities comes into better focus when we consider some of the central requirements of respect and recognition for cultural groups. As I suggested in chapter 1, a satisfactory conception of cultural pluralism must minimally recognize the following features:

(1) the importance and *value* to each individual of cultural identity and of membership in a respected cultural community;

(2) that liberal democratic states (and citizens more generally) have reasons to value, and to protect, cultural *diversity* within their boundaries;

(3) that respect and justice for cultural minorities includes their right to challenge and to help shape the public and political cultures of the society in which they live; and

(4) that liberal democratic states cannot justly define *which* differences they have reason to recognize politically without first deliberating with those involved.

In addition, I suggested that in order to contribute toward the development of concrete, democratic strategies for securing justice for cultural minorities, an adequate account of respect for cultural pluralism must provide:

(a) a satisfactory defense of the importance of some group cultural rights and limited forms of community autonomy and of the need for allocation of state resources to support these goals; and

(b) a good account of where to draw the "limits of tolerance" and of how we are to decide which differences democratic polities cannot protect or accept.

If we assess the arguments of proponents of toleration, neutral liberalism, and liberal perfectionism from the vantage point of the requirements noted above, we can see that many of their inadequacies reflect a failure to take seriously liberal norms of respect and consent. More generally, the arguments of those liberal thinkers examined in this book are limited by the thin conception of liberal democracy that their approaches presuppose. By contrast, a thicker account of democracy—one which envisages democratic practices even at the micro-level of society—would take seriously the demands of justice for all citizens, including members of cultural minority communities. A more robust and deliberative account of democracy that recognizes the importance of citizens' cultural identities and memberships to political life and acknowledges the need for some special arrangements and rights for such citizens would bring us closer to the goal of developing a truly inclusive democratic politics in culturally plural societies.

In chapter 2, I argued that political toleration, although an indispensable principle of democracies, cannot in itself fully meet minority groups' demands for positive forms of recognition and assistance. Long-standing national minorities, such as the Québécois and the Basques, seek not merely minimal toleration or noninterference by the state, but self-determination in the sense of enjoying greater control over the political institutions that bind them. Territorially dispersed ethnic minorities that are also immigrant groups—for example, South Asian Muslims in Britain—often seek greater voice and decision-making power within the institutions, such as local schools, that affect them directly. Toleration alone cannot deliver these forms of inclusion and community autonomy; nor can it help us to appreciate whether or why cultural identity and membership—much less the fact of cultural diversity—may be valuable and worth protecting.

Neutral or political liberals such as Rawls and Larmore, as we saw in chapter 3, surpass many of the limitations of strategies based solely on toleration insofar as they acknowledge both the importance and irreducible plurality of citizens' diverse moral and social views. These liberals advance principles of justice designed (at least in part) to secure maximum toleration and freedom for citizens' normative differences in their private and social lives. However, both Rawls and Larmore assume without sufficient warrant that reasonable citizens would consent to the introduction of norms and deliberative constraints in the public domain which incorporate a notion of neutral, public reason. Since this ideal requires citizens to bracket their deeply held comprehensive views when discussing and voting on matters of fundamental political importance—namely, public norms and "constitutional essentials"—I suggested that it is unlikely to meet with the agreement of members of cultural minority groups, many of whom do not readily separate their moral and religious views from their intuitions about justice. Simply assuming the political agreement of culturally diverse citizens, I argued, makes a farce of the principle of consent. This error compounds the failure of neutral liberals to take seriously those claims that are based on (or merely invoke) citizens' identities and constitutive attachments in political life. Contra these writers, I suggested that members of cultural minorities cannot enjoy equal concern and respect unless they are included in democratic deliberation and decision-making on terms that recognize the value and importance of their group identities.

Liberal perfectionists such as Joseph Raz and Will Kymlicka offer reasons why cultural membership and identity are valuable and important to individual citizens. Because liberal perfectionists do not place questions about individual well-being outside the realm of politics, they are able to consider how cultural identity and membership may contribute to a good life in critical respects. They are further able to reflect on whether, why, and how the liberal democratic state should help protect these features. Both Raz's and Kymlicka's proposals could help to secure a limited form of respect and recognition for certain cultural minorities. Nonetheless, both of these writers link the value of cultural identity and membership much too closely to controversial liberal goods, and in so doing, they restrict the possible scope of cultural recognition. In emphasizing that the value of cultural membership lies in the role that membership plays in fostering the personal autonomy of individual members, Raz and Kymlicka overlook other reasons why cultural identity and membership may be valuable to individuals and worth protecting. This foreshortened "view from autonomy" precludes adequate respect for more traditional cultural minority groups, especially nonliberal ethnic and religious minorities.

In addition to these blind spots of liberal theories based on toleration, neutrality, and liberal perfectionism, many liberals face specific conceptual limitations in thinking about social and cultural difference and diversity. In chapter 1, I sketched three main limitations of liberal thinking on difference, which help to explain why many recent liberal discussions have failed to give adequate consideration to the legitimate political significance of citizens' cultural identities, memberships, and attachments. I then suggested three conceptual shifts that political theorists will need to make if they are to contribute more adequately to debates about how to accommodate citizens' cultural differences.

The first of these shifts is the need to move from conceiving diversity in terms of interests, capacities, and beliefs of *individuals* to viewing politically important differences as also socially constituted and collective in form. Respect for our individual differences, I argued, cannot stand in for respect and recognition of citizens' cultural identities and memberships. A second shift requires that democratic political theorists cease thinking about pluralism strictly in terms of the diversity of citizens' individual *views, preferences, and interests* and recognize that these represent only a few of citizens' politically salient differences. Discussions of moral pluralism and differing individual conceptions of the good life do not exhaust the relevance or value citizens' cultural identities and memberships: these latter features also include differences in collective conceptions of value, in social and domestic arrangements, and in material and cultural practices. Finally, a third shift I suggest that political theorists need to make is to cease thinking about diversity strictly as a problem to be resolved and instead come to recognize that democratic states (and citizens generally) have reasons to value and protect existing forms of cultural diversity.[1] In addition, we would do well to remember that public acknowledgment of the value of cultural diversity is integral to many cultural minorities' claims for respect and recognition.

These proposed shifts and the requirements of respect for cultural pluralism set out above are not small amendments to otherwise satisfac-

---

1. I sketched some of these reasons in my discussion of the value of diversity in chapters 1 and 4 and also (briefly) in connection with the norm of respect in chapter 2.

tory liberal approaches to dilemmas of difference. Rather, if realized, they would signal important transformations in liberal political theory. These transformations are set in motion, I suggest, by moving toward a thicker conception of liberal democracy, one that takes serious account of the requirements of respect for cultural pluralism.

Justice Amid Diversity: A Perennial Problem for Political Theory?

Discussions by recent liberal and democratic theorists about the extent to which conceptions of justice should reflect the norms of citizens in a particular state or instead instantiate timeless, universal principles of right—or both—resonate with earlier debates in the history of political thought. Debates by early modern and modern thinkers about the philosophical and political significance of national and ethnic identities, local customs, and religious beliefs were not unlike some of today's discussions about the proper status of citizens' partial identities, attachments, and motivations in liberal and democratic theories of justice. Writers as diverse as Montaigne, Montesquieu, and Hume were concerned that the political principles and institutions governing a particular state should demonstrate an affinity with the national and regional customs, sentiments, and beliefs of citizens. Some of these thinkers, notably Hume, accused modern philosophers of foolishly assuming that ideal principles could stand over and above people's actual intuitions, attachments, and forms of practical reasoning.[2]

Hume's view that political philosophers should pay greater attention to people's sentiments and beliefs is echoed by numerous contemporary critics of liberalism. I count my own perspective within the ranks of immanent critics of liberalism who seek not so much to dispense with liberal principles as to make good their promise. Liberal political theory is much criticized for failing to give adequate consideration to citizens' ethnic and cultural identities, gender, religious views, and moral values. My discussion lends further support to these criticisms, but equally points to the need to radicalize liberal and democratic norms so as to render liberal democratic theory more responsive to the social realities of plural liberal states. In the course of assessing liberal responses to dilemmas of cultural diversity, I have come to the conclusion that liberals need to move toward a thicker account of democracy, one that takes seriously liberal principles of respect and consent.

2. David Hume, "Of a Particular Providence and of a Future State," sec. 11, *An Enquiry Concerning Human Understanding* (1748; Indianapolis: Hackett, 1977), 101.

Some of the liberal approaches examined in this book number among the best available discussions of issues of cultural identity and cultural membership in contemporary political theory. Raz and Kymlicka in particular provide some astute arguments for substantive, far-reaching collective rights for cultural minorities in democratic states. Their liberal arguments are far more convincing, for example, than opaque discussions of "difference" and "diversity" by certain harsh critics of liberalism.[3] But it would be a mistake to conclude from this survey of some of the best liberal discussions that there exists a growing consensus among these thinkers that cultural minorities deserve special recognition and collective rights to meet their claims for justice. Far from it. Indeed, there is a depressing abundance of examples of prominent liberals who vehemently reject suggestions that the plight of cultural minorities should lead us to rethink any aspect of liberal thought. Some of these views resonate with eighteenth-century liberal arguments for assimilation (not to mention the policies of certain modern states). For instance, Chandran Kukathas asserts that "there is ... no need to look for alternatives to liberalism or to jettison the individualism that lies at its heart. We need, rather, to reassert the fundamental importance of individual liberty or individual rights and question the idea that cultural minorities have collective rights."[4]

Although Kukathas's view stands at one extreme of possible liberal responses to the justice claims of cultural minorities, it is by no means atypical. Insofar as they address this issue at all, many contemporary liberal thinkers—notably neutral or political liberals such as Rawls—continue to assume that justice for cultural minority groups can best be met by ensuring that they enjoy the same rights, duties, and liberties as other citizens. The thought that so long as citizens are free to form, revise, and pursue their own conceptions of the good, their social identities and ways of life are in some sense "accommodated," remains a typical liberal refrain. Responses by neutral liberals to some of the dilemmas posed by social and cultural diversity reflect a tendency to treat the justice claims of ethnic, cultural, racial, and religious communities primarily as merely a problem of the inadequate *application* of ideal liberal principles and practices which, if realized, would secure justice for all citizens regardless of their social and cultural attachments. The overwhelming evidence that cultural minorities in liberal states—especially territorially concentrated national minorities—seek greater

---

3. I have in mind here Connolly's *Identity\Difference* and Honig's proposals for an agonistic politics of difference in her *Political Theory and the Displacement of Politics*.

4. Kukathas, "Are There Any Cultural Rights?" 107.

recognition, respect, and inclusion as members of minority communities, not merely as liberal citizens, illustrates the shortsightedness of such strategies.

The assumption by neutral liberals that cultural minorities' claims for respect and recognition can best be met within the framework of a neutral, liberal conception of justice ignores the deeper challenges that struggles for recognition pose for liberal theory and practice. These challenges come from diverse sources. The inequalities that are motivating territorially concentrated minorities' claims for national self-determination are poignant reminders that individual rights and freedoms—although essential features of liberal democracies—cannot in themselves secure substantive justice and equality for all citizens, especially for cultural minorities. Calls for devolution of power and community autonomy—for example, by Scottish and Basque nationalists and the Québécois—evince the need for a conception of citizenship and for political practices that take better account of the cultural identities and memberships of citizens. Even the more limited justice claims of recent immigrants underscore the importance of developing public respect for cultural communities and of coming to recognize their contribution *as groups* to the societies in which they live.

Shifting Frameworks: Thick Democracy

The specific problem of how to define and secure justice for cultural minorities in liberal democratic states is a comparatively new problem for political theory. Early modern liberal theorists sought to address the dilemmas and challenges of what were essentially nondemocratic societies, societies in which the idea of full citizenship rights for all was not yet a consideration, much less the prospect of special rights and arrangements for cultural minorities. Although contemporary liberal theorists presuppose universal rather than selective citizenship, they remain limited by a narrow or thin view of the requirements of democracy. The liberal perspectives examined in this book, like those of their early modern predecessors, draw an overly sharp distinction between that which is public and political and that which is private and social. This dichotomy has made it difficult for certain liberals to appreciate the importance of citizens' cultural identities, memberships, and attachments to political life. For these and other reasons, it should come as no surprise that some of the solutions proposed by recent liberals fall short of meeting the requirements of respect for cultural pluralism.

Whether or not the best available liberal responses to the myriad claims of ethnic and national minorities can supply compelling strategies for securing respect and recognition for cultural minorities groups remains to be seen. To the extent that a reformed and expanded liberalism can meet the challenges posed by the justice claims of cultural minorities—and I have tried to argue that it can—it will only be by deepening its commitment to democratic norms and practices. One route toward the thicker account of democracy that I have proposed—by far the most promising, so I argue—is to institutionalize aspects of a deliberative conception of democracy. This political model locates legitimacy in the actual agreement of citizens to particular norms and procedures, thereby necessitating much wider practices of public consultation and deliberation. Because deliberative democracy foregrounds political deliberation and decision-making by citizens and legislators alike and does not impose constraints on the kinds of arguments or reasons they can offer in public discussion, it may help to secure greater respect and recognition for citizens' identities and diverse perspectives.

These and other aspects of a thicker, more deliberative account of democracy, when combined with a modified and limited conception of differentiated citizenship, may go some distance in helping us to meet the many demands of cultural minorities for greater recognition and accommodation. Whether or not there exists a commitment in liberal democratic states to institutionalize practices and procedures that demonstrate respect for and inclusion of citizens of minority cultures is of course another story. What I have tried to show is that if political theorists are concerned to secure justice for all citizens, they cannot afford to ignore the justice claims of cultural minorities. By moving toward a thicker account of democracy and a more robust and demanding view of the requirements of liberal norms of respect and consent, we can come closer to meeting these claims.

Works Cited

Ackerman, Bruce. "Neutralities." In *Liberalism and the Good*, ed. R.B. Douglass, G.M. Mara, and H.S. Richardson. London: Routledge, 1990.

———. *Social Justice in the Liberal State*. New Haven and London: Yale University Press, 1980.

Appiah, K. Anthony. "Identity, Authenticity, Survival: Multicultural Societies and Social Reproduction." In *Multiculturalism: Examining the Politics of Recognition*, ed. Amy Gutmann. Princeton, N.J.: Princeton University Press, 1994.

Archard, David. "Political Philosophy and the Concept of the Nation." *Journal of Value Inquiry* 29, no. 3 (1995): 379–92.

———, ed. *Philosophy and Pluralism*. Royal Institute of Philosophy, suppl. 40. Cambridge: Cambridge University Press, 1996.

Arendt, Hannah. *The Human Condition*. Chicago: University of Chicago Press, 1958.

Aristotle. *The Politics*. Translated by T.A. Sinclair. New York: Penguin, 1986.

Asad, Talal. "Multiculturalism and the British Identity in the Wake of the Rushdie Affair." *Politics and Society* 18, no. 4 (1990): 455–80.

Audard, Catherine. "Political Liberalism, Secular Republicanism: Two Answers to the Challenges of Pluralism." In *Philosophy and Pluralism*, ed. David Archard. Royal Institute of Philosophy, suppl. 40. Cambridge: Cambridge University Press, 1996.

Ayer, A.J. "Sources of Intolerance." In *On Toleration*, ed. Susan Mendus and D. Edwards. Oxford: Clarendon, 1987.

Barber, Benjamin. *Strong Democracy*. Berkeley: University of California Press, 1984.

Barry, Brian. "How Not to Defend Liberal Institutions." *British Journal of Political Science* 20, no. 1 (1990): 1–14.

———. *Justice as Impartiality*. Oxford: Clarendon, 1995.

Baynes, Kenneth. "Liberal Neutrality, Pluralism, and Deliberative Politics." *Praxis International* 12, no. 1 (1992): 50–69.

Benhabib, Seyla. "Deliberative Rationality and Models of Democratic Legitimacy." *Constellations* 1, no. 1 (1994): 26–52.

———. "Judgment and the Moral Foundations of Politics in Arendt's Thought." *Political Theory* 16, no. 1 (1988): 29–51.

———. "Liberal Dialogue versus a Critical Theory of Discursive Legitimation." In *Liberalism and the Moral Life*, ed. Nancy Rosenblum. Cambridge, Mass.: Harvard University Press, 1989.

———. *Situating the Self: Gender, Community, and Postmodernism in Contemporary Ethics.* Cambridge: Polity Press, 1992.

Berlin, Isaiah. *The Crooked Timber of Humanity.* Ed. Henry Hardy. London: John Murray, 1990.

———. "Does Political Theory Still Exist?" In *Concepts and Categories*, ed. Henry Hardy. London: Hogarth Press, 1978.

Berlin, Isaiah, and Bernard Williams. "Pluralism and Liberalism: A Reply." *Political Studies* 42 (1994): 306–9.

Bickford, Susan. *The Dissonance of Democracy: Listening, Conflict, and Citizenship.* Ithaca, N.Y.: Cornell University Press, 1997.

Blum, Lawrence. "Multiculturalism, Racial Justice, and Community: Reflections on Charles Taylor's 'Politics of Recognition.'" In *Defending Diversity*, eds. L. Foster and P. Herzog. Boston: University of Massachusetts Press, 1994.

Bohman, James. "Public Reason and Cultural Pluralism." *Political Theory* 23, no. 2 (1995): 253–79.

Bonhôte, Françoise. "Réflexions sur la tolérance." *Revue de théologie et de Philosophie* 12, no. 6 (1994): 1–18.

British Commission for Racial Equality. *Schools of Faith: Religious Schools in a Multicultural Society.* London, 1990.

Brunton, Ron. "The Hindmarsh Island Bridge and the Credibility of Australian Anthropology." *Anthropology Today* 12, no. 2 (1996): 1–7.

Caney, Simon. "Anti-Perfectionism and Rawlsian Liberalism." *Political Studies* 43, no. 2 (1995): 248–64.

———. "Consequentialist Defences of Liberal Neutrality." *Philosophical Quarterly* 41, no. 165 (1991): 457–77.

Chambers, Simone. "Discourse and Democratic Practices." In *The Cambridge Companion to Habermas*, ed. Stephen K. White. Cambridge: Cambridge University Press, 1995.

———. *Reasonable Democracy: Jürgen Habermas and the Politics of Discourse.* Ithaca, N.Y.: Cornell University Press, 1996.

Chaplin, Jonathan. "How Much Cultural and Religious Pluralism Can Liberalism Tolerate." In *Liberalism, Multiculturalism and Toleration*, ed. John Horton. London: Macmillan, 1993.

Cohen, Joshua. "Deliberative and Democratic Legitimacy." In *The Good Polity*, ed. A. Hamlin and P. Pettit. Oxford: Basil Blackwell, 1989.

———. "Moral Pluralism and Political Consensus." In *The Idea of Democracy*, ed. D. Copp, J. Hampton, and J.E. Roemer. Cambridge: Cambridge University Press, 1993.

Cohen, Joshua, and Joel Rogers. "Associations and Democracy." *Journal of Social Philosophy and Policy* 10, no. 2 (1993): 282–312.

Connolly, William. *Identity \Difference: Democratic Negotiations of Political Paradox.* Ithaca, N.Y.: Cornell University Press, 1991.

Cooke, Maeve. "Habermas and Consensus." *European Journal of Philosophy* 1, no. 3 (1993): 247–67.

Crowder, George. "Pluralism and Liberalism." *Political Studies* 42 (1994): 293–305.

Dahl, Robert. *Democracy, Liberty, and Equality.* Oslo: Norwegian University Press, 1986.

Dallmayr, Fred. Introduction to *The Communicative Ethics Controversy*, ed. Seyla Benhabib and Fred Dallmayr. Cambridge, Mass.: MIT Press, 1990.

Deveaux, Monique. "Conflicting Equalities? Cultural Group Rights and Sex Equality." *Political Studies*.

Douglass, R. B., G. M. Mara, and H. S. Richardson, eds. *Liberalism and the Good*. London: Routledge, 1990.

Dryzek, John. *Discursive Democracy: Politics, Policy, and Political Science*. 1990. Cambridge: Cambridge University Press, 1994.

———. "Political Inclusion and the Dynamics of Democratization." *American Political Science Review* 90, no. 1 (1996): 475–87.

Dunn, John. *Rethinking Modern Political Theory: Essays, 1979–1983*. Cambridge: Cambridge University Press, 1985.

Dworkin, Ronald. "Liberalism." In *Public and Private Morality*, ed. Stuart Hampshire. Cambridge: Cambridge University Press, 1978.

Fletcher, George. "The Case for Tolerance." *Social Philosophy and Policy* 13, no. 1 (1996): 229–39.

Foderaro, Lisa. "Hasidic Public School Loses Again Before U.S. Supreme Court, but Supporters Persist." *New York Times*, 13 October 1999, 5.

Fraser, Nancy. "Recognition or Redistribution? A Critical Reading of Iris Young's Justice and the Politics of Difference." *The Journal of Political Philosophy* 3, no. 2 (1995): 166–80.

———. "Rethinking the Public Sphere: A Contribution to the Critique of Actually Existing Democracy." In *Habermas and the Public Sphere*, ed. Craig Calhoun. Cambridge, Mass: MIT Press, 1993.

———. "Toward a Discourse Ethic of Solidarity." *Praxis International* 5, no. 4 (1986): 425–29.

Friedman, Marilyn. "Beyond Caring: The Demoralization of Gender." *Canadian Journal of Philosophy* 13, suppl. (1987): 90–109.

———."The Impracticality of Impartiality." In *What Are Friends For? Feminist Perspectives on Personal Relationships and Moral Theory*. Ithaca, N.Y.: Cornell University Press, 1993.

———. "The Practice of Partiality." *Ethics* 101 (1991): 818–35.

Galeotti, Anna Elisabetta. "Citizenship and Equality: The Place for Toleration." *Political Theory* 21, no. 4 (1993): 585–605.

Galston, William. *Liberal Purposes: Goods, Virtues, and Diversity in the Liberal State*. Cambridge: Cambridge University Press, 1991.

Gardner, Peter S. "Tolerance and Education." In *Liberalism, Multiculturalism, and Toleration*, ed. J. Horton. London: Macmillan, 1993.

Goodin, Robert, and Andrew Reeve, eds. *Liberalism and Neutrality*. London: Routledge, 1989.

Gray, John. "Agonistic Liberalism." *Social Philosophy and Policy* 12, no. 1 (1995): 11–135.

Gutmann, Amy. "The Challenge of Multiculturalism in Political Ethics." *Philosophy and Public Affairs* 22, no. 3 (1993): 171–206.

———. "Civic Education and Social Diversity." *Ethics* 105, no. 3 (1995): 557–79.

———, ed. *Multiculturalism: Examining the Politics of Recognition*. Princeton, N.J.: Princeton University Press, 1994.

Gutmann, Amy, and Dennis Thompson. *Democracy and Disagreement*. Cambridge, Mass.: Harvard University Press, 1996.

———. "Moral Conflict and Political Consensus." *Ethics* 101 (1990): 64–88.

Habermas, Jürgen. "Citizenship and National Identity: Some Reflections on the Future of Europe." *Praxis International* 12, no. 1 (1992): 1–19.

———. *Moral Consciousness and Communicative Action.* Translated by Christian Lenhardt and Shierry Weber Nicholsen. Cambridge, Mass: MIT Press, 1993.

Haksar, Vinit. *Equality, Liberty, and Perfectionism.* Oxford: Oxford University Press, 1979.

Herman, Barbara. "Agency, Attachment, and Difference." *Ethics* 101 (1991): 775–97.

———. "Pluralism and the Community of Moral Judgment." In *Toleration: An Elusive Virtue,* ed. David Heyd. Princeton, N.J.: Princeton University Press, 1996.

Heyd, David, ed. *Toleration: An Elusive Virtue.* Princeton, N.J.: Princeton University Press, 1996.

Honig, Bonnie. *Political Theory and the Displacement of Politics.* Ithaca, N.Y.: Cornell University Press, 1993.

———. "The Politics of Agonism." *Political Theory* 21, no. 3 (1993): 528–33.

Horton, John. "Liberalism, Multiculturalism, and Toleration." In *Liberalism, Multiculturalism, and Toleration,* ed. John Horton. London: Macmillan, 1993.

Hume, David. *An Enquiry Concerning Human Understanding.* Indianapolis: Hackett, 1977.

Hurka, Thomas. "Indirect Perfectionism: Kymlicka on Liberal Neutrality." *Journal of Political Philosophy* 3, no. 1 (1995): 36–57.

———. *Perfectionism.* Oxford and New York: Oxford University Press, 1993.

Jacobsohn, Gary J. "Three Models of Secular Constitutional Development: India, Israel, and the United States." *Studies in American Political Development* 10, no. 1 (1996): 1–68.

James, Susan. "The Good Enough Citizen: Female Citizenship and Independence." In *Beyond Equality and Difference,* ed. G. Bock and S. James. London: Routledge, 1993.

Jones, Peter. "The Ideal of the Neutral State." In *Liberalism and Neutrality,* ed. Robert Goodin and Andrew Reeve. London and New York: Routledge, 1989.

Kant, Immanuel. *The Metaphysics of Morals.* Translated by Mary Gregor. Cambridge: Cambridge University Press, 1991.

Kekes, John. "The Incompatibility of Liberalism and Pluralism." *American Philosophical Quarterly* 29, no. 2 (1992): 141–51.

———. *The Morality of Pluralism.* Princeton, N.J.: Princeton University Press, 1993.

Knight, James, and Jack Johnson. "Aggregation and Deliberation: On the Possibility of Democratic Deliberation." *Political Theory* 22, no. 2 (1994): 277–96.

Kukathas, Chandran. "Are There Any Cultural Rights?" *Political Theory* 20, no. 1 (1992): 105–39.

———, ed. *Multicultural Citizens: The Philosophy and Politics of Identity.* St. Leonards, Australia: Centre for Independent Studies, 1993.

Kymlicka, Will. "Liberal Individualism and Liberal Neutrality." *Ethics* 99 (1989): 883–905.

———. *Liberalism, Community, and Culture.* Oxford: Clarendon Press, 1989.

———. *Multicultural Citizenship: A Liberal Theory of Minority Rights.* Oxford: Oxford University Press, 1995.

———. "Review, Justice and the Politics of Difference and Throwing Like a Girl." *Canadian Philosophical Reviews* 11, no. 6 (1991): 441–45.

———. "The Rights of Minority Cultures: Reply to Kukathas." *Political Theory* 20, no. 1 (1992): 140–46.

———. "Two Models of Pluralism and Tolerance." *Analyse & Kritik* 13 (1992): 33–56.

Langton, Marcia. "The Hindmarsh Island Bridge Affair: How Aboriginal Women's Religion Became an Administerable Affair." *Australian Feminist Studies* 11, no. 24 (1996): 211–17.

Larmore, Charles. "The Limits of Aristotelian Ethics." In *Nomos* 34, *Virtue*, ed. John W. Chapman and William A. Galston, 185–96. New York: New York University Press.

———. *Patterns of Moral Complexity*. Cambridge: Cambridge University Press, 1987.

———. "Political Liberalism." *Political Theory* 18, no. 3 (1990): 339–60.

Lijphart, Arend. *Democracies: Patterns of Majoritarian and Consensus Government in Twenty-One Countries*. New Haven: Yale University Press, 1984.

———. *Democracy in Plural Societies*. New Haven and London: Yale University Press, 1977.

Locke, John. *A Letter Concerning Toleration*. 1689. Ed. J. Tully. Indianapolis: Hackett, 1983.

MacCormick, Neil. "Liberalism, Nationalism and the Post-sovereign State." *Political Studies* 44 (1996): 553–67.

Macedo, Stephen. "Charting Liberal Virtues." In *Nomos* 34, *Virtue*, ed. John W. Chapman and William A. Galston, 204–32. New York: New York University Press, 1992.

———. *Liberal Virtues: Citizenship, Virtue, and Community in Liberal Consitutionalism*. Oxford: Clarendon, 1990.

MacIntyre, Alasdair. *After Virtue*. Notre Dame, Ind.: University of Notre Dame Press, 1981.

———. *Whose Justice? Which Rationality?* Notre Dame, Ind.: University of Notre Dame Press, 1988.

Mansbridge, Jane. *Beyond Adversary Democracy*. New York: Basic Books, 1980.

———. "Using Power / Fighting Power." *Constellations* 1, no. 1 (1994): 53–73.

Marx, Karl. "On the Jewish Question." In *Karl Marx: Selected Writings*, ed. David McLellan. Oxford: Oxford University Press, 1977.

Mason, Andrew. "Autonomy, Liberalism, and State Neutrality." *Philosophical Quarterly* 40, no. 160 (1990): 433–52.

McCarthy, Thomas. "Legitimacy and Diversity: Dialectical Reflections on Analytical Distinctions." *Protosoziologie* 6 (1994): 199–228.

Mendus, Susan. Introduction to *On Toleration*, ed. S. Mendus and D. Edwards. Oxford: Clarendon, 1993.

———. *Toleration and the Limits of Liberalism*. London: Macmillan, 1989.

———, ed. *Justifying Toleration: Conceptual and Historical Perspectives*. Cambridge: Cambridge University Press, 1988.

Mill, John Stuart. *On Liberty*. 1859. Indianapolis, Indiana: Hackett, 1985.

Miller, David. "In Defence of Nationality." *Journal of Applied Philosophy* 10, no. 1 (1993): 3–16.

Mohood, Tariq. "Kymlicka on British Muslims." *Analyse & Kritik* 15 (1993): 87–91.

———. "Race in Britain and the Politics of Difference." In *Philosophy and Pluralism*, ed. David Archard. Royal Institute of Philosophy, supp. 40. Cambridge: Cambridge University Press, 1996.

Montefiore, Alan. "Neutrality, Indifference, and Detachment." In *Neutrality and Impartiality*, ed. A. Montefiore. Cambridge: Cambridge University Press, 1975.

Moon, J. Donald. *Constructing Community: Moral Pluralism and Tragic Conflicts*. Princeton, N.J.: Princeton University Press, 1993.

———. "Practical Discourse and Communicative Ethics." In *The Cambridge Companion to Habermas*, ed. Stephen K. White. Cambridge: Cambridge University Press, 1995.

Moore, Margaret. "Liberalism and the Ideal of the Good Life." *Review of Politics* 53, no. 4 (1991): 672–90.

Nagel, Thomas. "Moral Conflict and Political Legitimacy." In *Authority*, ed. Joseph Raz. Oxford: Basil Blackwell, 1990.

———. *Mortal Questions*. Cambridge: Cambridge University Press, 1979.

Neal, Patrick. "Perfectionism with a Liberal Face? Nervous Liberals and Raz's Political Theory." *Social Theory and Practice* 20, no. 1 (1994): 25–58.

Nozick, Robert. *Anarchy, State, and Utopia*. New York: Basic Books, 1975.

Nussbaum, Martha. "Aristotelian Social Democracy." In *Liberalism and the Good*, ed. R. B. Douglass, G. M. Mara, and H. S. Richardson. London: Routledge, 1990.

———. "Human Functioning and Social Justice: In Defense of Aristotelian Essentialism." *Political Theory* 20, no. 2 (1992): 202–46.

Nussbaum, Martha, and Amartya Sen. "Internal Criticism and Indian Rationalist Traditions." In *Relativism: Interpretation and Confrontation*, ed. Michael Krausz. Notre Dame, Ind.: University of Notre Dame Press, 1989.

O'Neill, Onora. "Constructivisms in Ethics." In *Constructions of Reason: Explorations of Kant's Practical Philosophy*. Cambridge: Cambridge University Press, 1989.

———. "Ethical Reasoning and Ideological Pluralism." *Ethics* 98 (1988): 705–22.

———. "Justice, Gender, and International Boundaries." In *The Quality of Life*, ed. Martha Nussbaum and Amartya Sen. Oxford: Clarendon Press, 1992.

———. "Political Liberalism and Public Reason: A Critical Notice of John Rawls." *Philosophical Review* 106, no. 3 (1997): 411–28.

———. "Practices of Toleration." In *Democracy and the Mass Media*, ed. Judith Lichtenberg. Cambridge: Cambridge University Press, 1990.

———. "The Public Use of Reason." In *Constructions of Reason: Explorations of Kant's Practical Philosophy*. Cambridge: Cambridge University Press, 1989.

———. "Rights, Obligations, and Needs." *Logos: Philosophic Issues in Christian Perspective* 6 (1985): 29–47.

Okin, Susan Moller. *Justice, Gender, and the Family*. New York: Basic Books, 1989.

Paine, Thomas. *Rights of Man*. 1792. Ed. Eric Foner. New York: Penguin, 1984.

Parekh, Bhikhu. "Discourses on National Identity." *Political Studies* 42, no. 3 (1994): 492–504.

———. "Moral Philosophy and Its Anti-pluralist Bias." In *Philosophy and Pluralism*, ed. D. Archard. Royal Institute of Philosophy, suppl. 40. Cambridge University Press, 1996.

———. "Non-ethnocentric Universalism: A Preliminary Sketch." Paper delivered at a conference on Multiculturalism, Minorities and Citizenship, at the European University Institute, Florence, 1996.

———. "The Rushdie Affair: Research Agenda for Political Philosophy." *Political Studies* 38, no. 4 (1990): 695–709.

Paris, David. "The Theoretical Mystique: Neutrality, Plurality, and the Defense of Liberalism." *American Journal of Political Science* 31, no. 4 (1987): 909–39.

Pateman, Carole. *The Sexual Contract*. Stanford, Calif.: Stanford University Press, 1988.

Perry, Michael. "Neutral Politics?" *Review of Politics* 51, no. 4 (1989): 479–509.

Phillips, Anne. "Descriptive Representation Revisited." Lecture to the Seminar in Political Thought and Intellectual History, Faculty of History, University of Cambridge, 1995.

Index